Campfire Stew

FORT WORTH'S
GIRL SCOUT TROOP 11

Linda K. Wood

ISBN 978-1-64559-557-1 (Paperback)
ISBN 978-1-64559-558-8 (Digital)

Covenant Books, Inc.
11661 Hwy 707
Murrells Inlet, SC 29576
www.covenantbooks.com

In loving memory of Mrs. Minnie Ruth Elrod, Mrs. Thelma Still, Mrs. Jeanette Hudson, Mrs. Esther Killian, and all the parents of Girl Scout Troop 11.

CONTENTS

Appendixes

ACKNOWLEDGMENTS

No book is the work of just one person. *Campfire Stew* is no exception.

Certainly, all the women of Girl Scout Troop/Ship 11 contributed to the creation of *Campfire Stew*. All of them shared memories, many of which I didn't remember. Carole Capps Steadham, Wanda Elrod Crowder, Martha Still Littlefield, and Karyn Hudson Draper had saved mountains of reference materials from our years of Scouting and graciously shared these treasures with me. Almost every troop member dug in her cache of memorabilia and sent me photographs to include with the text. When I couldn't locate my copy of the *1950 Girl Scout Handbook: Intermediate Program*, Pat Cookus Haberman kindly sent me hers. Needless to say, I couldn't have put it all together without the considerable help from my Scout sisters.

Friends, Julia Sheppard and Suzanne Smith, both of whom possess superior editing and critiquing skills, poured over my manuscript with minute attention and gave me invaluable advice for improving it. My friends in Los Alamos Writers Group also listened to the work in bits and pieces and helped me mold it into a complete package. I am so grateful for the help and support of all these people. All the Scouts read the manuscript and made suggestions, but Ann Brown Fields scrutinized it in detail and improved the text considerably.

Julia Sheppard and Belen Cuenca Shiley used their artistic skills to create much-needed illustrations in places where they were seriously lacking. I am extremely grateful for their talents and gracious help.

My husband Gerry scanned and enhanced many old photographs, took new pictures, and helped me place all artwork in the text. I am so thankful for his loving expertise and constant support. He alone heard the cries of frustration when technology seemed above my reach and schedules seemed impossible to manage. Thank you so much, my forever friend.

Thanks to all the people at Covenant Books who made the production of this book a reality.

All mistakes are mine.

PREFACE

Fort Worth's Girl Scout Troop 11 has been together for sixty-two years. Twelve of us have gathered in our hometown for a weekend-long reunion in 2011.

Carole Capps Steadham, one of the twelve, has planned a marvelous Saturday of touring three of the city's outstanding museums. Elaine Walton Lofland, a troop 11 member and museum docent, is trying to shepherd us through the special traveling Caravaggio exhibit at the Kimbell Art Museum. She told us that we must be quiet and respect other museum visitors, that we can't get within two feet of any painting, and that we must stay in a group.

We are dressed in attractive pants outfits, appropriate for visiting museums. We have always been able to appear as if we know what to do.

As usual, there are stragglers. Some of us never could keep up with the group. That's why our Scout leader, Mrs. Minnie Ruth Elrod, had used the buddy system to keep us in tow when we were little.

Elaine has had to chide me twice not to get so close to the paintings: I am so enthralled by her excellent presentation that I get careless and lean in too much.

Soon, chattering and giggling come from the back of our group. Silence has never been our forte.

Elaine goes, "Shh!"

The giggling stops for a minute and then resumes.

Elaine says "Shh" again, giving her fellow Scouts her sternest look. The noise stops for a minute but starts up yet another time. Elaine shakes her head and gives up.

We are no longer six years old, sixteen years old, or even sixty-six years old, but…some things never change.

* * * * *

When I graduated from Fort Worth's Amon Carter-Riverside High School in 1961, I thought I was finished with Girl Scouts. Our troop had stayed together all through public school, a remarkable record in itself, but I was headed off to college and a new world. Surely, Girl Scouting—and everything it had entailed—was behind me.

However, I underestimated Girl Scout Troop 11.

Not having enough money to go away to college, I stayed at home my freshman year and studied at Arlington State College (ASC, now The University of Texas at Arlington). Arlington, now a metropolis of approximately four hundred thousand people but at that time a much smaller town, is situated east of Fort Worth and is part of the sprawling Dallas-Fort Worth Metroplex.

The first day at ASC and my new future, whom should I encounter in the cavernous student center but Carole Capps, the Girl Scout who would become the most instrumental in keeping troop 11 united for the rest of our lives. Carole and I didn't do any Scout stuff that year, but we did stay in touch, sometimes commuting together from northeast Fort Worth to Arlington, about a thirty-minute drive south.

I transferred to The University of Oklahoma (OU), Norman, in the fall of 1962 and, despite the Cuban missile crisis and the assassination of President John F. Kennedy, I managed to spent three marvelous years there. Most important, I met Gerry, my future husband. We made plans to marry in August of 1965.

Back in Fort Worth after graduation from OU, I employed a caterer for our wedding. She was none other than Girl Scout Troop

11's incomparable leader, Mrs. Minnie Ruth Elrod. She now owned her own florist and wanted to expand into catering. Mine was her first catered wedding. She did a beautiful job of helping me plan the big event and stay within budget. And when the ceremony took place at Riverside Church of Christ, her daughter Wanda Elrod Crowder and fellow Scout, Jacque (pronounced "Jackie") McNiel Winkler, attended. Wanda, Jacque, and Mrs. Elrod had been in my life since the autumn of 1948 when we girls entered kindergarten. Best friends forever—today's teenagers only think they know what that means.

After our wedding, Gerry and I attended graduate school at The University of Texas at Austin (UT Austin). I completed my MA in communication degree and worked as assistant editor of *Texas Medicine*, journal of the Texas Medical Association, while he earned his PhD in chemistry. In the rest of the country, protests against the war in Vietnam and civil rights demonstrations were taking place, but Gerry toiled in his laboratory, and I wrote and edited articles intended to aid Texas physicians. We did, however, experience terror on August 1, 1966, when fellow UT Austin student, Charles Joseph Whitman, climbed to the top of the twenty-seven-story campus bell tower, shot and killed sixteen people, and wounded thirty-two others.

One day in 1969, while reading the *Austin American-Statesman*, I learned that Charles Fields, husband of Girl Scout friend Ann Brown Fields, had died of a heart attack at the too-young age of twenty-nine. I knew that Ann was living in Austin, but I had lost contact with her.

I went to Charles's funeral at Austin's University Methodist Church. There I saw, of course, Girl Scouts who had driven down from Fort Worth. I would learn that troop 11 women always show up for each other when they can. It was my first lesson in "Girl Scouts Together," not only for twelve years, but for life. I also saw that Ann was pregnant. When Ann's beautiful daughter Charlotte was born, I went by Ann's house to see mother and baby.

Soon after my reunion with Ann, Gerry completed his work at UT Austin, and we moved to Los Alamos, New Mexico, for Gerry to do research at Los Alamos National Laboratory. More than fifty years later, we continue to reside in that pretty mountain town.

In the meantime, Carole was making it her mission to convene Girl Scout Troop 11 at least once a year. Annually, I'd receive a letter announcing the reunion. Los Alamos is about six hundred and fifty miles from Fort Worth. I had small children and, as a stay-at-home mom, limited funds, so I rarely made it to the yearly gatherings; but as many Scouts as could attend did so.

In 1999, Carole and the other women who remained in Fort Worth planned a weekend-long fiftieth anniversary celebration for the troop.

My phone began to ring.

First it was Ann: "The gatherings get more precious each time. Please come to the fiftieth."

Next it was Martha Still Littlefield, saying, "It's so good to hear your sweet voice. I've missed you."

Then it was Beverly Wilson Greene begging me to come.

Finally, Karyn Hudson Draper called to say, "We've been friends since kindergarten, and I've missed you so much. Please come to the fiftieth."

I assured them that I couldn't miss this milestone anniversary for the troop.

Karyn had spearheaded the establishment of a Minnie Ruth Elrod Endowment Fund to provide scholarships for needy girls to attend Girl Scout summer camp. We all contributed and raised money, accumulating $10,000 that year. We have continued to give to the fund regularly.

The anniversary weekend included a Friday night camp out, some Saturday activities, worship together and afternoon festivities on Sunday. Ann, now an ordained United Methodist Church minister, preached at the church service. Sunday afternoon, our spouses, children, grandchildren, and surviving parents joined us for the "main event." As we "girls" stood for group pictures, I regretted not having made the effort to attend earlier gatherings. We Scouts had shared a lot—we were cute little girls, cantankerous teenagers, and now rather amazing adults, and we'd done it all together. What a heritage. Ann was right: the gathering was indeed precious.

When our high school class has a reunion, Girl Scout Troop 11 also has one. So, in 2001, I attended our fortieth high-school-class reunion and the Girl Scout luncheon. The reunion weekend took place only a few weeks after terrorists had flown airplanes into World Trade Center buildings in New York City, the Pentagon in Washington, DC, and a field in Pennsylvania. Horrified at the carnage and shocked that such an event could happen, we found some solace in talking about these events with people we had known all our lives.

Martha hosted the Girl Scout luncheon at her mother's house on Sunday after we had attended worship at Riverside Christian Church. Mrs. Thelma Still had been our able assistant leader throughout our twelve years of public school.

In the spring of 2003, Carole e-mailed us that Mrs. Elrod was too ill to come to Fort Worth for the annual reunion. She was living with Wanda's sister Sharon Elrod Wallace in Lake Wales, Florida. Since Mrs. Elrod couldn't come to us, Carole reasoned, why didn't we go to her?

"You'll never guess what Carole has dreamed up now," I said to Gerry as I told him about the proposed trip.

"Well, we have a free ticket on Southwest Airlines," he replied. "Why don't you go?"

So I did, along with six other troop 11 Scouts and Mrs. Still.

We joined Sharon in giving Mrs. Elrod a party with her Florida friends. This party was an occasion that none of us will ever forget. It was also the last time we saw Mrs. Elrod. She passed away in November 2003.

"It was a God thing," I told Carole. "What if we hadn't done it? I'm so glad you had that crazy idea, and we made that trip."

I couldn't go to Mrs. Elrod's funeral, which took place in Fort Worth, but Carole wanted me, the professional writer, to pen the tribute from the troop. Ann, the minister, would read it.

Then in January 2004, it was my sad duty to walk into a chapel for my own mother's funeral. My mother had been living with us in Los Alamos, but she wanted to be buried with the rest of her family in Fort Worth, so we had her body brought to Lucas Funeral Home, which handled the arrangements. Sure enough, I looked back at the small crowd the day of the funeral and saw two whole pews full of Girl Scouts. "Girl Scouts Together." That's us. They simply don't go away, and I'm so glad they don't.

Well, it's now spring of 2019. Carole is still planning our gatherings, and I try to get there, no matter what. We aren't just friends now: we're sisters. We find a way to support each other in whatever situation we're facing, good or bad. Each "girl" is accomplished by herself, but united, we make something extraordinary—like our favorite camping delicacy, Campfire Stew.

We've celebrated more reunions, one or two a year, sometimes weekend-long affairs. We've traveled to Savannah, Georgia, to visit Girl Scout founder Juliette Gordon Low's homes. We've been honored in our native Texas, both in Girl Scout publications and at a lovely banquet in Arlington. We've even celebrated our seventy-fifth birthday year together in an all-day bash. And we're still going strong—well, strong for seventy-five and seventy-six year olds.

> Girl Scouts together. That is our song.
> Winding the old trails rocky and long,
> Learning our motto, living our creed,
> Girl Scouts together in every good deed.
> —Girl Scout official song
> Copyright Girl Scouts of the USA[1]

I couldn't have said it better myself.
—Linda Kay Killian Wood,
Los Alamos, New Mexico, 2019

---

[1] "Girl Scouts Together," official Girl Scout Song on Scout Songs.com website, https://www.scoutsongs.com/lyrics/girlscoutstogether.html.

ELLIE'S STEW

In the night, a young cook named Ellie had a vision. She was to find just the right assistants, and she was to make a magnificent stew. This was to be the high point of her life. The challenging aspect of creating this stew was that it would not be completed for forty to fifty years, maybe even more. In the vision, it was promised that both Ellie and her assistants would live to see this culinary masterpiece simmer to perfection.

The vegetables that Ellie selected had been planted and tended by privileged, loving caretakers.

When the plants began to blossom, Ellie took much care with them. Sometimes, an assistant would be a little harsh in the manner of gardening. The cook reminded her that if the hoe got too close to the root, it might be damaged. They must take the greatest care in nurturing these tender plants.

The vegetables began to ripen. The cook and her assistants had many talks about the handling and chopping of the fruit of their labor. The chef continued to remind the assistants that they must be patient and loving, so as never to lose the essence of any single plant of their yield. If the vegetables were handled too severely, they could be bruised and crushed: they would be unfit for the grand stew.

The cooks added the vegetables to the pot with care. They added liquid and lovingly stirred the stew…and stirred it…and stirred it… and stirred it.

After twelve years, the chief cook and assistants had done all that they could do. The stew must now be set aside so that it could rest for a season.

The cook and the assistants watched through the years as the stew delicately aged.

The time came when their concoction was to be appraised by some of the most discerning judges in the world. The judges tasted the stew and proclaimed that this was the most superb stew they had ever tasted.

"Yes," they said, "this stew is truly magnificent!"

"Ellie's stew is a masterpiece!"

—Wanda Elrod Crowder

Recipe for Ellie's Stew

Mrs. Minnie Ruth Elrod (Ellie), chef
Mrs. Thelma Still, Mrs. Jeanette Hudson, and
Mrs. Esther Killian, assistant chefs

Ingredients:

Marilyn Ball	Jacque McNiel
Linda Booker	Linda Simons
Ann Brown	Martha Still
Earline Campbell	Margie Stoddard
Carole Capps	Mary Stoddard
Pat Cookus	Donna Throckmorton
Diane Crawford	Joyce Wakefield
Wanda Elrod	Elaine Walton
Linda Heaton	Marilyn Weiss
Karyn Hudson	Beverly Wilson
Linda Kay Killian	

Directions:

Mix together ingredients when very young and fresh. Combine gently. Stir and simmer carefully, slowly, patiently, and lovingly for twelve years. Let mixture age for at least thirty-eight more years, longer if desired. Serve, savor, and enjoy a marvelous concoction.

PART I

First Grade through High School

CHAPTER 1

Seventy Years and Counting

In 2011, Carole Capps Steadham telephones the Modern Art Museum of Forth Worth to arrange a docent-led tour for Girl Scout Troop 11's sixty-second reunion. She tells the events coordinator, "Our Girl Scout troop would like to tour your museum."

The man is happy to accommodate her.

"We're sixty-eight," Carole says and hears through the phone a noticeable intake of breath.

"You want to bring sixty-eight Girl Scouts to tour our museum?" He is probably having visions of football-stadium-level noise and demolished exhibits in his very adult-oriented art museum. A free-standing ball and pipe exhibit particularly must come to his mind.

"No, we're sixty-eight years old."

"You're still Girl Scouts at sixty-eight years old?" This must call up images of old ladies on walkers and squeezed into out-grown green uniforms.

"Yes, we're having our sixty-second troop reunion. We have remained friends all this time, and we would like to tour your museum as part of our weekend activities."

The disoriented man somehow takes down the information and schedules the tour, promising to provide a guide to lead it.

Carole turns off her cell phone and smiles. Such a reaction is not unusual: she encounters it often. Nothing is ordinary about troop 11.

When we arrive at the Modern to take our tour, a host of museum employees "just happen" to be stationed at the entrance "to get a peek at the Girl Scouts" and to fill the entry hall with an unmistakable buzz.

* * * * *

In September 1949, Mrs. Minnie Ruth Elrod agreed to act as leader for Brownie Troop 11. We girls all lived in the Oakhurst/Riverside area on the northeast side of Fort Worth, Texas. Most of us attended Oakhurst Elementary School.

In 1949, the United States was well on the way to recovery from World War II. Most factories had retooled and were producing consumer goods again. America's entry into the Korean War had not yet begun. In Fort Worth, the average middle-class family had one vehicle, a modest two-bedroom house, and no television set. Most dads went to work daily; most moms, like ours, stayed home. Several troop 11 mothers made their daughters' clothes. The average family consisted of a dad, a mom, and two or three kids. We were living the 1950s version of the great American Dream.

Our neighborhood was white middle class. Its name describes it—located on the east bank of the Trinity River's West Fork, it contains lots of oak trees on its wooded land. On a bluff overlooking the river, Oakhurst/Riverside was and is 2.8 miles from downtown Fort Worth.[2] From some locations in our neighborhood, one can look out

---

[2] Libby Willis, *Fort Worth's Oakhurst Neighborhood* (Charleston, South Carolina: Arcadia Publishing, 2014), 7.

over the river and see the site where the US Army's original Fort Worth once stood, near the present site of the Tarrant County Court House.[3]

Wanda Elrod Crowder, Mrs. Elrod's daughter, insists that her mother intended from the outset that the troop would stay together through high school. However, it's doubtful that even "Ellie," as we girls would come to call her, could have imagined then that the troop would stick it out seventy years and more.

Altogether, twenty-eight girls joined troop 11 at one time or other. Some, like me, began in 1949 and stayed in the troop from first grade through high school graduation. Some came in from another troop that folded. Some joined at a later time simply because they wanted to. Others who began in 1949 didn't stay the entire twelve years. Twenty of us, however, became cemented as one unit for life.

At any time, the troop numbered seventeen or nineteen girls, never fewer; for when someone left, another girl filled her slot. From the outside looking in, troop 11 seemed to have so much fun that others wanted to join. Wanda thinks the core group mostly was formed by fourth grade. Linda Booker was the last to join, in tenth grade.

Mrs. Elrod—with assistant leaders Mrs. Esther Killian (my mother), Mrs. Thelma Still (Martha's mother), and Mrs. Jeanette Hudson (Karyn's mother)—seemed an unending resource of activity ideas to interest a bunch of rambunctious girls. Over the years, we camped, made crafts, performed community services, sang songs, earned merit badges, took classes, enjoyed field trips, sold cookies, and went on vacations—together.

---

[3] Mike Nichols, *Lost Fort Worth* (Charleston, South Carolina: The History Press, 2014), 11.

Photo courtesy of Martha Still Littlefield
Brownie Troop 11 began and ended each meeting with a flag
ceremony. The color guard changed each week. Left to right are
Diane Crawford, Kay Lynn Mills, Carole Capps, Wanda Elrod,
Elena Patterson, Martha Still, Karyn Hudson, Jacque McNiel, Linda
Kay Killian, Linda Heaton, Betty Bias, and Margie Stoddard.[4]

We were all white Anglo-Saxon—this was before racial integra-
tion in Texas schools. We all ranked somewhere in the middle class,
lived in single homes with yards, and played in our close-knit community. We walked to our neighborhood school.

But troop 11 was by no means a homogeneous group. In fact,
we were quite a hodgepodge. We had different interests, personalities, and abilities. Each girl was unique.

Wanda, who puts some stock in the birth-order theory, likes to
point out that most of us were either firstborn or "only" children. She's
mostly right; but four girls had older brothers and two had older sisters. The birth-order theory dubs firstborn children as achievers, babies

---

[4] Kay Lynn, Elena, and Betty would soon leave the troop to be replaced by other
    girls.

as clowns, and middle children as sometimes getting lost in the shuffle.[5] Troop 11 Scouts, regardless of their birth order, stood out always.

Wanda also likes to compare us to Campfire Stew, one of our favorite dishes when we went camping. We each brought a canned vegetable: we dumped the contents of the cans en masse into a big pot and added browned hamburger meat and chopped onions, potatoes, and carrots. It smelled yummy while it cooked and tasted yummy when we ate it. If each ingredient is one girl, then troop 11 *is* like Campfire Stew—good by herself but so much improved when put with the others. We believe Wanda is right: we do see ourselves as better together than when we are apart—and, because we liked Wanda's metaphor, we began to refer to ourselves as "Campfire Stew."

Names sometimes presented a problem in the troop. We had some multiple names to deal with: four *Linda*s (Linda Faye Booker, Linda Gay Heaton, Linda Kay Killian, and Linda Faye Simons), two *Marilyn*s (Marilyn Ball and Marilyn Weiss), and one set of twins (Margie and Mary Stoddard). Really there were five *Linda*s, but Lynda Pat Cookus always went by *Pat* and didn't contribute to the confusion.

The name situation didn't get easier in later years. Earline Campbell married Jerry Wood, and I married Gerry Wood, so we had two Scouts with the same last name and husbands with similar first names. Linda Booker married Mike Webb, and I married Gerry Wood, so two *Linda*s had last names beginning with *W*. We did and do refer to the *Linda*s as Booker, Heaton, Simons, and Linda Kay.

---

[5]   Dr. Kevin Leman, *The Birth Order Book: Why You Are the Way You Are* (Ada, Michigan: Revell, reprint edition, 2015), 16.

Photo courtesy of Karyn Hudson Draper
Troop 11 Christmas party at the Elrod home in 1951. Pictured,
left to right: front row, are Mary Lois Tucker, Carole Capps,
Donna McDowell, Karyn Hudson, Martha Still, Diane Crawford;
middle row, Linda Kay Killian; left to right, back row, Kay Lynn
Mills, Linda Heaton, Elena Patterson, Margie Stoddard, Wanda
Elrod, Mary Stoddard, Jacque McNiel, and Elaine Walton.[6]

Sometimes, most of us in troop 11 would admit to being bossy.
We had and still have strong personalities, and once we get our individual or collective minds set on something, it was and is difficult
to divert us. We were opinionated. Our independent streaks would
later take us into successful careers and far-flung enterprises when we
reached adulthood. Ann Brown Fields thinks that perhaps our strong
personalities came about because "we learned in Girl Scouts and in
our families that we could do anything."

Troop 11 girls didn't seem to have a lot in common, or so I
always thought. Some were athletic, some studious, some musi-

---

[6] Mary Lois, Donna McDowell, Kay Lynn, and Elena would soon leave the troop
to be replaced by others. Later, Donna Throckmorton would join the troop: she
is the Donna referred to in the rest of the book.

cal. That didn't matter so much in the elementary years, but in high school, our paths began to diverge. However, lack of common interests or not, troop 11 stayed together. We did so largely before high school graduation because Mrs. Elrod was resourceful and clever and, after graduation, because Carole Capps Steadham, with help from some others, made sure that almost nobody got away.

Individual talents caused troop 11 to be prominently represented in the student leadership of Amon Carter-Riverside High School. We were class favorites, cheerleaders, National Honor Society officers and members, sports team members, school newspaper and yearbook editors, student government and club officers, and choir soloists.

Troop 11 girls also took their share of the awards handed out in the spring of senior year. A troop 11 girl won the citizenship award from the local chapter of Daughters of the American Revolution. When the CHS faculty named "Who's Who" that year, three troop 11 members received awards: for leadership, school spirit, and citizenship. Another Scout received a scholarship award from a local secretaries' organization. The Tarrant County chapter of Theta Sigma Phi women's journalism fraternity named a troop 11 Scout as the county's top high school female journalism student. (Tarrant County includes Fort Worth, Arlington, and several other incorporated communities. It's a big county.) Twelve of us graduated high school with honors: one summa cum laude, eight magna cum laude, and three cum laude. Not bad.

Photo courtesy of Martha Still Littlefield
Troop 11 girls took a trip to San Antonio, Texas, as Senior Girl
Scouts. Pictured left to right, front row are Linda Kay Killian,
Martha Still, Donna Throckmorton, Mary Stoddard, Beverly
Wilson; second row, Linda Heaton, Linda's younger sister Jo Marie
Heaton, Wanda's younger sister Sharon Elrod, Jacque McNiel,
Wanda Elrod, Diane Crawford, and Joyce Wakefield; third row,
Pat Cookus, Ann Brown, Linda Simons, and Marilyn Ball.

Each troop 11 girl had her sights set on her future, and she
would move purposefully, actively, and steadily to carry out her plans.

Today we are unanimous in the belief that Scouting gave us a
head start on life skills—skills such as interacting with people, following through on projects until completion, having the confidence to
take the lead, having the willingness to try different things, and working compatibly on a team. We have a can-do attitude that began in
those formative days and has served us well throughout our lives so far.

The accomplishments of the troop 11 girls after high school
graduation are legion. Some of us earned advanced college degrees;
some of us didn't finish college, but every one of us succeeded in
our chosen fields. We became business executives, business owners,
accountants, office managers, sales managers, writers, public school
and college teachers and administrators, an editor, a pharmacist, a
nurse, and a Christian minister.

Most of us are retired now; but some continue to run companies, help their children in self-owned businesses, teach part-time, or do volunteer work. Until a year ago, one Scout helped her son-in-law in the office of his concrete business. Another runs her own architectural placement business. Yet another is a part-time librarian at an elementary school. One troop member teaches nursing classes. One is a docent at Fort Worth's renowned Kimbell Art Museum. Another works summers in US National Parks. Two of us are freelance writers. And four play in amateur golf tournaments.

Almost all of us have children and grandchildren, and some have great-grandchildren. We are deeply involved with our families, something we have always thought was even more important than our other accomplishments.

Stamina—that's what we have. That and the ability to get along in the world. Mrs. Elrod and our parents instilled in us confidence and competence. The adults also made sure that we Scouts learned to interact amiably with each other and serve people less fortunate than ourselves. Our parents interacted heavily with the troop: mothers and dads served as drivers, teachers, helpers, chaperones, and project leaders.

The girls of troop 11 were, are, and will always be Texas belles: visualize United States First Ladies Laura Bush and Lady Bird Johnson. All but two of us reside somewhere in the state and in fairly easy-driving distance of Fort Worth. Wanda and Linda Booker lived outside Texas for some years, but they moved back. Joyce Wakefield Burks lives in California. I live in New Mexico. Marilyn Weiss splits her time between Fort Worth and South Carolina. In my opinion, Texans don't transplant well. It's like that George Strait song, "I Can't See Texas from Here." We get homesick.

It's debatable whether our Texas heritage or the modeling and grooming classes we took through Scouting produced our sense of fashion. The rest of the world might not put Fort Worth in the same fashion category as her bigger sister Dallas, but people might be mistaken in that assessment, for Fort Worth women pay attention to fashion too. Because we know our fabrics, textures, and styles, we of troop 11 know how to dress appropriately and becomingly for whatever occasion we're attending.

Our ensembles are coordinated—always. Hardly a week goes by without someone in New Mexico commenting on how I "always match" and am "coordinated" in my dress. Well, when I'm in Texas, nobody ever says that to me. In Texas, especially the Dallas-Fort Worth Metroplex, coordination just is. Yes, we Scouts are fashionably coordinated: we'd receive comments in Texas if we weren't.

We try to dress age appropriately too. Carole describes her fashion sense:

> When I try on something, I ask myself, "Would my mother wear this?" If the answer is "Yes," I put it back on the rack. If the answer is "No," I ask, "Would my daughter wear this?" If the answer is again "No," and I like the outfit, I buy it. But if the answer is "Yes," I don't.

And it's not only the clothes, jewelry, and matching accessories that are correct for the occasion: our hairstyles are perfectly groomed in place and suitable for the individual women sporting them. We don't wear white gloves and hats anymore, but we did so when we were teenagers, and we'll do so again should fashion dictate it.

Each Scout also knows how to *behave* appropriately at any social occasion. We are equally at home addressing a room full of professionals, presiding over an afternoon tea, or yelling for our favorite football team.

All of us speak with Texas accents, even Joyce, who has lived out of the state for forty-nine years. Some of our accents are slightly "ranchy," while others speak pure refined Southern velvet. Carole, for example, sounds as if she belongs on the steps of Tara in a green-and-white-flower-print billowing dress. We know the language of Texas too, including the meaning of *fixin' to*, *over yonder*, and *cotton-pickin'*. And let me make it clear: *y'all* is plural, not singular.

Along with our Texas belledom, we are "Steel Magnolias," tough and competent on the outside but tender and compassionate on the inside. We know how to be gracious and loving, and we know how to withstand the deepest heartbreaks. Four of us—Beverly Wilson

Greene, Jacque (pronounced "Jackie") McNeil Winkler, Linda Booker Webb, and Margie Stoddard Terry—are now deceased. All but one of our parents are also deceased. Some of us have lost spouses, siblings, children, and grandchildren to death. Three of us have survived cancer; two did not survive it. Twelve have endured the heartache of divorce. We've also watched our children suffer every imaginable physical and emotional pain, and any parent knows how hard it is to endure your child's anguish. We Scouts have stood strong and courageous in the face of whatever life has dealt us. And we have striven to lift each other up in difficult circumstances. We have faced adversity together.

Most of us have always gotten our strength from our Christian faith, as well as from each other. The 1950s was an amazing time to grow up in Fort Worth. Yes, it was the time of rock and roll, poodle skirts, and tail-finned cars; but it was also a time when almost everybody worshiped in a Christian church. Certainly everyone in Girl Scout Troop 11 did so. Accordingly, troop reunions never fail to include attendance at a local church on Sunday morning, devotionals, and grace at meals. Why not? We were reared to think, act, and live as Christians, and we have honed our faith through the years.

The troop maintains an e-mail loop. When anybody needs prayer about anything, she sends her request out on the loop, and her Scout sisters direct their prayers heavenward. It never occurs to any of us to face life without our individual prayers or the prayers of each other. Wanda says she prays for every Scout sister every day. She also places Bible verses and other inspirational notices on Facebook for us to read. Carole gave us each a bracelet that reads "God is big enough."

It's hard to collect the memories of seventy years, even when we get together and work at it. The memories are numerous: we can stay up until the wee hours of the morning reminiscing. We began in 1949 as cute, active, and chatty little girls. We grew into teenagers who sometimes lacked social skills and didn't always get along well with each other. Now we are competent women, comfortable in ourselves, and "glued" to our Scout sisters for life. It's quite a story we have to tell—quite a Campfire Stew our leaders cooked up.

Photo courtesy of Karyn Hudson Draper
Troop 11 members gathered at Martha Still Littlefield's house in
Arlington, Texas, in May 1986. Left to right are, front row, Earline
Campbell Wood, Linda Heaton Leonhardt, Beverly Wilson Greene,
Martha Still Littlefield, Karyn Hudson Draper, Donna Throckmorton
Jones, and Diane Crawford Hill; second row, left to right, Pat
Cookus Haberman, Marilyn Weiss, Linda Booker Webb, Carole
Capps Steadham, and Ann Brown Fields; back row, left to right,
Wanda Elrod Crowder, Mary Stoddard Hitt, Mrs. Minnie Ruth
Elrod, Mrs. Thelma Still, Jacque McNiel Winkler, Elaine Walton
Lofland, and Marion Hardy of the local Girl Scout office.[7]

---

[7] All core troop members are present in this picture except Marilyn Ball Murray,
Joyce Wakefield Burks, Linda Kay Killian Wood, and the already-deceased
Margie Stoddard Terry. Note: Beverly and Karyn, at age forty-three, can still fit
into their Mariner and Senior Scout uniforms, a fact that astounded the rest of
us. Martha put her Brownie and Mariner Scout uniforms on a large teddy bear
and a rag doll.

CHAPTER 2

The First Years: Brownies in Beanies

Brownie Troop 11 is en route to day camp on the farm of Durward and Mary West, northeast of Fort Worth. We are traveling on a chartered Fort Worth city bus. We are yelling, wiggling, and bouncing on the seats.

Our leaders, fearing for the girls' safety and the bus driver's sanity, suggest that the group sing some songs. So we break into "The Lord Said to Noah," "John Jacob Jingleheimer Schmidt," and "If You're Happy and You Know It."

Someone yells "The Bus Driver Song." We give it our best effort:

> *I wish I had a little red box to put the bus driver in.*
> *I'd take him out and (kiss, kiss, kiss) and put him back again.[8]*

The surprised chauffeur, who, wonder of wonders, hasn't shut us completely out of his brain, smiles in the mirror and waves back to us. We giggle as if we are sure that we have "made the man's day."

Who knows, maybe we have.

* * * * *

---

[8] "The Little Red Box Song," a traditional children's song with variable lyrics.

Today, girls can begin in kindergarten as Daisy Scouts.

In the late 1940s, however, Daisies didn't exist. Girls didn't typically begin their Scouting experience until first grade as Brownies. Most were six years old. Girls remained Brownies for three years before "flying up" to Intermediate Girl Scouts.

We became Brownies in an initiation ceremony, part of which included a poem that we said and still remember. After saying the poem, a girl was a Brownie.

> Twist me and turn me and show me the elf.
> I looked in the mirror and saw myself.[9]

The "brownies" the girls represent are not square chocolate bars, but sprite-like helpful elves.

Photo courtesy of Wanda Elrod Crowder
Brownie Troop 11 at a typical meeting. The girls are, left to right, Linda Heaton, Jacque McNiel, Linda Kay Killian, Margie Stoddard, Wanda Elrod, Carole Capps, Diane Crawford, Martha Still, Elena Patterson, Karyn Hudson, Kay Lynn Mills, Betty Bias, and Mary Stoddard. Linda Heaton, Jacque, Linda Kay, and Karyn were the color guard of the day, hence the sashes.[10]

---

[9] Scouting Website: Online Resources for Scouting Volunteers, http://www.scoutingweb.com/scoutingweb/SubPages/BrownieInvestiture.htm.

[10] Elena, Kay Lynn, and Betty dropped out of the troop during the Brownie years. Ann, Donna Throckmorton, Joyce, and Marilyn Ball joined after this picture.

In fall of 1949, Brownie Troop 11's eighteen girls, like all Brownies, wore medium brown one-hundred-percent cotton belted dresses, brown shoes and socks. A dark brown beanie, brownie embroidered on the front, topped each head. A yellow handkerchief, also embroidered with a brownie, adorned the left breast pocket.

This era being before permanent press, the dress was hard to iron. Our mothers didn't look forward to the weekly uniform wearing: laundering the thing was a chore.

But we loved wearing our uniforms, which were more or less flattering to every girl, regardless of her size or shape—flattering, that is, if the color brown can be attractive for a young girl.

Meetings took place weekly on Friday afternoons in the fellowship hall of Oakhurst Methodist Church, an aging wooden white building on Sylvania Street. The church had the musty, somewhat natural gassy, smell of many buildings that stay empty and closed most of the week. All of us were chatterboxes, and the noise from the fellowship hall echoed throughout the building.

In nice weather and for the first six years, most of us walked to the church together from our nearby elementary school. Times were different then, and little girls could safely walk four blocks on a busy city street without their parents' worrying. Of course, neither we nor, apparently, our parents were aware that in the 1950s, gangsters on the FBI's most wanted list were operating full tilt in clubs on Fort Worth's Jacksboro Highway, the "Highway to Hell."[11] Safe or not, depending on how one perceived things, we generally walked in a clump because we enjoyed the company.

Each girl dressed in her Brownie uniform and brought two nickels: one for her weekly dues and one to buy an ice cream cone at Oakhurst Drug Store on the way. Chocolate was our favorite flavor, though I sometimes got strawberry. Mrs. Minnie Ruth Elrod wasn't happy about the ice cream delay, but she never managed to stop it entirely.

Throughout troop 11's growing-up time together, Mrs. Elrod insisted that the girls, when we went anywhere as a group, must go in uni-

---

[11] Mike Nichols, *Lost Fort Worth*. (Charleston, South Carolina: The History Press, 2014), 102.

form, and everything about the uniform must be correctly worn. So, on Fridays, approximately eighteen little Brownies showed up at Oakhurst Elementary School in their uniforms. Some of our class photographs must have been taken on Friday because they show us in Brownie attire.

We bought our uniforms at Stripling's Department Store in downtown Fort Worth, then the local headquarters for Girl Scout paraphernalia. Troop 11 members thought going to the Girl Scout department a special treat; our parents did not share the joy. We could be rather vocal about asking to buy the many tempting items on display.

"Mommy, can I have a Brownie doll? P-l-e-a-s-e!" I begged every time we went to Stripling's. When my mother gave in and got me the doll, I named her Jacque. The doll was a blue-eyed blonde with long braids, and the real Jacque McNiel was a brown-eyed brunette. Nevertheless, the name stuck. The doll is still in my collection.

Stripling's, like many local department stores, is no longer in business.

Photo courtesy of Gerry Odell Wood
My Jacque doll.

A typical Brownie meeting began with a flag ceremony performed by the color guard of the day. The girls, different each week, wore red sashes and carried the United States and Brownie Scout flags. The Veterans of Foreign Wars and their women's auxiliary had presented the flags to our troop in a special ceremony. Jacque had accepted the American flag for troop 11, and I had received the

Brownie flag. Jacque's dad, Mr. Jack McNeil, presented both to us. The flags would be the troop's to keep.

At meetings, we saluted the flags and recited the US Pledge of Allegiance. Then we sang songs, played games, made crafts, viewed films, and learned Girl Scout history.

One craft we made was puppets. Each puppet represented a different country.

Illustration by Belen Cuenca Shiley
One of the puppets, this one from the Netherlands. One finger in a cardboard tube "worked" the puppet.

The puppet's head was a solid rubber ball, 2 1/2 inches in diameter, in which Mr. Rudy Still, Martha's dad, had drilled a finger hole. The Brownie placed a cardboard tube in the hole, covered her ball with a sock, drew a face on the sock, glued on yarn hair, and sewed on the correct costume for the puppet's country. Our moms had to help big time.

Wanda Elrod's puppet was Bella from Hungary, Karyn Hudson's was Giovanna from Italy, Martha Still's was "Gypsy Rose" from Spain, and mine was Rana from India.

Mother and I didn't know what Indian women wore. I'm pretty sure Rana didn't wear a sari. She had dangly earrings and long black yarn hair, so we got those parts right.

Every girl researched her puppet's country in an encyclopedia. Martha's dad built a puppet stage. We presented a puppet show at a city-wide Scout exhibition in which each "puppet" told about her country.

Photo courtesy of Wanda Elrod Crowder
Brownie Troop 11 girls pose in front of our puppet stage. They are, front row, left to right, Beverly Wilson, Pat Cookus, Martha Still, Linda Kay Killian, Mary Lois Tucker, Wanda Elrod, Elaine Walton, and Karyn Hudson; second row, Linda Simons, Mary Stoddard, Margie Stoddard, Linda Heaton, Diane Crawford, Carole Capps, Elena Patterson, Jacque McNiel, and Joyce Wakefield.[12]

Another craft we Brownies made was "sit-upons" for use at day camp. These were slick oil-cloth rectangles folded in half and stuffed with newspapers. We sewed three sides together with yarn through punched holes about an inch apart.

---

[12] Mary Lois also soon would drop out of the troop.

Photo courtesy of Wanda Elrod Crowder
A sit-upon made by a girl in Brownie Scout Troop 11.

It was hard for little fingers to weave the yarn in and out to close the cushions: getting it tight enough and keeping it from tangling were tricky.

"Ms. Elrod, my yarn is knotted up," Diane Crawford complained. Mrs. Elrod or one of the assistants helped Diane get her yarn unknotted. As soon as Diane's yarn was fixed, Beverly Wilson needed help. It went on like that the entire meeting until each girl had finished her "sit-upon" and the long-suffering leaders needed to take some aspirin.

It's a wonder any of us ever sewed a stitch after that, but in time, our fingers became more agile, and in later years, we would sew gifts, clothes, and hammocks.

Another item that we had to make for camp was a lanyard. This cord-like holder hung from our necks and kept our pocket knives handy. To craft these, we had to do some creative braiding of plastic vinyl strips. We began with a metal clip fastener and wove the strips into a long cord to go around our necks. The most difficult part was making the slide that enlarged or reduced the size of the neck opening.

Photo courtesy of Wanda Elrod Crowder
A lanyard, this one holding a whistle.

The lanyards, which came in a variety of color combinations, were quite attractive. It was an intricate craft, but every girl managed to finish one and attach her knife to her lanyard. We who were fortunate enough to prevail upon our parents to buy us official green Girl Scout knives really felt special. We of troop 11 wore our lanyards for years and on numerous camping trips: we had done a good job of putting the lanyards together, and they performed well.

Craft sessions were usually fun and productive, but that was not always true. Ann Brown Fields remembers getting into trouble during craft time. The scene went like this:

> "Ms. Elrod, Ann is swinging her foot and hitting the table leg. She made me mess up the design on my box," Elaine Walton wails.
>
> "Please try to keep your foot still, Ann," Mrs. Elrod says.
>
> But the swinging foot does not stop.
>
> Suddenly, the table lurches sideways. We all gasp, and a jar of tempura paint clatters to the floor. Paints splatter everywhere, and the leaders have a significant mess to clean up, which they patiently do.

Ann's chagrin is sufficient for her to remember the episode for life. Mrs. Elrod, Mrs. Thelma Still, and Mrs. Esther Killian simply took more aspirin.

At every meeting, after we cleaned up whatever mess we had made—the mess was usually less disastrous than spilled paint—we retired the colors. Following this flag ceremony, we girls stood in a circle, holding hands with arms crossed, and sang "Taps."

> Day is done, gone the sun,
> From the lake, from the hills, from the sky;
> All is well, safely rest,
> God is nigh.
>
> —bugle call,
Music by US Army Brigadier
General Daniel Butterfield,
Lyrics by Horace Lorenzo Trim[13]

After the song, we broke hands, gave a two-fingered Brownie salute, and in unison yelled, "'Bye, Brownies." Then we took off noisily in eighteen directions.

Sometimes, during meeting time, we went on field trips to local factories or businesses. Our parents dutifully took turns driving carloads of girls to these activities. We learned a lot on these outings and created, as always, significant girlish chatter.

We enjoyed touring Mrs. Baird's Bakery, Fort Worth's local bread and cake company, where we were treated to free chocolate cupcakes. Mrs. Baird's is in business today, with bakeries located throughout Texas, and distributes products in Texas and neighboring states. It is now a division of Bimbo Bakeries USA, which distributes numerous brands, including Sara Lee, Oroweat, and Entenmann's.

Another favorite excursion was to the Dr Pepper Bottling Company, where we received complimentary bottles of the beverage

---

[13] "Taps," Wikipedia website, http://en.wikipedia.org/wiki/Taps, copyright Pennsylvania Military College.

right off the assembly line. Some people say they like hot Dr Pepper, but I don't. The lukewarm beverage at the factory that day sealed my preference for *cold* Dr Pepper. Dr Pepper, though it is the unofficial favorite soft drink of Texans, no longer is bottled in Fort Worth.

Every time troop 11 went anywhere, even if it was just to play in a park, we used the buddy system. A girl chose or was assigned a buddy with whom she walked in a line two-by-two. We stayed with our buddy throughout the day's activities. This system helped leaders keep up with eighteen little girls and prevented anyone's getting lost. If anybody was injured, her buddy would notify an adult. The plan mostly served us well.

Of course, no system works if you don't use it. We did like to walk in bunches to our Friday meetings, but once we must have forgotten to choose buddies. Ann remembers getting lost that time and entirely forgetting to go to the meeting.

In summers, Brownie Troop 11 went to day camp at the Durward and Mary West farm on North Beach Street. The farm back then was out in the country northeast of Fort Worth. If it's still there—as a few farms are—it has been engulfed by a sprawling city and has houses and businesses surrounding it. Some of us have tried to locate it in recent years, but, so far, Karyn is the only one who thinks she has done so. She says part of the farm is now Buffalo Ridge Park with an assisted-living facility next to or on the property. The area is now mostly housing developments and shopping centers.

The West family graciously provided part of their land annually for use by both the Boy and Girl Scouts. They even had a shelter on the farm that was dedicated to the Boy Scouts. We used it for craft projects.

West family members dropped by during our camp days to interact with us, to lend a hand with camp chores, and to answer questions about permissible activities on their property. We all remember the Wests as kind and friendly.

Photo courtesy of Wanda Elrod Crowder
Mrs. Minnie Ruth Elrod, Mrs. Jeanette Hudson, and Mrs.
Frances Swanson, camp nurse, pose by the Durward and
Mary West plaque on the West Farm Boy Scout shelter.

To and from day camp, we rode on a chartered Fort Worth city bus. To keep us relatively calm and corralled, our leaders or the more leadership-oriented (to be translated "bossy") girls led songs. We sang at the top of our voices until we were hoarse—almost.

Lack of vocal training or musical excellence never daunted us, for we loved to sing—and we still do. Ask us today, and, without hesitation, troop 11 Scouts can sing a beloved song for you. If you can stand it, we can sing songs until we're hoarse.

"We don't sound any better now," Jacque told a Fort Worth *Star-Telegram* reporter at the troop's thirty-eighth-year reunion in 1986.

I think she was wrong. In fifth grade, I would sing a solo, "Oh, Holy Night," five times in the much-presented Oakhurst Elementary chorus Christmas program. Five of us would sing in the Amon Carter-Riverside High School (CHS) chorus and the Fort Worth High School all-city chorus. Wanda and Ann would sing in the CHS girls' sextet. But perhaps our vocal refinements came later. As rendered by us in Brownie days, song tunes were barely discernible. Jacque was right about that.

Photo courtesy of Karyn Hudson Draper
Karyn Hudson, wearing her pocket knife on her lanyard, baits
her hook in preparing to fish in Fossil Creek on West Farm.

Day camp activities included making crafts such as sun-leaf pictures on both colored paper and plaster of Paris, fishing, hiking, and eating a sack lunch—no Campfire Stew yet. We also enjoyed dangling our bare feet in the chilly water of Fossil Creek.

At day camp, we learned about "stinky" latrines, a new experience for us city dwellers, but if you had to go, you had to go. Latrines had to be dug and cleaned up. Our latrine was a hole in the ground with a canvas "tent" around it, kind of like a tiny tepee.

We learned to clean up carefully at camp and to leave the premises as if we'd never been there—well, almost as if we'd never been there. At this stage, the leaders did most of the campsite building, restoration, and serious cleanup, including digging and covering up the latrines. I do remember "helping," if you could call it that.

"Linda Kay, please put the glue, glitter, and paper in that box and carry it to the bus," Mrs. Still would tell me. "Martha, we need to pick up that trash by the trees."

Even at this early stage, our leaders organized us for cleanup and other duties. They used what they called "Caper Charts" to assign us tasks. The first caper chart was much simpler than the one we'd use later at Camp Timberlake on Eagle Mountain Lake. We talked about the chart at our regular meeting and learned how we would use it.

Early caper charts were made of poster board. A small round poster board circle rotated on a large poster board. The larger poster board had the jobs listed around the outside. Inside the small circle were group numbers or names (bluebirds, mockingbirds, cardinals, for example). The smaller circle rotated. When it stopped, the groups and jobs were matched up, and each girl had her assignment. Every day or meal, the wheel turned one space around the chart, thus changing everyone's jobs. Depending on the number of girls and camp days, jobs could be combined or added.

At day camp, our jobs included cleaning up trash in our area, unpacking craft supplies in the morning, packing them up again for transporting home, and carrying supplies to the bus.

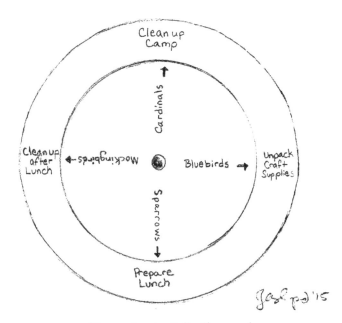

Illustration by Julia Sheppard
An early troop 11 caper chart.

Troop 11 women remember the Brownie years as mostly fun, partly learning, some mischief-making, and lots of singing. We know that we found Brownie Scouting special enough to cause most of us to stay with the troop until it was time to "fly up" to Intermediate Girl Scouts.

> I've got something in my pocket that belongs across my face.
> I keep it very close at hand, in a most convenient place.
> I'm sure you couldn't guess it if you guessed a long, long while.
> So I'll take it out and put it on, it's a great big Brownie Smile!
>
> —"Brownie Smile Song"
> Harriet F. Heywood, late 1920s
> ©Girl Scouts of the USA[14]

---

[14] Scout Songs.com, Virtual Songbook, http://www.scoutsongs.com/lyrics/browniesmilesong.html.

CHAPTER 3

The Intermediate Years: Girls in Green

"Mrs. Elrod! Mrs. Elrod! Come quick! Wanda just stepped on a copperhead!"

Girl Scout Troop 11 is camping in the Pioneer Unit at Camp Timberlake on Eagle Mountain Lake, west of Fort Worth. This unit comprises tents perched on wooden platforms with steps up to them. They were probably built high to protect the wood from ground moisture and occupants from snakes that inhabit Texas woodlands. Each tent-house provides beds for four to six girls.

Wanda Elrod exits her tent. She steps on the first step. On the next step lounges a peacefully sleeping snake—peacefully sleeping, that is, until Wanda, who doesn't see the snake, puts her other foot down on it.

Wanda screams. The others in her tent scream. Mr. Snake slithers away at warp speed.

Mrs. Minnie Ruth Elrod grabs her first aid and snakebite kits and comes running.

We girls hover around with our incessant questions.

"What did the snake look like?"

"Was it big?"

"Where is it?"

"Did it bite her?"

"Is she going to die?"

Wanda chews her lip and tries to push back tears.

Ellie carefully examines Wanda's legs and, seeing no fang marks or raised red areas on her skin, determines that the girl was not bitten.

Mrs. Thelma Still finds and kills the snake. We can always count on Mrs. Still for strength, resourcefulness, and action.

After everyone's pulse returns to nearly normal, Mrs. Elrod explains to the troop that this situation could have been horribly bad. Her words strike home in every little-girl heart.

From this moment on, we will carefully watch where we step, and Mrs. Elrod will never be more than an arm's length from her snakebite kit.

* * * * *

On March 13, 1953, in Fort Worth's Riverside Junior High School auditorium, Brownie Troops 11 and 214 "flew up" together to become Intermediate Girl Scouts. It was a dignified occasion—at least as dignified as nine-year-olds could manage.

One by one, the girls, dressed in pine-green uniforms, traversed a wooden bridge, received their Girl Scout pins, and gave three-fingered Girl Scout salutes.

We took turns lighting white taper candles and mounting them on a two-foot-wide greenery-surrounded gold Girl Scout trefoil displayed on a table. A trefoil is a three-lobed design. The word means "three leaves." The Girl Scout symbol has always been a trefoil: each "leaf" stands for a part in the Girl Scout promise. In the fly-up ceremony, every candle had a particular meaning too: in this instance, the three candles at the top represented the three parts of the Girl Scout promise; the other ten candles stood for the Girl Scout laws. The smoke from the lighted candles emitted a slight fragrance.

Photo courtesy of Gerry Odell Wood
The Girl Scout trefoil pin as it appeared in the 1950s.

The Girl Scout Promise

On my honor I will try to do my duty to God and my country,
to help other people at all times, to obey the Girl Scout laws.

Promise from 1953 edition *Girl Scout Handbook: Intermediate Program*, property of Pat Cookus Haberman

The Girl Scout promise as said in the 1950s. It is slightly different today.[15]

We girls recited from memory the promise and the laws in unison.

---

[15] The Girl Scout Promise in the 1950s, *Girl Scout Handbook: Intermediate Program*, 1953 ed. (New York: Girl Scouts of the U.S.A.), ii.

The Girl Scout Laws

1. A Girl Scout's honor is to be trusted.
2. A Girl Scout is loyal.
3. A Girl Scout's duty is to be useful and help others.
4. A Girl Scout is a friend to all and a sister to every other Girl Scout.
5. A Girl Scout is courteous.
6. A Girl Scout is a friend to animals.
7. A Girl Scout obeys orders.
8. A Girl Scout is cheerful.
9. A Girl Scout is thrifty.
10. A Girl Scout is clean in thought, word, and deed.

Laws from 1953 edition *Girl Scout Handbook: Intermediate
Program*, property of Pat Cookus Haberman
The Girl Scout laws as they read in the 1950s.
These too are different today.[16]

After the ceremony, three girls from each troop posed by the candle-bedecked trefoil for a picture to be published in the neighborhood newspaper, the *Riverside News*. The three members from troop 11 were Wanda Elrod, Martha Still, and I because our mothers were at that time troop leader and assistant leaders.

---

[16] Ibid.

Photo by Pat Sneed Photography

Three girls from each troop pose by the trefoil. Troop 11 Scouts are on the right. Left to right are Wanda Elrod, Linda Kay Killian, and Martha Still.

Then the entire troop posed with our three leaders. We still numbered eighteen, and what would always remain the core group was now almost established.

Soon after this time, Mrs. Esther Killian, my mother, a divorced mom who worked full-time to support us, resigned as assistant leader. Mrs. Elrod and Mrs. Still, however, persevered the twelve years of troop 11's public school life. At some later time, Mrs. Jeanette Hudson, Karyn's mother, joined them.

Photo by Pat Sneed Photography
Troop 11 girls and leaders pose for post-fly-up picture. We are, left to right, front row: Ann Brown, Mary Stoddard, Margie Stoddard, Beverly Wilson, Marilyn Ball, Donna Throckmorton, Martha Still, Linda Simons, Linda Heaton, and Jacque McNiel; second row, Pat Cookus, Linda Kay Killian, Elaine Walton, Karyn Hudson, Diane Crawford, Wanda Elrod, Joyce Wakefield, and Carole Capps; third row, Mrs. Esther Killian, Mrs. Minnie Ruth Elrod, and Mrs. Thelma Still.

Girl Scout Troop 11 now began a new chapter in its long life. We would camp more, work more, learn more, and bond into ever-deeper relationships. Probably nobody yet imagined that the group would continue to be close friends—if anything, closer friends—when we reached age seventy and beyond, but the foundation was building way back then.

The new uniforms seemed to bring new responsibility.

Ann Brown Fields says, "I loved every uniform troop 11 ever wore."

However, some girls were getting style-conscious—we were Texans, after all—and grumbling about the uniforms did occur. We were now in the 1950s and had televisions in our homes, but permanent press fabric still didn't exist, so mothers continued to iron.

Now, what Karyn Hudson Draper dubs "that ugly green dress" was to be worn on all troop occasions. "Like that awful ugly yellow tie would make it look better…and those matching green socks."

The dress opened down the front with dark green trefoil-decorated buttons. We wore a yellow tie, with a green embroidered "GS" in a trefoil on each end, and tied it in a square knot at the neck and topped the knot with the Girl Scout pin on the knot. A dark green belt defined the waist. Dark green berets perched on our heads, and our feet sported two-toned green socks.

Our leaders, as always, were determined that our uniforms would be worn exactly as prescribed in the *Girl Scout Handbook*. Mrs. Still stopped as many of us as she could. "Let me pin your tie in the proper flared-out position, so it doesn't droop," she'd say.

Photographs of the troop show both a long-sleeved and a short-sleeved version of the green dress. Possibly, one reason we preferred the short-sleeve style was because we could wear badge sashes with that version instead of sewing badges on our sleeves.

Photo by Pat Sneed Photography
Troop 11 girls in their short-sleeved uniforms a year after the fly-up ceremony. They are, left to right, front row, Earline Campbell, Linda Heaton, Beverly Wilson, Martha Still, Karyn Hudson, Donna Throckmorton, Diane Crawford, and Linda Simons; second row, Pat Cookus, Linda Kay Killian, Marilyn Ball, Margie Stoddard, Carole Capps, and Ann Brown; third row, Wanda Elrod, Mary Stoddard, Joyce Wakefield, Mrs. Minnie Ruth Elrod, Mrs. Thelma Still, Jacque McNiel, and Elaine Walton.

Martha says, "I think the long-sleeved dress was for winter, the short-sleeved one for summer. We didn't have a lot of cold weather in Fort Worth, and the short-sleeves looked better. Maybe that's why we wore the short sleeves most of the time."

We troop 11 Scouts enjoyed our regular meetings, but we loved parties even more, and Mrs. Elrod was good at planning them. In fall 1953, we celebrated our troop's fourth birthday. Only half of us showed up in our uniforms. Why? Nobody recalls.

Photo courtesy of Wanda Elrod Crowder
Troop 11 celebrates its fourth anniversary in 1953. We are, left to right, first row, Joyce Wakefield, Linda Simons, Beverly Wilson, Donna Throckmorton, Linda Heaton, Jacque McNiel, and Karyn Hudson; second row, Carole Capps, Earline Campbell, Ann Brown, Linda Kay Killian, Diane Crawford, Margie Stoddard, Mary Stoddard, and Martha Still; third row, Mrs. Minnie Ruth Elrod, Wanda Elrod, and Mrs. Thelma Still.

Troop 11 worked on crafts in the intermediate years. Our finger dexterity improved with physical growth, and crafts became easier.

We made all kinds of gifts for our families at Christmas, Mother's Day, and Father's Day, and we made Christmas decorations.

In the 1950s, milk came in glass bottles with foil lids. Mrs. Elrod obtained at the local Boswell's Dairy long foil strips from which the lids had been cut. We cut the strips apart, rolled them around pencils, and tied them in bunches to make ornament balls. The balls came in red, green, purple, and silver with red stripes. Every year, I hang the balls I made on my Christmas tree or arrange them in a centerpiece. They bring back memories of Christmases past, for these ornaments always adorned the trees in our house when I was growing up. Like most crafts we made in Girl Scouts, they held up well. At sixty-plus years old, don't they deserve heirloom status?

One year for Christmas, we pinned sequins, beads, and braid into medium-sized Styrofoam bells. Mother displayed the bell I made until in her nineties when she quit decorating for Christmas. I still hang that bell, now a little worn-looking, each Christmas.

Photos courtesy of Gerry O. Wood
Troop 11 made milk-bottle-top balls and decorated
Styrofoam bells for Christmas.

Several of us remember making candles that looked like Christmas trees: we poured hot green-tinted wax into cone-shaped molds. When the wax hardened, we removed the molds and stuck various shapes of sequins, beads, and braid into the wax with straight pins. We never burned my candle: my mother and I considered it too pretty to destroy.

Linda Heaton remembers making stuffed bunny brooches of pink felt. "That's when I learned how to do the embroidery blanket stitch," she says. These were to be pins for our mothers.

Each year, troop 11 girls made Christmas gifts for our parents. These treasures included decorated coffee mugs, etched glass goblets with "Mom" and "Dad" on them, hand-painted ceramic fish, etched and fluted aluminum trinket trays, and gold-painted Sucrets® lozenge tins.

Photo Courtesy of Earline Campbell Wood
The etched-glass goblets we made for "Dad" and "Mom."

The first difference Karyn remembers about being a Girl Scout is working on proficiency badges. "That's when we got serious and really earned all those badges. One would think Mrs. Elrod was receiving prize money the way she lined up so many activities for us to do to fulfill some badge requirement." Of course, we know Ellie wasn't getting compensated for her efforts. She just loved doing it. If she didn't *always* love doing it, she did it anyway, and we benefited.

Indeed, Mrs. Elrod seemed constantly to spawn ideas for badges and ways to earn them. Her creativity knew no limits. So all the girls filled the fronts of their badge sashes and some filled half the back side too. The sash, a four-inch-wide dark green fabric strip, draped across the right shoulder and hung over the left hip. Our mothers sewed on the colorful one-inch-diameter embroidered circles, making the sash real needlework art.

Photo courtesy of Earline Campbell Wood
Karyn Hudson's and Martha Still's badge sashes.

In the fall of 1953, troop 11 took cooking classes at the Lone Star Gas Company in downtown Fort Worth. In a state-of-the-art classroom/test kitchen, we made such delights as biscuits, cakes, spinach with cheese sauce, and hamburger patties with bacon bits. These classes helped us earn our cook badge. The aromas of baking biscuits and sizzling hamburgers made us eager to consume our culinary creations. I learned to like spinach: cheese sauce made it good. I still think cheese makes almost everything better.

Photo courtesy of Wanda Elrod Crowder
At Lone Star Gas Company cooking class, Beverly Wilson and
Linda Heaton discuss how much cinnamon to put on biscuits, as
Linda Simons and Wanda Elrod carry out their calculations. Linda
Kay Killian and Joyce Wakefield work in the background.

In 1954, troop 11 girls took roller-skating lessons at Moran's Skateland on Fort Worth's North Main Street. We learned to skate backward and forward and to assume a stability position to keep from falling when standing still. We also learned to "shoot the duck," a maneuver requiring the skater to squat with one leg suspended in front and skate forward on the other leg. We made short skating skirts for ourselves, with a lot of help from our moms. After we completed the class, we each received our skating badge.

I remember rushing home from skating class to watch singing idol Pat Boone on WBAP-TV's *Teen Times* show: the future movie and recording star, in college then, hosted the local Fort Worth show. Later, he made many hit records and several movies.

Today, Moran's Skateland no longer exists.

Every troop 11 girl remembers working on the photography badge. Mrs. Elrod turned her kitchen into a developing center, for these were the days of film photography.

"Did you ever wonder what the Elrod family did for meals during that time?" I once asked Ann. "Did they eat a lot of sandwiches? Did they dine out all the time? Did they eat a lot of carry-out Texas-style barbecue?"

Whatever their sacrifices, we successfully snapped our pictures, developed our film, printed our pictures, and even made picture Christmas cards for our families to send.

Photo courtesy of Linda Killian Wood
Jacque McNiel's Christmas card she made in
earning her photography badge.

During these Intermediate Girl Scout years, troop 11 began taking the many swimming classes that would culminate eventually in the swimmer, lifesaver, canoeing, and boating badges. At this young level, we took summer outdoor Red Cross swimming lessons at Fort Worth's Sylvania Park pool and winter indoor lessons at Texas Christian University's pool. We moved up through the ranks of Red Cross swimming, and all of us became proficient.

The troop also loved swimming at Girl Scout Camp Timberlake on Eagle Mountain Lake.

Photo courtesy of Wanda Elrod Crowder
Headed for swimming at Camp Timberlake are, bottom,
Linda Simons; second row, left to right, Wanda Elrod, Diane
Crawford, Beverly Wilson, Donna Throckmorton, and Linda
Kay Killian; top row, Karyn Hudson and Jacque McNiel.

We still remember one swimming adventure at Timberlake.
Wanda relates it.

> When we returned from swimming one day,
> we changed into our shirts and shorts and hung
> our swimsuits to dry on a rope strung between
> two trees. By the time we retrieved our suits the
> next day, a honeybee had taken residence in my
> swimsuit.
> It didn't start stinging me until we were on
> the road waiting for the bus to take us to the
> lake. I was embarrassed and didn't want to strip.
> Mama finally put a large towel around me, and I
> removed the suit.

The bee escaped.

Mama applied to the obvious sting something soothing from her ever-present first aid kit. I examined my suit for more bees, found none, and put the suit on again.

"Here comes the bus," Jacque announced. We climbed in, and the swimming outing continued as planned.

When we got back to camp, Mama applied more medicine to my sting. Fortunately, I wasn't allergic to bee venom.

Poor Wanda. She had some hard times at camp. She never lost her love for camping though.

After becoming Intermediate Girl Scouts, troop 11 began camping in earnest. Our leaders still did the lion's share of the planning and work, but we girls had to pitch in and do our part too. We learned how to build fires, cook food on them, make bedrolls, and assemble camping equipment we could carry. We learned to use our knives safely, to cover up with mosquito repellent, and to recognize and avoid poison ivy and poison oak.

Our leaders did a good job of getting us ready to go into the wilderness to camp—in summer in above-ground tents at Camp Timberlake and in winter in Twin Oaks Lodge, which had four enclosed walls and a fireplace, but no indoor bathroom facilities.

Riverside News staff photo
Some of troop 11's camp outings got coverage in the
Riverside News. Here Mrs. Jeanette Hudson helps Karyn
Hudson (standing) and Martha Still build a campfire.

Camping required us to learn basic knots for securing various items to one another. The square knot, the one we used for the yellow ties on our uniform, was the first knot we learned. It was a practical, all-purpose knot that served us well in many kinds of situations. To this day, my knot of choice for almost everything is a square knot.

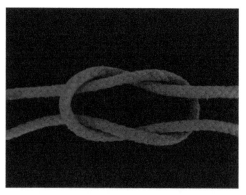

Photo courtesy of Gerry Odell Wood
The square knot.

But the square knot was only the beginning. We learned other rarely used knots.

One, however, the clove hitch, we used often in camping. It fastened a rope to a ring, post, or tree, and it kept boats from floating away and hammocks from falling.

Photo courtesy of Gerry Odell Wood
The clove hitch knot.

The first overnight winter camping trip troop 11 made to Camp Timberlake—the first one we recall anyway—turned out to be quite memorable indeed. This time, we stayed inside the Twin Oaks Lodge. All of us remember the incident.

It is Elaine's story, and she describes it like this:

> With bellies full of Campfire Stew and S'mores, the nine-year-olds of troop 11 huddled around the fireplace in their PJs, ready to be bedded down for the night. A blue Texas norther blew a howling cold wind outside the old lodge at Camp Timberlake.
>
> The unexpected drop in temperature made the outside latrine seem a million freezing miles away. Squeals of laughter rang through the shadowy old lodge, as Miz [sic] Elrod instructed her

girls in how to use the big enamel cooking pot she placed at the end of a row of cots. Each girl lined up for her turn to "tinkle" in the "potty."

The last little girl, dressed in a red flannel nightgown, was enjoying the kidding that her bright outfit evoked as she settled over the nearly-filled potty and contributed her share. Finishing, she sprang from her squat. The tail of the gown, which had caused so much ado, caught the lip of the potty, and what a mess we had!

I remember how Miz Elrod laughed about the mishap. I remember her asking why I had to be the last in line, but I don't remember her losing her good humor—not that time or any other.

Miz Elrod and Miz Still magically made the mess disappear (as they so often did through the years), and we continued with our first overnighter. We giggled, we sang, we told ghost stories. Wanda crooned "Baby's Boat," and we fell asleep by the fireplace where Miz Elrod and Miz Still kept the fire burning all night.

Photo courtesy of Wanda Elrod Crowder
Mrs. Minnie Ruth Elrod organizes troop 11's
cup rack at Twin Oaks Lodge.

Camping meant that we had duties to perform: it wasn't all fun. To distribute the duties equitably, our leaders used the aforementioned caper charts. When camping became more sophisticated, the jobs on the caper chart grew more rigorous. Typically, caper chart lists included the following:

- fire building (gathering wood, building correct type of fire, putting it out when finished, and leaving the area ready for the next fire),
- cooking (preparing and cooking food, setting table, serving food, and choosing the grace to be sung before the meal),
- cleanup (washing and putting away dishes, cleaning all cooking and eating areas, and leaving the area ready for the next meal), and
- cleaning latrines (cleaning sinks, showers, toilets, trash cans, adjoining area; assuring everything was working, turned off, and equipped with toilet paper and soap). When the "toilets" were just holes in a cabineted wooden shelf that opened into the sewer, we only had to clean the shelf and mop the floor.

While early Caper Charts were made of poster board, later Mr. Rudy Still, Martha's dad, made us another one of wood. We used the wooden chart throughout our troop's subsequent camping experiences. The wooden board employed the same rotating wheel, with removable masking tape indicating the groups and their appropriate jobs for the day or meal. Mr. Still lovingly built several items for the troop: he was a treasure.

Every girl did a turn at each chore and, depending on the length of the camp out, perhaps she performed the chores several times. Everybody got to do the more pleasant duties and had to do the not-so-pleasant ones, and we *did do* them all.

As camping became the favorite activity of most troop 11 girls, Campfire Stew and S'mores took their places as our perennial favorite menu choices.

We made Campfire Stew by dumping tin cans of food—each can with different contents and brought by one girl—into a big pot and cooking it all together. Before filling the pot, we soaped its outside to make cleanup easier.

We used ground beef, browned with onions, and drained. The meat was added last after a vegetable portion had been removed for Carole Capps, who disliked hamburger meat.

"I had to feed raw ground meat to my pet turtle, and the meat smelled so bad to me that I have never been able to eat hamburger," she explains.

The meat was always the same, but the stew contained different vegetables every time. The more exotic veggies, like okra, spinach, and hominy, usually were not included, because several of us didn't like them. Staples were vegetable soup, green beans, corn, pinto beans, and tomatoes. Chopped carrots, fresh or canned, and potatoes often were dumped in also. Cooked on an open fire and eaten outdoors, the stew was always yummy, satisfying to our taste buds and our tummies.

Ann and Martha and their families have Campfire Stew on camping trips today. I have fixed it for Wednesday night supper at our church in Los Alamos, New Mexico.

A similar camp meal included "tin-can casserole." We filled large coffee cans with seasoned browned hamburger meat, carrots, onions, and potatoes. One can was allotted to each girl. We placed the cans on the campfire until their contents cooked thoroughly. Then we pulled the cans out of the ashes with long tongs, let the cans cool enough to handle safely, and spooned out melt-in-your-mouth deliciousness.

Another variation was "hamburger stew in the coals." This stew used much the same ingredients. We tightly closed individual servings in foil squares and cooked the packages on the coals after a campfire had burned down. We ate the stew out of the cooled foil packets. Yum.

S'mores have been favorites with Brownies and Girl Scouts all over America for many years. In fact, their popularity is almost universal. Troop 11 was no different. This delicacy is always a crowd-pleaser, especially when the crowd sits shivering around a campfire. When troop 11 gathers for reunions in the twenty-first century, we still have a campfire at our bed-and-breakfast and eat S'mores. They're easy to make, warm, messy to eat, delicious—perfect for a camp outing with youngsters. Sticky fingers and lips lead to happy mouths and tummies. Included here is the recipe troop 11 has always used.

S'more *(serves 1)*

4 squares plain chocolate (thin)
2 squares graham crackers
1 marshmallow

Toast a marshmallow slowly over coals until brown. Put chocolate on a graham cracker, then the toasted marshmallow on top, then another graham cracker. Press gently together, and eat.

Recipe for S'mores, Girl Scout Troop 11 style.

Troop 11 always sang grace before meals. After trying several graces, we settled on "Johnny Appleseed" as our favorite. We hold hands, bow heads, and sing it at meals today—in restaurants, homes, picnics, or wherever.

> The Lord is good to me, and so I thank the Lord
> For giving me the things I need—
> The sun and the rain and the apple seed.
> The Lord is good to me.
> —Swedenborgian hymn, Johnny
> Appleseed's traveling song[17]

---

[17] Johnny Appleseed. February 7, 2014, in Wikipedia online. From Mae Beringer. "The Memory of Johnny Appleseed Lives On." Cornell University.

Wanda has a memory box with the Johnny Appleseed grace and apples painted on it. Elaine, our troop artist, made it for her.

Photo courtesy of Wanda Elrod Crowder
Wanda Elrod Crowder's memory box that
Elaine Walton Lofland made for her.

A favorite camping activity for troop 11 was drama night. Each tent of girls would plan and act out a skit for the evening's entertainment. Sometimes, when several troops were camping at Timberlake at the same time, all the troops did skits.

One of our troop's skits involved the traditional American folk song, "Pick a Bale of Cotton." We sang it with body actions and hand motions. And we knew how to act out picking cotton, as we had done this job once on a real cotton farm as a requirement for some milestone Mrs. Elrod had set for us.

Sometime in these Intermediate Girl Scout years, we began using an alphabetical telephone "chain" so that everyone would be informed or reminded of activities. One of the leaders called Marilyn Ball, Marilyn called Ann Brown, Ann called Earline Campbell, and so on all the way to Marilyn Weiss calling Beverly Wilson. Phone chain announcements included reminders of meetings, instructions on items to bring to events, and cancellations of activities. If, after two or three tries, you didn't reach your assigned person on the phone chain, you called the next person after that. We had no e-mail, Facebook, or answering machines in those days, but the phone chain worked reasonably well most of the time. Maybe we hadn't activated it at the time of the fourth-anniversary party, or maybe we activated it immediately *after* half of us showed up out of uniform.

As I look back on those particular years of Scouting, I see that we learned a little bit about a lot of things. Mrs. Elrod gave us the opportunity to explore many areas of life. Learning varied skills, however rudimentary, helped me decide what I would like to do in my life and what I didn't care to explore further. Troop 11's program helped develop the all-around girl. We all benefited from the diversity of projects we dabbled in, no matter what courses our lives took later.

And as for camping, while we troop 11 members mostly remember carefree happy days in the out-of-doors, Mrs. Elrod might recount more serious memories, such as her constant fear that a girl would get bitten by a snake. Thankfully, though, she never had to use her snakebite kit, except for that one incident with her own daughter.

CHAPTER 4

Senior Scouts: Trying to Grow Up

"Now I don't want to see you girls parading around in your nudidity.*"*

Troop 11 is on one of many weekend excursions to Camp Timberlake. The speaker is Mr. Jack McNiel, Jacque's dad. As he instructs us Scouts in proper female teen behavior, Jacque rolls her eyes and turns red.

"Oh, Daddy, please," she mutters under her breath, "this is the umpteenth time you've told us."

Mr. McNiel, a kind but outspoken no-nonsense veteran of World War II, wants us to learn modest behavior and consideration for the dads who are chaperoning the camping trip. He wants us to realize that we are not little girls any longer and that our womanhood is beginning to blossom. So he coins the new word, nudidity, *to impress on our minds that he means business.*

Ann Brown, appropriately impressed, incorporates nudidity *into her vocabulary and will use it for the rest of her life.*

* * * * *

It was 1955. Troop 11 had now been together six years. We were growing up, but we weren't doing it as fast as we thought we were.

Most of us had now reached the age of twelve. We were students at Riverside Junior High School in Fort Worth. We were beginning to get hooked on rock and roll, poodle skirts, and ponytails.

We had watched, both at Scout meetings and in public school physical education classes, the 1946 Walt Disney film *The Story of Menstruation*.[18] We had read the film's companion book, *Very Personally Yours*.[19] Most of us considered both the movie and the book to be rather stupid, but we got the point. Change was coming to our bodies. Some of us already had started our menstrual periods, and we were growing breasts and other feminine curves.

Hormones played havoc with us in other ways too. We were emotional. We didn't always get along well with each other. The seemingly most innocent word or look could be—and was—misunderstood, misinterpreted, and overreacted to. We had discovered boys. Some of us were becoming quite pretty and, consequently, were popular at school.

Troop 11 had progressed to be Senior Girl Scouts. The uniform was now a white blouse, with the inevitable yellow tie at the neck, and an A-line dark green skirt. The whole outfit was topped with the badge sash, which displayed more and more badges as time went on. On our heads, we wore a dark green flight or service cap similar to that worn by many military personnel. We pretended that we were airline stewardesses (now called flight attendants).

---

[18] *The Story of Menstruation* (Burbank, California: Walt Disney Productions and International Cellucotton Company, 1946).

[19] Marion Jones, ed. *Very Personally Yours* (Neenah, Wisconsin: Kimberly-Clark Corporation, 1946).

Photo courtesy of Donna Throckmorton Jones
Donna Throckmorton and Marilyn Ball in Senior Girl Scout
uniforms await the beginning of a ceremony at Camp Timberlake.

The uniform actually wasn't too bad, but a lot of us griped about it: we were not only Texas girls, but *teenage* Texas girls who were very style conscious. Some no longer wanted to wear our uniforms everywhere we went, and we for sure didn't wear them to school and troop meetings. The complaining reached such a level that Mrs. Minnie Ruth Elrod worried that some of the Scouts would leave the troop. She would solve the problem, but not just yet.

We now met weekly at the Elrod home on Aster Street. The house was located closer to the junior high and high schools than was the Methodist church so we could walk there more easily. We would gather at "Ellie's house" almost every week for six years: it would become a second home to us. It was especially a second home to me as I stayed with the Elrod family several times when my mother had to go out of town on business.

The troop continued to work on proficiency badges and make crafts, doing both with increasing sophistication. Each year brought a Christmas, and each Christmas meant a handmade gift for our families. We learned to value such gifts: they have love in them, not just money.

In the autumn of 1955, as seventh graders, troop 11 went to Clifford Herring Sound Studio, west of downtown Fort Worth, to make a seventy-eight rpm record to give our parents for Christmas. This was a world before compact disks and even cassette tapes. The phonograph record ruled our world. These records were a big, big deal to American teens of the 1950s.

We Scouts saw ourselves as exceedingly grown-up to be making a record. Who knew? Maybe Elvis Presley had started this way. We didn't yet know about Memphis and Sun Records.

On our record, we sang two Christmas carols, "O Little Town of Bethlehem" and "Silent Night," for the front side of the record. The flip side, as the back side of a record was called, contained two favorite Girl Scout songs, "Girl Scouts Together" (for the words, see page 14 of this book.) and "White Coral Bells," which we sang in a round.

White Coral Bells

White Coral Bells upon a slender stalk.
Lilies of the Valley deck my garden walk.
Oh, don't you wish that you might hear them ring?
That will happen only when the fairies sing.

The second song, sung in a round, on the flip side of our record.[20]

After we finished singing, each girl said her name; and in unison, we yelled a hearty "Merry Christmas!" Our voices sounded really

---

[20] Traditional English round. New York: Metropolitan Museum of Art Website, http://blog.metmuseum.org/cloistersgardens/2009/05/15/white-coral-bells/.

sweet and young, like elementary-school age, another indication that we were growing but not yet grown.

Today, most of us in troop 11 have no machine that plays a seventy-eight rpm record, so my husband Gerry used his computer skills to convert the record's contents to something we could all listen to on our computers. When we heard the production again after so many years, almost everyone agreed that the thing we loved most was hearing each girl say her name, especially the ones who are deceased and no longer with us.

Photo courtesy of Gerry Odell Wood
Troop 11's seventy-eight rpm record produced in 1955.

It was during this Senior Scout period that the Girl Scouts of Fort Worth and Dallas took a train trip to San Antonio, Texas, to visit several of that historic city's tourist attractions and watch the Texas Cavaliers River Parade on the San Antonio River. The Texas Cavaliers is a charitable organization that seeks to help those in need, especially children. Every year, the Cavaliers sponsor the river parade, which features more than forty-five decorated floats.

The trip began for us early in the morning at Fort Worth's Texas and Pacific Railroad passenger station, which sadly no longer provides passenger train service. Troop 11, dressed in our appropriately laundered and pressed uniforms, boarded a modern, comfortable silver train.

Photo courtesy of Wanda Elrod Crowder
Troop 11 waits to board a train at Fort Worth's Texas and Pacific Railroad passenger station. Faces shown are, front row, left to right, Margie Stoddard and Carole Capps; second row, Pat Cookus and Earline Campbell; third row, Martha Still and Mary Stoddard, left of Margie, Jacque McNiel right of Earline. The adult is my mother, Mrs. Esther Killian.

That train transported us the thirty-two miles to Dallas, where we transferred to an older train with seats that didn't adjust, restrooms that were dirty, and air-conditioning that didn't work well. We rode to San Antonio and back to Dallas on the "prehistoric train," as we called it. Actually, the train was probably early 1900s vintage, and we now pay premium prices to ride such a train in, say, Chama, New Mexico, or Durango, Colorado. On arriving back in Dallas late that night, we transferred again to the modern train for the short ride to Fort Worth.

We never figured out why the train transfer occurred. Did the railroad want to hide from Fort Worth parents the true condition of the train their children would ride on the twelve-plus-hour round trip to San Antonio? Did Fort Worth Scouts get a better deal than Dallas Scouts, who didn't get to ride a modern train? Whose idea was it to use the older train: the Dallas-Fort Worth Girl Scout councils or the railroad? It is a mystery troop 11 has never solved.

Photo courtesy of Linda Kay Killian Wood
Martha Still in Senior Scout uniform on the
"prehistoric" train to San Antonio.

But the uncomfortable train didn't mar our youthful enjoyment of the marathon day. The trip definitely imprinted fond memories in our heads.

After touring the ancient Alamo, we posed together for pictures in front of the famous battle site. Well, those of us who could be rounded up posed for the picture. Some were probably still in line at the gift shop to purchase souvenirs. I remember the line was r-e-a-l-l-y long.

Photo courtesy of Wanda Elrod Crowder
Troop 11 girls stand for a picture in front of the Alamo. We are, left to right, Linda Heaton, Linda Kay Killian, Wanda's younger sister Sharon Elrod, Martha Still, Marilyn Ball, Beverly Wilson, Ann Brown, Jacque McNiel, Wanda Elrod, Diane Crawford, Margie Stoddard, and Carole Capps. Pat Cookus, Joyce Wakefield, and Mary Stoddard also were there.

Next, we took a bus to the old Spanish Mission San Jose, where we marveled at the ornate Rose Window, and to the city's Breckenridge Park, where we visited the San Antonio Zoo and the Chinese Gardens. Back downtown, we explored the oddities of the historic Old West's Buckhorn Saloon, marveled at the gorgeous floats in the Texas Cavaliers "Festival of Lights" river parade, and clapped to the Mexican dances performed at the limestone amphitheater on the stage across the river from where we were sitting.

This excursion predated the building of the renowned San Antonio River Walk but nevertheless, we Scouts remember the whole experience as grand, simply grand.

As Senior Scouts, we continued to work on earning badges, but now the badge requirements were more sophisticated and more demanding.

Troop 11 girls, in addition to our own troop camping experiences, served as day-camp counselors in summers. One year, while doing this, we earned our pioneer badge.

First, we had to make hammocks to sleep in. Mrs. Elrod always worried about snakes, so we had to sleep at least three feet above ground. No sleeping bags were allowed, unless they lay atop hammocks. Each girl made her own hammock at the home of Karyn's mom, Mrs. Jeanette Hudson. We used thick, stiff ecru-colored canvas—sturdy and hard to sew through.

Ann remembers breaking several of Mrs. Hudson's sewing-machine needles, a possibility Mrs. Hudson undoubtedly prepared for by stocking extras.

Pat Cookus Haberman describes her hammock-constructing experience this way:

> Making the hammocks, oh my. I thought Mrs. Still was going to lose her mind during that process. She stood over me until mine was finished, but I'm sure she went straight home to bed afterward. We made the hammocks well enough to sleep in, though—even in the rain once, as I recall.

The hammocks had to be hemmed on both sides and both ends, then double-sewn on the ends. We threaded ropes through holes in the poles and the sides of the hammocks, then tied knots on both sides of each end of the poles. We left several feet of rope at both ends for attaching the hammocks to trees. We used the clove hitch knot to tie each hammock between two trees.

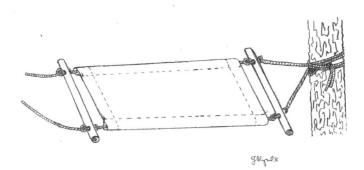

Illustration by Julia Sheppard
Hammock construction.

After constructing our hammocks, we wrote our names on them, rolled them up until they looked like large biblical scrolls, and tied them with the end ropes to be taken to West Farm.

Photo courtesy of Donna Throckmorton Jones
Carole Capps prepares to hang her hammock at West farm.

We slept in our hammocks, which held strong throughout the week of rustic camping: no hammock dumped out its occupant. More amazing, we slept well. Perhaps we were ultraexhausted when we retired for the night, or maybe our homemade sleeping accommodations really were comfortable.

Wanda Elrod and Karyn Hudson hung their hammocks close together. Wanda remembers it like this:

> We watched a "spacecraft" moving across the sky.
> We just lay there and talked and watched it.
>   Even though the idea of a weather balloon
> or whatever it was did enter our minds, the idea
> of an alien spaceship was more exciting.

She expresses an introspection to which all of us concur: "I loved our hammocks. I wish I still had mine. In my mind, it wouldn't be rotten."

We used our hammocks on other camp outs too.

Once Marilyn Ball "just laid a hatchet on Jacque's hammock rope," and the hatchet was so sharp, it cut the rope. Naturally, Jacque was in the hammock at the time. "I did not mean to cut it," Marilyn maintains to this day.

Photo courtesy of Donna Throckmorton Jones
Top to bottom, Beverly Wilson, Jacque McNiel, and Marilyn
Weiss enjoy an afternoon rest on their hammocks. Note
wooden poles at ends and ropes stretching to trees. The poles
kept the hammocks from folding up on us like cocoons.

Sleeping was one thing. Eating was another.

For this primitive camping trip and others to follow, we made Buddy Burners on which we could presumably cook our breakfast. Buddy Burners were large tin cans from juice, shortening, or coffee. We cut holes in the sides at the bottom and the top. We placed these large cans over small tuna cans filled with a long strip of corrugated cardboard coiled inside and covered with melted paraffin. When the paraffin was set on fire, heat escaped through the holes at the top of the larger can. The cans got extremely hot, and we could, if we were lucky, cook eggs, bacon, and pancakes on them. One Buddy Burner served two girls; hence, its name.

Photo courtesy of Gerry Odell Wood
A Buddy Burner with a pancake on top. We used tuna-can, paraffin and corrugated cardboard "candles" as the heat source inside the can.

Some of us remember Linda Heaton crying when she flipped her pancake, missed the top of her Buddy Burner, and deposited the pancake into the dirt. But she wasn't the only one to have trouble with cooking pancakes on the uncooperative cans.

Martha Still Littlefield recalls her personal nightmare:

Mastering the art of using the buddy burner—now that was a skill.

Keep in mind that pancake batter can be a little runny.

Beverly was my buddy. We learned quickly why the cans needed to be flat on the ground. When we finally got our can flat, we poured too much batter on it, and some spilled to the ground. We had some trouble, but we were getting better.

Jacque was next to us, and she thought she had it mastered. She took some of our batter and got Beverly's pancake done.

Everyone else went off to eat while I put the rest of the batter on to cook. What a wonderful smell and, oh, how hungry I was. I went to flip my pancake and, bingo, perfectly in the dirt.

Ellie to the rescue: silently, quickly a beautiful pancake appeared on my empty plate. I ate a perfect pancake that day and never forgot how much a helping hand can mean.

Martha also remembers an outing when Ann mostly covered the bottom of the kitchen sink at a Camp Timberlake lodge with paraffin from a Buddy Burner.

"Mrs. Elrod, I just spilled hot paraffin in the sink!" Ann moans.

"Okay, let's sing 'Taps,' and you can clean it up after," Ellie says.

"But I have to go home right now. My dad's in a hurry."

"Well, we'll see about it after 'Taps.'"

We girls make a circle and cross our hands to sing "Taps."

When the song is over, Ann quietly disappears and is nowhere to be found.

Mrs. Elrod asks Donna and Martha to clean up the now-hardened paraffin.

"Hey, look," Donna whispers, "we can carve pictures in the hard wax with a spoon handle." She carves a heart and puts an arrow through it.

Martha takes the spoon and makes a picture of a dog.

The girls are giggling and having fun drawing more pictures when Mrs. Still discovers what they are doing and orders them to clean up for real.

Ah, Mrs. Still, always, always the "bad cop."

Yes, the Buddy Burners provided many cooking adventures for our troop. Between outings, Mrs. Still kept the miniature stoves in her garage so they could be used often.

During the West Farm primitive camping expedition, we also used other utensils to cook. We cooked some of our meals on a campfire. Of course, the cast-iron pot over a traditional fire produced the inevitable and beloved Campfire Stew, a mainstay of any troop 11 camping trip.

We fished in Fossil Creek and even reeled in some fish big enough to eat, which we did. Mine, however, was a teeny little thing that had to be thrown back, much, I'm sure, to the relief of the poor fish. He or she was terrified: I could see it in his or her eyes.

We also made coals by burning wood branches. Then we cooked "hamburger stew in the coals" in the pit we had created.

We also baked peach cobbler in a reflector oven in the sun, though it did require an additional heat source: it was the most delicious cobbler we ever ate. We remember.

At camp, we took a "shower" at night. The makeshift shower stall comprised lengths of brown burlap wrapped around three trees. We crawled under the burlap "walls" to get inside and crawled under again to get out. We had to dress and undress in the "shower." Water came from large tin coffee or juice cans: after soaping her body, each girl poured water over herself in a hopeful attempt to rinse off. The water was cold, but it *was* summer in Texas, so none of us got frostbite. We each were allowed two cans of water—one to wet ourselves and one to rinse. We learned to use the soap sparingly.

Troop 11 spent the entire week at West Farm, teaching classes and otherwise supervising younger Scouts and Brownies during the day and then camping out at night.

Fort Worth *Star-Telegram* staff photo
At Girl Scout day camp, Wanda Elrod, center front,
teaches a Brownie how to tie a square knot. Left to right,
Karyn Hudson, Marilyn Ball, Jacque McNiel, Donna
Throckmorton, Linda Heaton, and Beverly Wilson watch.

Everything considered, troop 11 has happy memories of that week camping at West Farm. We learned to do things we'd never dreamed we could do or wanted to do. We taught skills to younger Scouts. We survived living in the open—actually enjoyed it.

As Senior Scouts, the entire troop earned our Curved Bar Rank, and we did it all together as a troop. Mrs. Elrod saw to that. The Curved Bar was the highest rank in Girl Scouting at that time, and a candidate had to complete specific requirements to attain it. The *Girl Scout Handbook* lists those requirements as:

1. Complete the first-class rank.
2. Earn at least four badges from one of the following groups, none of which you earned before.[21]

The four categories were the arts, citizenship, homemaking, and out-of-doors.

We aren't agreed now about the category in which we completed our requirements, the reason being that we earned badges in each group. The consensus is, though, that out-of-doors was our official selection. Within the out-of-doors classification, we met requirements for campcraft, outdoor cook, pioneer, adventurer, and explorer badges.

It was unusual then and now that the whole troop earned this highest Girl Scouting award as a group. The award is now called the Gold Award, and a girl does a special community service project to earn it, much like the Eagle Scout Rank in Boy Scouting. Rarely, if ever, do entire troops attain the rank at the same time. Wanda says:

> It was very important to my mother for all of troop 11 to receive the Curved Bar together. She had somewhat the motto of "No girl left behind." This was extremely important to her. If even one girl was ready

---

[21] Curved Bar Rank Requirements, *Girl Scout Handbook: Intermediate Program*, 1953 ed. (New York: Girl Scouts of the U.S.A.), 106–07.

to receive an award, Mother waited to acknowledge it until all the girls were ready to receive it.

Now in our seventies, we continue to do many things together as an entire group. Perhaps we got the idea from the Curved Bar experience.

Curved Bar pin as it was in the late 1950s. It was the highest rank in Girl Scouting at that time.

Upon receiving the Curved Bar award, troop 11 again posed for a picture to be published in the Fort Worth *Star-Telegram*.

The Senior Scout period too was when some girls performed their most notable antics.

Jacque developed a reputation for short-sheeting the beds of her tent mates.

Joyce Wakefield took to signing her name as Nosmo King (no smoking).

Ann convinced Carole Capps that if she continued to drink the juice out of olive jars, her blood would dry up.

"I believed her because, of course, she was always smarter than I was," Carole quips.

Then there were the numerous camp stories.

Once Margie and Mary Stoddard and Donna Throckmorton slept in a Western Unit covered-wagon tent at Camp Timberlake. They awoke to find a mouse perched on Margie's toe. Their screams drove the mouse to safety and awakened the rest of us.

Fort Worth *Star-Telegram* staff photo
Troop 11 posed after receiving the Curved Bar rank. We are,
front row, Carole Capps; second row, left to right, Ann Brown,
Beverly Wilson, Donna Throckmorton, Mary Stoddard, Linda
Kay Killian, Joyce Wakefield, and Earline Campbell; third row,
Diane Crawford, Wanda Elrod, Martha Still, Marilyn Ball, Linda
Simons, Linda Heaton, Margie Stoddard, Karyn Hudson, and
Jacque McNiel. Not pictured are Marilyn Weiss, Linda Booker,
Elaine Walton, and Pat Cookus, who also earned this award.

When we learned to change a car tire at camp, Linda Booker
swore she'd never be a mechanic. The tires *were* heavy, and Booker
became a schoolteacher, not a mechanic.

If there was a leftover dessert at camp, we troop 11 girls played
a game to see who could claim the goody. The game was Ein, Zwei,
Drei, Horsengoggle. Everyone stands in a circle with fists pointing
into the circle. When the counselor says, "Horsengoggle," the partic-
ipants throw out a number of fingers. The counselor adds the number of fingers in the circle, counts around the circle from a person
designated as the beginning point, and awards the dessert (or other
prize) to the person who is in the number position of the finger total.
Complicated, but fair.

Another favorite camp game was Spoons, a Crazy-Eights-type draw-and-discard game in which the first person to get four matching cards (aces, kings, queens, or the like) picks up a spoon from a pile in the center. When the first person grabs a spoon, everyone else scrambles to claim the others. The pile of spoons contains one less spoon than the number of players. The person left without a spoon gets an S. When a person gets all the letters in SPOON, she is out of the game. The game continues until only one player, the winner, is left. Troop 11 likes to play Spoons at our reunions, and the game gets as rowdy as ever. Watch out for your fingers: you might lose one in the melee.

At week-long troop camp one year, Joyce, Elaine Walton, Diane Crawford, and Wanda formed an "exclusive" club called the Doodlebugs. Elaine remembers it as Doojibugs. They camped in the same tent, had their own Doodlebug jewelry pins, and wrote their own club song. They gathered wood and built fires together.

"Our club song was a little bit ugly to others," Wanda remembers, "saying, 'We have more fun than you ever can.' I don't think it bothered anyone very much: they pretty much ignored it. And I don't think anybody else particularly wanted to be in our club."

Photo courtesy of Wanda Elrod Crowder
The Doodlebugs—Joyce Wakefield, Diane Crawford, Elaine Walton, and Wanda Elrod—build a fire at Camp Timberlake.

Photo courtesy of Martha Still Littlefield
The Doodlebugs at troop 11's fiftieth anniversary. Left to
right are Diane Crawford Hill, Wanda Elrod Crowder,
Joyce Wakefield Burks, and Elaine Walton Lofland.

In the last year of our Senior Scout period, the Soviet Union launched the first-ever space satellite, Sputnik. That event rocked our world. The Soviets were ahead of the United States in the space race, and a frightened America made preparations to try to catch up. With the Cold War always in the back of our minds, Girl Scout Troop 11 marched on through their teens.

We learned many varied things in those Senior Scout years. We began learning how to cope with growing up. We learned to take responsibility and handle it reasonably well. We, more or less, learned how to handle our hormones. Although somebody was almost always in a tiff about something, we mostly learned how to get along with each other and "get over it."

And, thanks to Mr. McNiel, we learned not to "parade around in our *nudidity*."

CHAPTER 5

Taking Classes: Galaxies to Glamour

It's troop 11's 2012 reunion on the anniversary of our sixty-third year together. We have just finished our tour of Fort Worth's Amon Carter Museum of American Art. We viewed the special traveling exhibit, "To See as Artists See: American Art from the Phillips Collection," and the museum's permanent collection of Charles Russell and Frederick Remington paintings and sculptures. We soaked up a pot-load of culture.

As always, we are dressed appropriately in fashionable pants outfits. We feel pretty good about ourselves.

The museum is on a hill west of downtown and presents probably the best panoramic view anywhere of the Fort Worth skyline. A succession of steps leads down from the museum to the parking lot.

We are about to descend the steps when Carole Capps Steadham reminds us to step sideways as we go down.

"What?" we ask in chorus.

Carole is aghast. "Don't you remember from our modeling class? You are always supposed to walk down a flight of stairs sideways: it's the proper way, and, besides, it's safer."

We do not remember, but, in deference to what we are sure is her infallible memory, we all float down the steps with our feet firmly planted sideways on each step. Surely everyone who happened to be in the parking lot was impressed with our proper form and elegance—and that none of us fell flat on our faces.

* * * * *

Girl Scout Troop 11 took a variety of classes together in our twelve years of public school. I have already mentioned the cooking course at the Lone Star Gas Company, the roller-skating class at Moran's Skateland, and the numerous swimming classes in various locations. Those were just a few of our educational endeavors.

Mrs. Elrod never ran out of ideas for learning opportunities, and I can't say that I ever regretted participating in any of them. In fact, I think the variety of things we delved into helped me develop the broad background of knowledge needed for a career in communication. I don't know *a lot* about a lot of things or even a lot about a few things, but I know *a little* about a lot of things, and such knowledge gave me head starts on conversations, interviews, or research into subjects I needed to write about. I am so grateful for being introduced to the different subjects we studied as Girl Scouts: the variety proved to be excellent preparation for my future life and work.

What did we learn that was so valuable?

Well, we're all rather good cooks, though Diane Crawford Hill and I have given up cooking in our "maturity." We didn't learn to make Campfire Stew in the Lone Star Gas Company cooking class, but we did expand our repertoire a bit.

I love to watch ice-skating on TV or in person. In fact, I talked my husband into taking me to the 2002 Olympics in Salt Lake City, where we witnessed America's Timothy Goebel win a bronze medal in the men's singles final. My teen experiences on roller skates taught me to appreciate the difficulty of the positions, moves, and jumps world-class ice-skaters perform—on blades, not rollers. I can also tell the difference between a triple axel jump and a triple lutz.

And the swimming classes? Well, I believe that if we are ever on a cruise ship—as Linda Heaton Leonhardt often is—and there's an accident, most of us can probably tread water until we're saved or manage to swim to shore if we're near a shore. That's assuming, of course, that we're not in icy waters like those in which the *Titanic* sank.

In one of the classes we took, the sky was truly the limit. We took an astronomy class at Fort Worth's Forest Park under the excellent tutelage of Mrs. Charlie Mary Noble, for whom the city's Noble Planetarium is named. She was undeniably Fort Worth astronomy royalty, and we were privileged to study under her.

In this class, we learned about the Southern summer constellations and how to spot them. The only one I'm still able to identify with complete certainty is the Big Dipper, but maybe with a little refresher course, I could probably also find some others.

The main thing I do remember from the class was the shadow boxes we made from shoeboxes. We made "slides" from cardboard, each one punched with holes in the shape of a constellation. We partially cut one end out of the box and placed a "slide" in the hole. A flashlight inside the box behind the slide illuminated the constellation when viewed from outside. The box lid was placed on top. The shadow box worked really well at night or in a dark room.

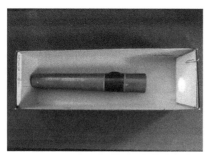 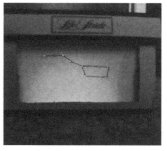

Photos courtesy of Gerry Odell Wood
Astronomy class-made shadow box with "slide" showing the Big Dipper.

Elaine Walton made her box and carried it through several transfers on a Fort Worth city bus, presenting it intact at astronomy class.

Another benefit of the class for me is that I can at least ask intelligent questions when my husband, Gerry, gets to talking about astronomy, one of his interests, and when he comes home excited about something he's learned in an astrophysics class.

A completely different class was the sewing class we took at the Singer Sewing Machine Company in downtown Fort Worth.

In this class, we made our own sewing kits from cardboard cigar boxes. We covered the boxes with scrap fabric, usually a print, and lined them with contrasting fabric, most often a solid color. Then we put our scissors, pincushion, tape measure, thimble, and hand-sewing needles inside the box for carrying to and from class.

Photo courtesy of Martha Still Littlefield
Martha Still's sewing box made for class at Singer Sewing Machine Company. The fabric-covered cigar box held sewing notions as pictured.

I used my sewing box until it wore out, but I followed it with a succession of similar boxes that have served me well right up to the present.

But the most important thing we learned in the sewing class was how to use a sewing machine. We threaded machines and their bobbins, sewed more or less straight seams, and assembled simple garments. Our most prized accomplishment was the dark green skirts we made and wore as part of our Senior Girl Scout uniforms.

Photo courtesy of Martha Still Littlefield
Troop 11 girls pose by our sewing machines upstairs at Fort Worth's Singer Sewing Machine Company. They are, left to right, front row, seated, Linda Kay Killian, Wanda Elrod, and Ann Brown; standing, left to right, Jacque McNiel, Beverly Wilson, Marilyn Ball, Linda Simons, and Martha Still. Sadly, we have forgotten the teacher's name.

What did I personally take away from this class? For years, I made my own clothes, my children's clothes, Christmas decorations, and many gifts. The first major purchase Gerry and I bought after our marriage was a sewing machine. I prefer to spend my time on other things now, but I continue to mend items other people would likely throw away. I also help with our church's prayer quilt ministry.

And don't forget that we Girl Scouts later made hammocks for our camping trips, hammocks that really did hold together for multiple nights of sleeping. In addition, the hammocks and the astronomy class allowed Wanda Elrod and Karyn Hudson to lie next to each other, name the stars, and imagine an alien spaceship flying over.

So, hurrah for the rudimentary skills we learned in this Singer Sewing Machine Company class that started us off on the grand sewing adventure.

Sewing machines and habits have changed a lot in sixty years, and the downtown Fort Worth Singer Sewing Machine Company does not exist today. Companies that sell sewing machines and parts now are located mostly in the city's suburbs.

To prepare us for public service projects we would later perform, we took a first aid class at the Elrod home. We learned how to make and use a triangular bandage, treat burns, splint a broken limb, and even treat a snakebite.

For our final exam, the instructor asked each girl a random question about how to treat a particular malady. The girl demonstrated the correct procedure on another Scout. If a girl needed to apply a particular bandage, she would have to know which one, demonstrate how to fold it, and correctly put it on a "patient."

My question was, "Your friend has been bitten by a poisonous snake. What do you do?" My injured "friend" was Pat Cookus. I pretended to cut slits in her leg with a knife and to suck the venom out of her leg and spit it out of my mouth. The idea was that snake venom was not poisonous to the mouth but was poisonous to the blood. Pat was glad that I didn't actually cut her leg, suck on it, or spit on her, and I passed the test. First aid instructors today would cringe at the idea that cutting flesh and sucking was ever actually taught in the 1950s. Medical advances do occur as time goes by.

Today, the patient would be kept lying supine and still with the feet elevated about twelve inches. The aid worker would cover the wound with sterile bandages or make a loose splint to keep the area immobile. One should monitor the victim's vital signs, and if the area around the wound is swelling and changing color, try to suck the venom out with a pump created for that purpose. In other words, have Mrs. Elrod's snakebite kit handy. If possible, it's best to wait for emergency personnel to arrive. The bite of a venomous snake will require antivenin treatment and a tetanus shot.[22,23]

Some of our classes were fun, practical, and artistic.

Such a class was flower arranging. A member of Riverside Garden Club taught this one. When the garden club held its autumn show, each troop 11 girl made a flower arrangement to enter in the competition. Jacque McNiel, Martha Still, Wanda Elrod, and Linda Heaton won first-place ribbons for their arrangements.

Photo courtesy of Wanda Elrod Crowder
Linda Heaton, Wanda Elrod, Martha Still, and Jacque McNiel pose with their winning flower creations displayed on middle shelf.

22 "Snakebite Treatment," WebMD Website, http://www.webmd.com/first-aid/snakebite-treatment.

23 "Snake bites," MedicinePlus Website, http://www.nlm.nih.gov/medlineplus/ency/article/000031.htm.

Ceramics, another fun class, we took at the Fort Worth Recreation Department.

Most of us made and painted some kind of fish. Martha's sailfish reside today in her vacation house at Possum Kingdom Lake. My flounders remained in my mother's bathroom for fifty-five years.

Photo courtesy of Martha Still Littlefield
The sailfish Martha Still made hang on the wall in her lake house.

Mrs. Elrod must have really enjoyed the ceramic and flower-arranging classes herself. Perhaps these classes were the beginning of her successful florist and ceramist career after her days as Girl Scout leader were done.

When troop 11 members went to visit her in Florida in 2003, her friends, the "Keenagers," a church organization Ellie had organized, showed us the floral arrangements and ceramic pieces she had taught them to make. They sold their creations to benefit charity, and we each bought something to help out.

Ellie didn't have any ceramic pieces on display that day, so I bought a cream-colored, green-dotted teapot and matching mug from one of her friends. I display and treasure this set as a beautiful remembrance of Ellie and that last special time we had with her and her friends.

Photo courtesy of Gerry Odell Wood
The handmade ceramic teapot and cup purchased by Linda
Kay Killian Wood on troop 11's 2003 Florida trip.

And finally came the grooming and modeling classes.

We took a class on makeup and hairstyling from a professional hairdresser. She taught us to apply makeup so as to enhance our natural beauty and not look "painted."

Also in that beauty class, we learned about different shapes of faces people have and the hairstyle that looks best on each one. As we were Texas belles, we paid attention to these beauty lessons and tried hard to apply the information we received.

Though page-boy hairstyles were quite the thing in Texas for girls in our teen years, some of us had the nerve to wear short hairstyles on slender faces and longer styles on round faces, as we were taught in this class. If we had high foreheads, we chose bangs to give the illusion of a shorter face. But ponytails hardly ever waned in popularity.

The modeling class we took at a studio in downtown Fort Worth. None of us can remember the name of the studio, and it's most likely not there anymore. So many such businesses have left downtown for the suburbs.

Yes, we learned to stand tall and hold our shoulders back—no slouching allowed.

Yes, we learned how to walk with books on our heads so as to hold up our chins.

Yes, we learned the proper model stance with the heel of one foot backed up into the middle of the other foot so as to provide graceful and secure balance.

Yes, we learned to sit like ladies—with our knees always together, either crossed or uncrossed, but always together. And no slouching while sitting either.

Yes, we learned to gesture gracefully with our hands, like the queen of England.

Yes, we learned to look people in the eyes when we talk to them and to smile.

And, yes, as Carole insists, we learned to walk down stairs sideways.

Photo courtesy of Wanda Elrod Crowder
Even doing dishes in Carole Capps Steadham's kitchen in 1996,
Pat Cookus Haberman assumes a proper model stance.

Photo courtesy of Wanda Elrod Crowder
Wanda Elrod Crowder and Linda Heaton Leonhardt sit
correctly at a troop 11 gathering in 1996, so perhaps the
modeling class was a success. Ann Brown Fields also was
sitting properly, but she leaned over to be in the picture.

Obviously, the classes we took in Girl Scouting proved useful to
us in our lives after active Scouting days ended. We had dabbled in
several things, each one leaving its bit of knowledge with us to use in
our future lives. I, for one, was glad that Scouting for troop 11 wasn't
only camping and knots. In addition to the actual knowledge gained
in the classes, I gained the confidence to try new things.

And, yes, from now on, I intend to remember to walk down
steps sideways. Texas belle that I am and always will be, I want to
seem poised, refined, and elegant. Besides, it might prove disastrous
for a woman in her seventies to tumble headfirst down a flight of
steps and smash into whatever lies at the bottom of the stairs, be it
wood floor or cement sidewalk or paved parking lot. I need no broken bones, thank you.

CHAPTER 6

Public Service: Bedpans and Birdcages

It is a summer afternoon in 1958 at Fort Worth's Cook Children's Hospital.

In the 1950s, Cook Children's is not the multi-facility medical giant that it will become—a center serving a geographic area larger than New Mexico and sick children from across the country.

No, in the 1950s, Cook Children's is one small semicircular, two-story Italian Renaissance building that looks more like a setting for a garden party than a seventy-two-bed medical treatment facility. The attractive building is situated in a wooded area on West Lancaster Street, and its very appearance promises comfort, serenity, and tranquility to its ailing patients.

Diane Crawford, Ann Brown, and Linda Heaton are downstairs cleaning birdcages. They are fifteen years old. The day will come when they will gleefully point out to the rest of us that they are the youngest ones in troop 11, but today they aren't so thrilled about that fact because they need to be sixteen years old to work on the floors with the patients.

"I wonder what the others are doing upstairs," Diane says as she reaches into a canary's cage.

"*Probably having a lot more fun,*" Ann responds. *She is eyeing the scattered brown bird seed and white bird excrement adorning the bottom of her parakeet's cage.*

Heaton's canary isn't singing a pleasant tune, and it won't let her catch him to put him in a holding cage while she cleans up his mess and gives him fresh food and water. He knows the drill; he's been through it all before.

"*Oh, squawk, squawk. Come here and cooperate,*" *she orders him.*

"*I wish I were sixteen,*" *Ann says.* "*Then I could work upstairs and do more important stuff.*" *One-handedly she grabs the newspaper from the bottom of her parakeet's cage and carefully folds it so the contents won't spill. When she has the paper small enough to suit her, she slowly maneuvers it out through the miniscule cage door.*

Diane's canary nips her on the finger. "*Ouch! You brat! Keep your beak to yourself! Hasn't anybody taught you any manners?*"

Finally, she manages to grab him and pull him through his cage door. She places him in his "holding cell" and slams the door in his face, wrinkling her nose in response to his angry eyes. Failing to find blood on her sore finger, she sucks on it.

"*I never knew birds were so messy,*" *Heaton comments as she tackles a particularly crusty piece of poop on the inside edge of the cage.* "*He completely missed the paper with this deposit.*"

"*Wouldn't it be nice if we could teach them to use toilets?*" *Ann says.* "*It would make our lives so much easier.*"

"*Fat chance,*" *Heaton retorts.*

Diane has just about had it with her cantankerous bird, who continues to squawk at her with murder in his eyes. She puts her hands on her hips and asserts, "I'm never going to have a bird!"

But, at a later time, she does get one: it is a green-and-yellow parakeet named Tweety, and she does lovingly clean his cage.

* * * * *

Girl Scout Troop 11 performed our share of public service projects in our twelve years of active troop participation. Our leaders wanted us to learn that, while none of us could have been considered rich, other people existed who were much less fortunate than we were. And these women wanted us to develop sympathetic hearts for suffering people.

As Intermediate Scouts, we helped with citywide recycling drives. This was in a time long before recycling became popular or considered necessary. Most people hadn't begun to think about reusing waste materials yet. We traversed our neighborhoods collecting used glass bottles, cans, and newspapers. By so doing, we helped clean up the areas we lived in, provided materials for recycling, and eliminated some waste. It was a save-the-environment push way ahead of its time, and it probably helped make us become more environmentally conscious as adults.

Photo courtesy of Wanda Elrod Crowder
Girl Scout Troop 11 waiting to place gathered recycle materials on a truck for transporting the items to a recycling center. The girls are, left to right, front row, Carole Capps, Martha Still, Jacque McNiel, Linda Simons, Linda Kay Killian, Margie Stoddard, and Beverly Wilson; second row, Ann Brown; third row, Karyn Hudson, Elaine Walton, Donna Throckmorton, Marilyn Weiss, Linda Heaton, Wanda Elrod, Joyce Wakefield, and Pat Cookus.

When we grew older and were Senior Scouts, troop 11 public service projects became more frequent, more difficult, and more complicated.

One afternoon, Mrs. Minnie Ruth Elrod and several parents transported us all to a local-area farm, where we picked cotton for several hours. We didn't do it the modern way with machines. We did it by hand with long burlap sacks placed over our shoulders and trailing behind us as we plodded down the rows. Visualize scenes from the movie *Gone with the Wind*. The bags were heavy, scratchy, smelly, unwieldy, and often snagged on the cotton plants as we inched forward. Needless to say, we complained a lot, both mentally and verbally.

The goal was for each girl to pick nine pounds of cotton that afternoon.

The cotton fiber grows around a seed on the plant until the protective hull bursts, and white fluff oozes out. At this point, the cotton can be picked and taken to a cotton gin for removing the fiber from the rest of the boll. Then the fluffy fiber goes to a textile mill for weaving into cloth.

That day, we picked the white cotton bolls one by one: the hull parts had stickers on them and scratched our hands and arms. We had to bend over constantly, and soon our backs hurt. The Texas sun was hot beating down on us, and we got very thirsty. We thought about singing the folk song, "Pick a Bale of Cotton," but soon we were too tired to consider singing anything. We would save the song for drama night at camp. This was agonizing work, and we wouldn't come anywhere close to picking a bale that day.

But the most disappointing thing for me was that when my cotton sack was weighed, I'd only picked eight pounds. I wanted to cry. I'd worked so hard and still hadn't reached my goal. Wanda Elrod, however, picked ten pounds, so I guess that made up for me.

Maybe the "cotton-pickin'" cotton-picking exercise gave some help to the farmer who owned that field, but I suspect Mrs. Elrod mainly wanted us to learn how hard farm work is. Today cotton is, of course, mostly picked by machine, which, I would think, makes the job easier and faster.

I know that I, for one, never again wore a garment containing some percentage of cotton without remembering the discomfort I endured in the cotton field that day and without being grateful for the workers who made my clothes possible. I no longer take for granted anything that comes from a farm because I know people have worked hard to produce it. If all of us Scouts feel that way, Mrs. Elrod accomplished her purpose in making us aware.

Another public service project we did was to make stuffed dogs for the orphans at Lena Pope Home for children in west Fort Worth. Yes, we'd had our Singer sewing class, but that didn't mean we were up to doing the twists and turns on a sewing machine to make little legs, ears, noses, and tails of stuffed dogs.

It was an interesting experience, probably the *most* interesting for Mrs. Elrod and Mrs. Thelma Still. Somehow, the two women had managed to gather several sewing machines, tables, and chairs, and organize a minisewing factory in a room of Mrs. Still's house. Just the organizing was amazing, but the executing of the project was absolutely arduous. The leaders had chosen what they thought was a simple pattern that we novice seamstresses could follow. Maybe, maybe not.

There we gathered. Some girls were assigned to cut out material from patterns, others assembled the cut pieces on the machines, and still others stuffed the animals and finished them by hand-sewing. This last group turned the animals right-side-out, stuffed them with cotton batting, sewed up the seams on their tummies, and attached buttons for eyes and felt tongues where the dogs' mouths were supposed to be.

I was one of the Scouts assigned to assemble the animals on a sewing machine. I had considerable trouble turning the fabric under the machine needle to make the legs of equal size. Attaching the ears was no picnic either: they had to be equal-sized and balanced on the sides of the face. Some of my dogs had short, fat tails, while others had long, skinny tails. Some had one long leg and three short ones or three long legs and one short one.

Jacque McNiel, who was on the stuffing crew, let me know about the flaws in clear terms. "These are going to be awfully strange-looking dogs, Linda Kay."

"Well, you be sure you get two buttons the same color for the eyes," I retorted as I rubbed the finger I'd managed to puncture under the sewing machine needle.

Most of the dogs, when standing, looked lopsided. The unequal-sized ears were unevenly spaced on each side of their foreheads. The stuffing jobs were lumpy and amateurish. Needless to say, we didn't put the Ideal Toy Company out of business. In reality, the pups were rather sad-looking, but we did make eighteen of them for the orphans and delivered them to the Lena Pope Home.

We could only hope that these precious little kids weren't picky about how great their stuffed doggies appeared. We wanted our creations to bring some joy to the children. We really did try our best, but at this stage, our best simply wasn't so great. Nevertheless, our leaders expressed pride in us for our efforts and lovingly took the dogs to the orphans' home. I don't recall that we received overwhelming expressions of gratitude from the kids. Oh well. That's not hard to understand.

Sewing wasn't something we all took to, but it did turn out to be "my thing." The day would come when I would make stuffed animals for my own children. They loved them and slept with them until, after several years, the poor little creatures fell apart. Maybe at least some of the orphans felt the same way about the stuffed dogs we made. As I say, we can hope.

Perhaps we should have taken the orphans a pot of our famous Campfire Stew instead. *That* we knew how to make, and it would have tasted good. They would have liked it.

Our next stitching endeavor would be our hammocks, and that would wrap up troop 11 sewing.

But the ultimate service project was working as nurses' aides at Cook Children's Hospital. The first aid class helped, and we received on-the-job training at the hospital. We learned how to make beds with hospital corners, wash bedpans, and feed patients.

This project required yet another uniform—a one-hundred-percent cotton persimmon-colored jumper dress with a white blouse underneath. The outfit was similar to the red-and-white candy-striper ones used in later years. We wore little pointed nurse caps on our heads. We had to wear closed-toe shoes, and in those days, that often meant saddle oxfords or penny loafers.

We looked like nurses, and we felt like nurses. We embraced this project with enthusiasm.

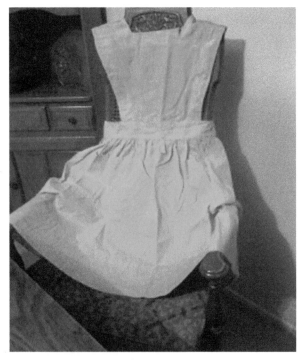

Photo courtesy of Earline Campbell Wood
Martha Still's nurses' aide uniform.

Cook Children's had a rule that no one under sixteen years old could work on the hospital floors with patients, so those who weren't yet sixteen got stuck in the basement cleaning birdcages. The birds undoubtedly brought joy to the young patients at the hospital, but the girls who had to clean the birds' cages didn't appreciate their feathered "friends" very much or enjoy those cleaning jobs. Indeed, they still complain today.

As for us older troop 11 members, we didn't think working on "the floor" was so marvelous either. We had to wash bedpans, change patients' clothes and bed linens after they had vomited or defecated on them, and bathe patients who had vomited or defecated. Sometimes we got to wheel the book cart from room to room and read to the children, and that was fun. Sometimes we delivered flowers and gifts to them: seeing their smiles was rewarding. And sometimes we actually were asked to help nurses and doctors with procedures they performed—holding their supplies and handing them things.

And sometimes our hearts were broken by the suffering we saw.

To this day, Wanda Elrod Crowder tears up when she talks about a little baby who was having an emergency procedure performed.

"I was rocking the screaming baby, and it had gone to sleep. I can see that they felt I was spoiling it, but the baby had no parents there: it was alone and hurting."

A nurse took the baby from Wanda and put it back in the crib. Wanda left the room, and the baby began to cry again. "The doctors and nurses wouldn't let me in the room. The baby just cried and cried. It was so sad. I'll never forget it."

Karyn Hudson Draper remembers being asked to change the diaper of a tiny infant who had a tube going into her head.

"I was so afraid that I'd cause the tube to come out."

She was also asked to help change bandages on a burn victim. This involved removing old bandages that covered most of the child's body, then laying hot bandages from a sterilizer on the exposed wounds. Karyn remembers fearing that the hot bandages would cause more pain to the child. Our nurse Scout, Marilyn Ball Murray, says this procedure is not used today. Rather, treatment includes briefly applied cool compresses, aloe vera and other soothing preparations, and frequent changing of gauze bandages.

So, birdcage cleaners, just so you know, we didn't have a lot of "fun" on the patient floors either.

Nevertheless, we thought that we were filling a need. None of us has ever forgotten the skills and compassion we learned while doing this particular public service project. I can still make hospital corners on a bed, though I rarely do them.

It was anticlimactic and definitely not as important as the help we rendered or the lessons we learned, but in serving as nurses' aides, we earned two more merit badges: first aid and home nurse.

Troop 11 performed other public service projects too. Mrs. Elrod frequently signed us up to sing at a dedication of some local memorial, to usher at some charity show, or to help with some neighborhood fund-raiser. These projects certainly didn't harm us any because in the process we learned to compassionately care about helping others—something it never hurts for teenagers, who can tend to be self-centered, or anyone else to learn.

Today we are all involved from time to time in public service activities of various kinds. In her early seventies, Ann participates in charity biking marathons in Austin. I help with Hope Pregnancy Center fund-raisers in Los Alamos. Almost every one of us do charitable work through our churches. We maintain a Minnie Ruth Elrod Endowment Fund to help needy Girl Scouts participate in camp activities. And, of course, we all try to be there for each other when we have health or other needs. We learned the sensitivity and compassion for others that our leaders wanted us to learn. They would be happy.

"On my honor, I will try to do my duty to God and my country, *to help other people at all times*, to obey the Girl Scout Laws."[24]

Even if it means cleaning birdcages and bedpans.

---

[24] The Girl Scout Promise in the 1950s, *Girl Scout Handbook: Intermediate Program*, 1953 ed. (New York: Girl Scouts of the U.S.A.), ii.

CHAPTER 7

Adventures in Cookie Selling

Linda Heaton is selling Girl Scout cookies with her younger sister Jo Marie. They approach a house and ring the doorbell. Their mother is waiting for them in her car.

Local children's television personality Bobby Peters comes to the door. Heaton recognizes him and feels like fainting, but she manages to sputter out her practiced cookie-selling spiel.

Peters says, yes, he'll buy some cookies and goes to get his money.

Heaton runs to the car, leaving Jo Marie and cookies on the porch.

"Mother, it's Bobby Peters's house! He's going to buy cookies!"

Her calm mother says, "Well, then, you'd probably better get back up there and take his money."

"Oh, yea."

Heaton runs back to the Peters porch to find the bewildered TV star and Jo Marie standing there staring at each other. Heaton takes the man's money and thanks him. Peters invites the girls to come on his WBAP-TV Channel 5 show the following

Saturday and talk about Girl Scout cookies, which they do.

Peters buys two boxes of cookies, and Linda Heaton will never forget her brush with TV fame.

* * * * *

Today, the national Girl Scouts of the USA Internet website states that selling cookies is about more than bringing in money for Scout projects: it's about the skills a girl gains from interacting directly with people. "It's about the experience of running her own cookie business and working with others."[25]

In the early days of Scouting, the girls actually baked the cookies themselves and sold the treats they had made. The baking-selling movement began in 1917 in Oklahoma, spread to Illinois and to New York, and finally took off in the rest of the country. The successful long-term annual fund-raising project was up and running.[26] One hundred years later, the annual Girl Scout cookie sale is still an established event. Today, they sell more items than cookies—nuts, trail mixes, chocolates, and even magazine subscriptions.

The girls no longer bake the cookies they sell, and the mass-produced varieties change often enough to keep the delicacies tasty, interesting, and sought-after.

Troop 11 participated annually in the nationwide Girl Scout cookie sale. However, we never baked any cookies to sell, except for special projects, such as raising money for the Minnie Ruth Elrod Endowment Fund or our troop trip to Colorado. By the time we became Scouts, the national Girl Scout organization had contracted with large companies to produce the cookies and box them in packages that advertised Girl Scouting. Almost every cookie variety in the 1950s had a Girl Scout trefoil emblem on it.

---

[25] "Ready for Cookies?" https://www.girlscouts.org/program/gs_cookies/find_cookies.asp.

[26] Stacey A. Cordery, *Juliette Gordon Low: The Remarkable Founder of the Girl Scouts* (New (New York: Penguin Group, 2012), 282.

Our first year, 1950, the cookies sold for forty cents a box.

I remember taking a coin purse full of jingling dimes for change when people gave me a fifty-cent piece or two quarters.

Selling cookies was how Ann Brown first learned that a dime, a nickel, and a quarter add up to forty cents.

Wanda Elrod Crowder laments that her favorite, the vanilla and chocolate trefoil-decorated cream-filled sandwich cookies, aren't among today's Girl Scout cookie offerings. At least, they don't appear on the current Scout website, and they aren't available in any of the areas where we live. "They were way better than Oreos," Wanda says. We agree. The creaminess just isn't the same. At least, that's what we remember.

I do have to say, though, that today's Girl Scout S'mores and Savannah Smiles can truly melt in the mouth. And, when you open the boxes, they smell *so* good.

Back in the 1950s, girls didn't do so much selling to friends at church and at tables in front of grocery stores, and the idea of selling cookies to send to US troops hadn't occurred to anyone yet. I should say that I don't remember selling in any of these ways, but Ann does remember selling at a grocery store one year. Most of the time, in order to sell our cookies, we girls went door-to-door to homes. Naturally, we trudged off dressed in our Brownie, Intermediate, Senior Scout, or Mariner uniforms, depending on our age and current rank in Scouting.

Riverside News staff photo
Sharon Elrod and big sister Wanda head out to sell Girl Scout cookies.

Even though life seemed safer in those days, our leaders insisted that a parent accompany us and stand on the sidewalk or wait by the curb in a car. Often, we went two-by-two to sell, taking turns at receiving profits and credit for sales. Yes, it was a gentler time, but the adults always adhered to a "safety first" policy for the girls of troop 11. And, as it turned out, this supervisory-and-togetherness rule was a sound one. Going house-to-house with a buddy was more fun anyway.

Wanda remembers being transported to sell cookies in parts of Fort Worth not assigned to any other troop, particularly near what was at that time Harris Methodist Hospital (now Texas Health Harris Methodist Hospital). "I loved the doorbells on some of the old houses there. They were round, and you had to turn them or pull them to make them ring. I thought they were beautiful, and I loved their sounds."

Karyn Hudson Draper recalls selling in exclusive neighborhoods and being amazed when maids answered the doors. "We didn't see that in our homes."

Martha Still Littlefield remembers pulling her cookie-box-filled toy red wagon from house to house in her grandmother's neighborhood. Her cousins went with her. "I remember how very, very large some of the houses were and how long the walkways were up to them. Some had so many stairs that I had to leave my wagon at the bottom."

Martha had quite a sales pitch. "I remember how I introduced myself and what I was selling, showing the boxes, describing them, explaining how it would help our troop with whatever goal we were working toward, and for only $__ a box."

Pat Cookus sold cookies in different types of neighborhoods, knocking on all kinds of doors, and meeting numerous types of personalities. "Some people looked forward to seeing us, some didn't. One time, I knocked on a door where the man who answered flipped his false teeth out at me. I didn't know I could run so fast."

Me? I was as dutiful a cookie seller as anyone. It wasn't my favorite Scout activity, but I did it.

One time, I went to a house where a grumpy old man answered the door. I had my spiel halfway out of my mouth when he frowned and interrupted me. "I don't want none," he barked and slammed the door.

Always a bit too sensitive for my own good, I was crushed. It's okay not to want to buy something, but you don't have to be mean about it—or so I reasoned. My mother always said, "It takes all kinds of people to make a world." I thought maybe the world could do without grumpy old men who slammed doors in the faces of little Girl Scouts.

But, again, I did learn a lesson. Ever since that day, I have tried to be courteous to salespeople wherever I encounter them, whether it be a fast-food restaurant, a retail store, on the telephone, or at the door of my house. I don't want to be the one person who ruins their day by acting nasty and whom they remember when they are in their seventies.

Troop 11's cookie-sales money over the years was used by the county Girl Scout council in several ways, among them to help less fortunate Scouts attend Camp Timberlake and to build a swimming pool on the camp premises. Every time we saw that swimming pool, we felt pride. We also enjoyed swimming in it, of course.

In raising money for the pool, one year in high school, Joyce Wakefield and Ann sold enough cookies to have their names put in a time capsule that was buried near the pool. In 2012, Camp Timberlake went into coownership with the Tarrant Joint Regional Water District. Personnel in the local Girl Scout office think the capsule was auctioned off at a "Farewell to Camp Timberlake" event in 2015. Anyway, it's gone.

Troop 11 always sold its assigned quota of cookies—and more. Mrs. Minnie Ruth Elrod saw to that. In fact, we sometimes went way over our quota. In 1951, the troop won second place in Brownie sales in Tarrant County. We received a cash prize from the Fort Worth Girl Scout Council, Inc., to be spent on supplies or equipment for the troop.

Again in 1956 as Senior Scouts, the troop qualified for prize money.

Fort Worth Girl Scout Council, Inc.

1414 PENNSYLVANIA AVE. — PHONE FA-1266 — FORT WORTH 4, TEXAS

April 23, 1951

Troop 11
2701 Quinn
Fort Worth, Texas

Dear Troop 11:

Enclosed is your prize money for winning Second place in the Brownie division of the Girl Scout Cookie Sale. You did a splendid job and we are delighted to present you with this prize and hope you will enjoy your winnings immensely.

You understand this prize money is to be used for a troop project or troop equipment.

Sincerely,

Mrs. Warren D. Sorrells
Mrs. Warren D. Sorrells
Cookie Chairman

WDS/jw

Letter courtesy of Wanda Elrod Crowder
Letter congratulating troop 11 on winning second place in the Brownie Division of the Tarrant County's Girl Scout cookie sale in 1951.

Neither congratulatory letter mentions the award's amount, and none of us remember how much they were. Neither do we remember what the money bought. However, knowing our leaders' frugality and the love they lavished on us, we have no doubt that they spent the money on something worthwhile to benefit the entire troop.

Yes, like it or not, we each sold our quota of Girl Scout cookies every year, even when, as teenagers, we thought it was silly to do so. Most of us, especially those not particularly inclined toward salesmanship, looked upon the annual cookie sale as a chore we had to do, not something we really enjoyed doing.

Nevertheless, we learned a lot of things from the experience.

For one thing, we learned that sometimes in life, you have to do things you don't necessarily want to do. So you do them anyway. In fact, you give them your best effort. Sometimes you get a reward, and sometimes you don't. That's life.

Also, some of us did accrue some business and salesmanship skills, as the Girl Scout Internet website suggests. Carole Capps Steadham, Elaine Walton Lofland, Earline Campbell Wood, Karyn, Marilyn Weiss, Pat, and Wanda successfully ran their own service and retail businesses in later years.

Finally, we learned that many kinds of people inhabit the world, and you encounter them when you knock on their doors.

And to illustrate that point, I recount a story Ann tells that, I think, tops them all. It also may explain why few Girl Scouts sell cookies door-to-door any longer.

> Joycie and I were selling cookies together. We knocked on one door. A man answered.
>
> I said, "Would you like to buy some Girl Scout cookies?" And then, we *ran like hell* because the man was completely naked.

Yes, selling cookies was another of troop 11's Girl Scout experiences. And, to be sure, cookie-selling was always an adventure, even though every girl didn't encounter TV celebrities or naked men.

CHAPTER 8

Colorado or Bust

It is July 1958. Most of the girls of Girl Scout Troop 11 are fifteen years old.

We are in Santa Fe, New Mexico, on the last leg of a journey to and from Colorado, and we are enjoying a stroll on Santa Fe's historic downtown plaza. We admire the handmade jewelry and pottery Native Americans are selling from blankets spread out on the porch of the Palace of the Governors on the plaza's north side. Some Scouts, ones who have money left, make purchases.

Carole Capps decides to pull out her Kodak Brownie camera and snap a picture of a Native American man in traditional attire. He sees her do it and runs after her.

Terrified, she flees as fast as her legs can carry her to the bus the troop is traveling in. The bus is parked about a block from the plaza. The man pursues her all the way to the vehicle.

As Carole climbs inside, Ann Brown meets her at the door and tells her that she needs to pay the man. Carole fumbles in her purse, pulls out her last fifty cents, and gives it to him.

"You should have asked permission," he growls at her and, shaking his head, stalks away.

Carole collapses breathless, trembling, and tearful on a bus seat. Everyone tries to comfort her.

We learned later that some Native Americans believe that having their pictures taken takes away their soul. Maybe Carole was fortunate to get the picture for only fifty cents.

It is a gut-wrenching experience she will never forget, but Carole still has the picture she took that day. It's in one of her photo albums.

* * * * *

The idea for the Colorado trip grew out of a troop conversation at Camp Timberlake in the summer of 1957. Leaders and girls were gathered around a campfire after enjoying Campfire Stew and S'mores. Somebody says, "Why don't we take a trip together?"

Mrs. Minnie Ruth Elrod must have shuddered, rolled her eyes, and thought, "Oh, I can't wait to plan and organize such a thing." But it was dark, and we couldn't see her do any of these things. At least, she didn't immediately squelch the idea. She just listened. Today we wonder how our leaders had the gumption to take us on that long bus trip. Even so, Ellie listened.

The ideas continued to flow. "We can stay in campgrounds along the way." "We can buy groceries and make our own meals." "We can raise the money we'll need by doing odd jobs and having fund-raisers."

The plan was already taking shape, and we hadn't yet left camp. By the time school started in the fall, it seemed as if the adventure might really happen.

Troop 11 girls were now in the ninth grade, which at that time in Fort Worth was junior high school, though ninth graders earned high school credits. We also were Senior Scouts.

Plans for the trip did indeed begin to develop. Mrs. Elrod figured out an itinerary and approximately how much money the group would need, of course, adding in extra funds for unforeseen expenses. She polled the troop to find out who was serious about going and began to look for a bus and a driver to get us to Colorado and back.

We girls brainstormed for ways to raise money.

We held a rummage sale of clothes we had outgrown and whatever else we could get friends and family to donate; it took place at the Elrod home.

The troop put on an ice cream supper at Riverside's Sylvania Park, selling ice cream for fifty cents a bowl and fresh-baked cupcakes and cookies at appropriate prices. We made the ice cream ourselves in our families' freezers and baked the other items.

"My arm's so tired, it's going to fall off," Jacque McNiel complained as she hand-cranked a freezer full of chocolate ice cream.

"It's worth it to go to Colorado, though," Beverly Wilson said through clenched teeth as she too cranked by hand her freezer.

We mowed yards, served as babysitters, and cooked for bake sales. Karyn Hudson Draper remembers organizing and hosting a neighborhood pancake breakfast.

We sold newspapers and magazines to a recycle firm. We filled the trunks of our parents' cars, which were weighed with trunks full, then with trunks empty. Karyn thinks we made only "a couple of bucks for a trunk load—hard work for so little money."

These activities took place during our ninth grade year. We worked so hard that we convinced Mrs. Elrod we were serious about the trip.

In the end, ten troop 11 members, four members from other troops, three female adult chaperones, and one male bus driver (poor man) departed for Colorado. The troop 11 girls were Marilyn Ball, Donna Throckmorton, Jacque, Beverly, Wanda Elrod, Karyn, Joyce Wakefield, Ann, Carole, and Earline Campbell. Linda Booker, who would later join our troop but who was then in another troop, also went. Troop 11's adult leaders/chaperones were Mrs. Elrod and Mrs. Jeanette Hudson. The bus driver was Mr. Creecy. Nobody recalls his first name, and we haven't been able to track down his family.

We made a big oilcloth sign and tied it on the side of the bus. It said "Girl Scout Troop 11: Colorado or Bust." On a July morning, we embarked on this fun-filled and scenic trip.

The bus wasn't air-conditioned, which wouldn't be a problem once we reached the cool, dry air north of Albuquerque, New Mexico, but certainly was a problem in a Texas July. Nevertheless, excitement trumped discomfort, and an atmosphere of jubilation filled the bus.

Photo courtesy of Wanda Elrod Crowder
Troop 11 in full Senior Scout uniform before boarding the bus for Colorado. They are, left to right, Beverly Wilson, Carole Capps, Marilyn Ball, Earline Campbell, Donna Throckmorton, Wanda Elrod, Ann Brown, Jacque McNiel, Karyn Hudson, Joyce Wakefield, and Mrs. Minnie Ruth Elrod. Mrs. Jeanette Hudson or Mr. Creecy must have taken the picture.

Along the way, we would sing "The Bus Driver Song" many times to Mr. Creecy, who good-naturedly smiled and waved at us. He'd also daily greet each girl with, "Good Morning, Glory."

Karyn describes Mr. Creecy as "a very nice, clean, polite, always smiling man—and have we also said *patient*." A unanimous opinion.

Ann adds, "He was, indeed, our long-suffering and eternally pleasant driver."

He must have been a most exceptional man to put up with us. Our teenage years, in some ways, were not our "finest hour."

That July morning, as we departed Fort Worth, we were beginning an adventure that we would remember and talk about the rest of our lives. Our leaders were giving us yet another precious gift that would teach us togetherness, interpersonal skills, and responsibility—and would also be a lot of fun.

Certainly, we had bumps along the way. We got weary of sandwich meals. We got burned out on having to fix our own meals when we were already tired and hungry. We got so tired of *each other* that we started hiding behind our seats on the bus. But we also learned that "everything is not about me" and maybe a little bit about how to behave ourselves when interacting with different cultures. For sure, we would never be the same after this trip.

The bus headed west toward New Mexico and the first major stop, Carlsbad Caverns National Park. The weather outside the caverns was warm, hot even, but inside the enormous caves, the temperature steadily became cooler as we walked down the distance of about one thousand feet from the entrance. The grade on the trails was not terribly steep, and a National Park Service ranger led our tour. At the bottom, it was so cool in the cave that we needed sweaters.

We walked from the cave entrance to the Big Room, the lowest point on the public tour. Along the way, we marveled at the gigantic stalactite and stalagmite water-created formations. We especially liked the Hall of the Giants and the King's Palace, but a true highlight of the tour was when the rangers turned out all the lights in the Big Room. We stood around the underground lake there and, in utter darkness, sang the Christian hymn, "Rock of Ages." Not considered politically correct, this exercise is not done today. Also, the lake is mostly dry.

We had a box sandwich lunch at the snack bar near the Big Room before making the uphill trip to the cave's opening.

"It must have been some job carving those restrooms out of the cave walls and installing the plumbing that works," Joyce marveled as we gave our thighs a good workout on the climb.

"Yeah, how about those elevators?" Ann chimed in. "That was an engineering feat too." Silently, she wondered why we didn't take the elevators to the top to go out.

At dusk in some months, the hordes of bats that inhabit the cave fly out into the night to hunt for food. Seventeen species of the tiny creatures with large wings put on quite a show. Amazingly, their flight is almost silent. On this trip, we didn't stay to see them. Those of us who have been fortunate enough to return to the caverns have made sure to treat ourselves to this unforgettable spectacle.

Ann was so impressed with the majesty of Carlsbad Caverns that she wrote a poem about the place, entitled "The Caverns." She remembers the first four lines.

> I felt so small as I stood there
> Before the entrance, old and wide,
> Remembering in silent awe
> The marvels I had seen inside.

Our visit to Carlsbad Caverns provided us with the first of many memories we would store away on this amazing trip.

Photo courtesy of Wanda Elrod Crowder
In 1958, the visitors' entrance to underground cave area
at Carlsbad Caverns National Park. Visitors can still go
down this way, but most now take the elevator.

Our second major stop was Colorado Springs, Colorado, where we stayed at Hamp Hut, a Girl Scout-owned lodge in the Garden of the Gods Park, a national natural landmark. The lodge had sleeping quarters for all of us. We cooked our breakfasts and some of our dinners there. We Texans, accustomed to brutally hot summers, couldn't believe how cool the weather was—at night, we again needed sweaters—and how comfortable Hamp Hut was without air-conditioning.

Upon arrival in Colorado Springs, we stopped at a grocery store. Karyn recalls, "We were delighted to discover another Scout troop that would be staying in the park, a troop of the 'boy' variety. While our leaders purchased groceries for us, we surrounded the boys on the parking lot." She adds, "We weren't boy-crazy. Of course not."

We had a flag ceremony each morning and evening. At campfires some nights, we ate Campfire Stew and S'mores. A little homesick, we sang "Deep in the Heart of Texas."

Photo courtesy of Wanda Elrod Crowder
Donna Throckmorton, Marilyn Ball, Wanda's sister Sharon Elrod, Carole Capps, and Ann Brown pose after a flag ceremony at Hamp Hut.

The formations in Garden of the Gods are awe-inspiring.

"I hope that thing named Balanced Rock doesn't fall down and crush somebody while we're here," Donna said with a little fear in her voice.

The rock didn't fall. In fact, it's still standing there today, even now threatening to topple over at any minute. I can't help but wonder whether someone cemented the enormous monolith in place at some previous time.

Another formation we loved was Steamboat Rock, a massive boulder.

"It really does look like a ship," Marilyn Ball exclaimed.

We climbed to the top of it and posed for a picture.

Photo courtesy of Wanda Elrod Crowder
Girl Scout Troop 11 atop Steamboat Rock in
Garden of the Gods, Colorado Springs.

Today, visitors are not allowed to climb on Steamboat Rock. It's there, but the railing is gone, and signs make the message clear: "Climbing is prohibited."

We stayed in Garden of the Gods five days. What a lovely place it was, with such beautiful scenery. It was a relaxing place too, not at all like the bustling city in which we lived. It was close in to Colorado Springs, but it seemed as if it were in the wilderness.

Hamp Hut is still located in Garden of the Gods, and Girl Scout troops continue to stay there. Colorado Springs has grown up really close to the park, but there remain trails for hiking, a nice visitor center and museum, and roads to the amazing formations.

From our base in Garden of the Gods Park, we traveled to other tourist sites near Colorado Springs. Favorites were Pike's Peak, Santa's Workshop/North Pole Christmas theme park, and Royal Gorge Bridge and Park.

At Pike's Peak, we rode the famous cog train up to the top of the mountain.

"The ride up (and down) was jerky but fun," Wanda says.

We heard that the drive up to the peak is spectacular too, but we were glad to take the train. The bus had lost its fascination for us, and the road appeared steep and winding. Mr. Creecy was probably glad not to have to drive it in a bus.

Photo courtesy of Wanda Elrod Crowder
Troop 11 girls on cog train ascending Pike's Peak. They are, left to right, first row, Marilyn Ball and Donna Throckmorton; second row, Joyce Wakefield and Jacque McNiel; third row, Wanda Elrod and Ann Brown.

The scenery at the top of Pike's Peak was indescribable. We were fortunate to have a clear day so that we could enjoy the amazing views.

"You could see forever in every direction—maybe to Kansas, Wyoming, and Utah, certainly to Denver," Carole remembers with fondness.

"It was also quite windy up there—and cold. Wow! What a difference from the heat of Texas. Could July weather really be like this?" Earline wondered. "We'd worn sweaters and scarves, but we needed to huddle together for warmth."

The wind was so strong that Jacque and Joyce almost lost their cowgirl hats.

The cog train continued to be a popular attraction up until 2018. When it reached the top, the conductor said, "Congratulations! You've just climbed one of Colorado's Fourteeners." A "fourteener" is a fourteen-thousand-foot-high mountain, and Colorado has many of them.

Unfortunately, the train is not now running. Inspection rendered the equipment and infrastructure to be unsafe. Railroad operators are making repairs and hope to reopen in 2021. At present, visitors have no option but to drive or ride up on the winding road. It's pretty much a universal hope that the train will reopen: it was an unforgettable experience.

At North Pole/Santa's Workshop, we shopped in cute little stores, rode on fun rides, and took turns having our pictures made sitting on Santa's lap. Park employees told us about a permanent ice pole (the North Pole), situated in the park's central area, that never melts. We touched it to make sure it was really ice, but we were smart enough not to lick it and get our tongues stuck.

"Do you believe that?" Linda Booker asked, shaking her head. It *was* something we found hard to believe, but sixty years later, the frozen pole remains there. North Pole/Santa's Workshop is there too; kids and their parents continue to enjoy it. My husband and I accompanied our son and his family there in 2016, and the vintage amusement park remains a delightful experience: it has rides you don't find in many other places.

Photo courtesy of Karyn Hudson Draper
Wanda Elrod and Karyn Hudson, wearing matching bandana shirts
Mrs. Jeanette Hudson had made for them, sit on Santa's lap at North
Pole/Santa's Workshop Christmas theme park near Colorado Springs.

Whereas at Pike's Peak we had ridden *up* the mountain, at Royal Gorge Bridge and Park, we rode a cable car *down* to the bottom of the gorge. Both rides were different from anything we'd ever done before. The scenery was, needless to say, again spectacular.

Royal Gorge is 956 feet deep. The bridge at the top is a quarter of a mile long and one of the world's highest suspension bridges.[27]

We posed for pictures both at the top of the gorge on the bridge and at the bottom of the canyon.

Visitors cannot take the ride down into the canyon today. A wildfire that swept through the area in 2014 destroyed the cable car, and it has not been rebuilt. It is also not possible now to walk out on the bridge at the top or even get a good view of it without paying a fee. It's a good thing we went there when we did. Today's visitors can, however, ride a train through the bottom of the gorge and enjoy some amazing scenery en route.

---

[27] "Royal Gorge Bridge," Royal Gorge Bridge website, http://www.highestbridges. com/wiki/index.php?title=Royal_Gorge_Bridge.

Photo courtesy of Wanda Elrod Crowder
Troop 11 at the bottom of Royal Gorge. Left to right are Mrs.
Jeanette Hudson, Joyce Wakefield, Karyn Hudson, Wanda
Elrod, Donna Throckmorton, Ann Brown, Marilyn Ball, Sharon
Elrod, Linda Booker, Carole Capps, Beverly Wilson, Pat Pittman
and Toni Bosch from other troops, and Jacque McNiel.

One night, we dressed up in western wear and attended a chuck wagon dinner. The food was delicious, though the barbecue was somewhat different from what we were accustomed to in Texas, and we didn't like it quite as much. By the twenty-first century, we have learned that barbecue, like Mexican food, varies in taste and preparation in different parts of the United States. Back then, however, we thought barbecue everywhere was Texas-style. So another fact we learned on this trip was that barbecue isn't prepared as beef brisket and ribs everywhere. Some places, it's pork or wild game.

After dinner, we square-danced and two-stepped with local people. Being Texans, we knew how to do these dances. Some of the girls went horseback riding with some boys (while some of the others were jealous and our leaders worried).

Photo courtesy of Wanda Elrod Crowder
Dressed in western regalia for a chuck wagon dinner are, left to
right, Donna Throckmorton, Jacque McNiel, Beverly Wilson,
Wanda Elrod, Karyn Hudson, Joyce Wakefield, Ann Brown, Pat
Pittman, Carole Capps, Toni Bosch, Sharon Elrod, Linda Booker,
and Earline Campbell. Marilyn Ball is just out of the picture at left.

One Sunday morning, troop 11 had a worship service in full uniform by ourselves. Another Sunday, we attended "the first church we came to," which happened to be a Baptist church near Colorado Springs. We all were some kind of Christian—Baptist, Methodist, Presbyterian, Independent Christian Church, Church of Christ— and we were taught not to take "vacations" from worshiping when we traveled. We reasoned that God didn't ever take a vacation from caring for us. So we managed to worship on the Sundays in Colorado and everywhere else we went. We even worshiped on our weekend camping trips: we did not forget God—ever, and we continue to lean on Him quite heavily now.

At our troop worship services, Ann frequently led the devotional message. She would later become an ordained Methodist church minister. Perhaps some early training came from speaking to us.

Photo courtesy of Wanda Elrod Crowder
Headed to Sunday morning worship service are, left to right, Jacque
McNiel, Karyn Hudson, Beverly Wilson, Earline Campbell, Linda
Booker, Pat Pittman, Joyce Wakefield, and Wanda Elrod.

After our fun time in Colorado, we headed home, making one
last major stop—in Santa Fe, New Mexico. We found Santa Fe to
be picturesque and every bit as wonderful as the sites we had seen
in Colorado. Santa Fe bills itself as "The City Different," and it certainly is. Rocky Mountain states' cultures were new to us Texans, and
we loved learning about the different people and customs.

In future years, Carol and her husband would purchase a cabin
in Red River, New Mexico, to escape the Texas summer heat. Earline
would call New Mexico her favorite travel destination. Ann would
work in Colorado's national parks. And I would live in Los Alamos
near Santa Fe, where the summers are, indeed, comfortably cool
most days. We have no air-conditioning in our home.

We Scouts hadn't realized before our trip that Santa Fe is the oldest capital city in the United States. Nor had we realized how charming its pueblo architecture is. The Santa Fe plaza is both Spanish and Native American in design.

Photo courtesy of Wanda Elrod Crowder
In 1958, Native Américans sold their handcrafts in front of Santa Fe's Palace of the Governors, just as they do today.

The mountains of New Mexico's high desert are spectacularly beautiful, and the air is so clean. We wanted to somehow package the invigorating cool dry air and take it home with us. We were amazed to discover that our bus was quite comfortable without air-conditioning. Also, the air smelled different—clean, piney, and fresh.

However, on the trip home, we were not nearly so delighted with the bus experience as we had been going out. We got hot while traveling through West Texas. And we were really sick of leftover food, especially bologna sandwiches, a sentiment most zealously expressed by Carole. Tempers were short, and girls were pouty.

The ride back to Fort Worth taught us another lesson, though: sometimes you have to forgo your own desires and do what's good for the group. We were pretty miserable, but we'd survive.

And we did manage to get home with no major mishaps, no physical injuries, and no documented incidences of heat stroke.

The experience was an educational one in several ways. We had no idea that places in our neighboring states were so different from places in our own. So on this trip through New Mexico and Colorado, we experienced not only new geographical sites but also new—to us—cultures. You can read about these places in books, but you can learn so much more by actually visiting them.

The heavily Spanish culture of Northern New Mexico is somewhat different from the Mexican heritage in which we had grown up in Texas: the *conquistadores* of Spain had populated this area and left a distinctly Hispanic mark here. Their descendants are proud of their Spanish—not Mexican—heritage. The New Mexican food also is different from the Tex-Mex variety we were accustomed to. New Mexico has a state question, "Red or Green?" which refers to the two main chili sauces that grace the food. Green chili is made from the chili peppers while they are still green. Red chili is made from the fully ripened and sometimes dried red peppers. New Mexican food has a fresh taste. Even fresh ground red chili powder has a different taste and color from the canned varieties in grocery stores.

The Native Americans were also new to us. Their distinctive crafts, architecture, costumes, and food fascinated us. These people had been here even before the Spanish came. We'd never heard of yummy Navajo tacos before, not to mention calabacitas (a green chili, corn, and squash dish) and fry bread.

So it had been a journey back in time for us. While the rest of the world was watching the European Economic Community begin to function; Fidel Castro's revolutionary forces capture Havana, Cuba; the United States launch its first space satellite, Explorer I; and Texan Van Cliburn become the first American to win the Tchaikovsky competition in Moscow, Girl Scout Troop 11 was getting to know their historic neighbors to the West. These people had lived in the area that is now New Mexico and Colorado before the coming of our English ancestors.

And besides learning to interact with cultures different from our own, we practiced getting along with each other. We matured and broadened our thinking, at least a little. And we're best friends in our seventies, so personal relationships didn't suffer.

And, of course, Santa Fe was where Carole learned that some Native Americans don't like having their pictures taken—period. But some will let you take pictures if you ask permission and pay them. I have never tried to photograph Native Americans without asking, so I don't know whether this custom has changed in the years since our trip. Of course, it never hurts to ask first anyway.

CHAPTER 9

Mariner Scouts in Landlocked Fort Worth

"Demonstrate bow position, now the pushover, now the draw. Good. Now the sweep. Good. Now the backwater stroke. Good."

Beverly Wilson, Martha Still, and Donna Throckmorton are in a canoe on Eagle Mountain Lake near Camp Timberlake and Fort Worth. They are taking a test to pass requirements for their canoeing badge. They are in deep water. The instructor, in another canoe, is barking instructions at them through a megaphone. Lifeguards are in the instructor's canoe and watching to ensure that nobody drowns.

"Paddle in stern position on a triangular course of 440 yards." The girls do this. One is paddling on the left side of the canoe, and two on the right side. After this task is completed, the instructor yells the next direction.

"Capsize canoe." The craft rocks violently as the Scouts stand up, lean to the right, and fall out of the craft, which turns bottom side up. Arms, legs, bodies, and paddles go flying into the water in all directions. The splash is loud and big. Beverly gets a

scrape on her leg as the canoe hits her when it turns over.

"Reposition and reenter canoe." The girls, who have surfaced and are treading water by now, swim to the craft and, heaving in unison, manage to get it upright again while trying not to "ship" water. Then, one at a time, they climb back into the canoe, while the others hold the craft steady. This time, Donna bruises her knee by contact with the side of the canoe as she hurls herself over.

Next, the Scouts paddle with their hands in unison to recover the wooden paddles lost in the "accident."

"Excellent! You pass," yells the instructor. "Return to shore. Next group."

The waterlogged three paddle back to the dock, exit the canoe, grab towels to warm themselves; and three others climb into the canoe to take their test.

"I thought I was going to drown out there," Donna mutters.

"But we didn't! We passed!" says Martha, always our troop 11 optimist. The girls, realizing their need for jubilation, unite in a wet, slippery, and shivery jumping-up-and-down yelling group hug.

* * * * *

Mrs. Minnie Ruth Elrod had solved the uniform problem. In 1958, she offered troop 11 the option of becoming either Mariner or Aviator Scouts. The sixteen-year-old Scouts took one look at the spiffy Mariner Scout uniforms and voted unanimously to go nautical.

The uniform was a tailored royal-blue sailor-style two-piece dress that had white piping around the square collar and the sleeve cuffs. The long-sleeved sailor blouse, which sported a black tie at the neck, eased into the fitted waist of an A-line skirt. For accessories, the girls wore white gloves, royal-blue sailor hats, and black dressy, high-heeled, pointed-toe, pump-style shoes.

"I feel stylish," Karyn Hudson said.

"And grown-up," Carole Capps added.

And Mrs. Elrod smiled a lot because she never again heard a complaint about wearing the uniform.

Personnel at Girl Scout headquarters in New York City must have done a double take in 1958 when they saw an application for a Mariner Scout troop from Fort Worth, Texas. Actually, troop 11's application was not the first. There was already a Ship 7 that was active for a long time, taking in new members as older members graduated from high school. Undoubtedly, though, the Mariner Scout program had been designed with the ocean- and river-rich United States east coast in mind.

Anyone who views a map of Texas sees that Fort Worth is landlocked.

The city *is* situated on the west fork of the Trinity River, which in 1949 overflowed its banks and flooded several sections of the city. And the Trinity River *does* flow to the Gulf of Mexico, leading some civic-minded types to talk from time to time of dredging the river and making Fort Worth an inland seaport, like Houston. But after the 1949 flood, engineers rechanneled the river, installing flood-control measures. Talk of making the river navigable to Fort Worth lessened considerably, as the waterway became in some places concrete-enclosed and more docile.

Fort Worth *is* blessed with several nearby lakes. Girl Scout Camp Timberlake is located on such a reservoir, Eagle Mountain Lake.

So Mrs. Elrod, Mrs. Thelma Still, Mrs. Jeanette Hudson, and the girls reasoned that they could fulfill Mariner Scout requirements by using area lakes. Probably because another troop had preceded us, the New Yorkers approved troop 11's request.

Thus, Girl Scout Troop 11 became Mariner Scout Ship 11, and the troop forged ahead toward new nautical adventures. We learned expert swimming, lifesaving, canoeing, and sailing skills. The sailing was, of course, in small-lake boats, not tall ships, but it counted for Scout requirements. We followed the handbook instructions carefully. Our leaders saw to that.

Mariner Scouts don't exist today in Girl Scouting. Girls who are interested in boating and sailing are permitted to join with Boy Scouts of America groups who also want to sail.

But in the late 1950s and early 1960s, ship 11 happily honed aquatic skills.

Photo courtesy of Martha Still Littlefield
Ship 11 members look very grown-up in Mariner Scout uniforms. They are left to right, Margie Stoddard, Wanda Elrod, Diane Crawford, Donna Throckmorton, Jacque McNiel, Mary Stoddard, Beverly Wilson, Joyce Wakefield, Martha Still, Ann Brown, Carole Capps, and Mrs. Minnie Ruth Elrod. Not pictured, but also Mariner Scouts, are Marilyn Ball, Linda Booker, Earline Campbell, Pat Cookus, Linda Heaton, Karyn Hudson, Linda Kay Killian, Linda Simons, Elaine Walton, and Marilyn Weiss.

To participate in sailing activities, we had to earn our lifesaving badge. The final exam required each girl to fall fully clothed into the lake, disrobe while treading water, and swim to shore. We had our swimsuits on under our clothes. This procedure was harder than one might think. I got awfully tired while trying to take off my jeans, shirt, lace-up shoes, and socks. Then I had to retrieve all my clothes and swim with them to the dock.

Ann Brown Fields remembers that Eagle Mountain Lake was low that year, so we had to fall off the dock into only four feet of water. We had to keep our legs curled up to keep from touching bottom and "cheating." That made it harder to get all the clothes off.

Anyway, we all passed the test and the class.

As Mariner Scouts, we studied all kinds of nautical subjects, learning new knots and new sea terms, and actually spending time on the water. We never did anything that would qualify us for the America's Cup, but we certainly enjoyed bragging about sailing.

Mrs. Elrod was delighted: the troop would stay intact through high school graduation, something that had always been her dream.

Photo courtesy of Wanda Elrod Crowder
Ship 11 Scouts prepare to launch canoes onto Eagle Mountain Lake.

While some of us were just "sticking with" Scouting until graduation, others were taking on ever-increasing roles. Four girls were becoming active in Girl Scout leadership on the county, state, and national levels.

In 1959, Wanda Elrod and Ann were selected to attend the Girl Scout International Roundup near Colorado Springs, Colorado. Ann says of this event:

This was a formative event in my life. I am still friends with one of the girls I met, who was from Scarsdale, New York. I had never had a Jewish friend before, and I loved getting to know her and her religion. Participating in the July 4 flag ceremony, raising the Texas flag alongside the flags of the other forty-nine states and numerous foreign countries was something I would never forget. That was the day that the Alaska state flag was first raised. I still remember with a full heart ten thousand girls from all over the world singing in harmony in a natural amphitheater on a ranch north of Colorado Springs.

Ann was also elected to the Tarrant County Girl Scout Council and served as vice president and later president of the planning board. She held these positions in her junior and senior years in high school.

Beverly, Joyce Wakefield, and Ann took a counselor-in-training course and worked as counselors at Camp Timberlake summer camps in 1959 and 1960.

And in 1960, Ann was one of four Tarrant County delegates to the Girl Scout National Convention. The theme for that year was "Use Us or Lose Us."

"We were on fire to continue to be ambassadors for the Girl Scout movement in any way in which we could," Ann recalls.

Later, Ann would work as a professional in the Austin, Texas, Lone Star Girl Scout Council.

On March 16, 1961, Ship 11 gathered with several other Fort Worth area Brownie and Girl Scout troops to celebrate the forty-ninth birthday of Girl Scouting. The theme of the night was "Today's Scouts—Tomorrow's Career Women."

As it turned out, *we* were the honorees of the evening. Ship 11 was already famous in Fort Worth for making it through to our high school senior year. And as we were about to end our Scouting careers and head out into the world, the other troops perceived us as the epitome of the event's theme. The younger girls who came behind us thought we were inspiring. Yes, us!

It was such a fun experience watching younger troops reenact events in our troop's history. The presentation, entitled "This Is Your Life, Ship 11," was patterned after Ralph Edwards's then-popular national television program, *This Is Your Life.*

First, troop 125 depicted us making some of the many crafts we produced for gifts, hospitals, nursing homes, children's homes, and overseas packets. The narrator said, "I am sure these would number in the hundreds." Hundreds? Maybe, maybe not.

Next, troop 40 showed us cooking and sewing in commemoration of the classes we took at the Lone Star Gas Company and the Singer Sewing Machine Company.

"Don't burn the biscuits," a little girl playing Linda Heaton ordered, pretending to smell something.

"Ouch! I just ran the sewing-machine needle over my finger," another, impersonating Jacque McNiel, wailed.

Troops 250 and 179 portrayed our excursion to San Antonio and the touristy things we did there.

"Didn't you love the Rose Window at Mission San Jose?" a pint-sized Linda Kay Killian exclaimed.

"Yes, but the Alamo is *really* special," a blonde Wanda said.

"I'll never forget the rickety train ride," a girl playing Joyce said.

Troop 275 relived some of our camping experiences, including fifteen-degree nighttime temperatures, snake incidents, drama nights, and our beloved Campfire Stew.

"It's absolutely yummy," Martha's counterpart said.

"Please leave out the hamburger," a younger Carole pleaded. "It makes me sick."

Our Colorado trip couldn't be left out. Troop 489 depicted scenes at Pike's Peak, Royal Gorge, and Garden of the Gods Park in Colorado, and on the Plaza in Santa Fe, New Mexico.

Another troop, number 65, demonstrated our making bandages and taking temperatures, in honor of Ship 11's public service activities.

"I hate cleaning bird cages," a diminutive Diane Crawford wailed.

Finally, the night ended with a Court of Awards ceremony for all the troops. Even this turned out to be in commemoration of the many awards ship 11 had received over the years. The younger Scouts and their leaders were particularly impressed that we had received our second- and first-class ranks, our Curved Bar, and our senior scout graduation into Mariner Scouts. It was not so much that we had done these things, but that we had achieved each milestone together as an entire troop: that was outstanding and unusual.

The memorable evening deeply touched our hearts. We felt awed and humbled to realize that younger Scouts had been watching us, looking up to us, and hoping to become like us.

"I can't believe they admire us so much," Ann said. "We're just us, a bunch of ordinary girls doing our own ordinary things."

It was a lesson to us as spunky, hardheaded, and self-centered female teenagers.

"I'm going to try to be half the woman these younger Scouts think I am," Karyn resolved.

That's the way the entire troop felt. Sometimes we'd live up to this objective, and sometimes we wouldn't, but at least we'd try.

Yes, it was 1961. John F. Kennedy was president of the United States. IBM unveiled its selectric typewriter. Roger Maris broke Babe Ruth's long-standing home run record. *West Side Story* won the Academy Award for best motion picture of the year. *Bonanza* and *Route 66* were popular TV shows. "Crying" by Texas's own Roy Orbison placed high on the pop music charts. Troop/Ship 11 girls were buying forty-five-rpm vinyl records on at least a weekly basis. We were "twisting the night away" to Chubby Checker's "Let's Twist Again," and other such songs. We would graduate from high school in June.

If truth be told, most of us were developing interests beyond Scouting. Oh, we still met every week at Ellie's house. We dabbled in crafts and went camping. We sold Girl Scout cookies and ate them, even though we considered ourselves too old to be bothered with the selling endeavor.

"I feel silly selling cookies now," Jacque said. "People must say to themselves, 'Why are you big old things selling Girl Scout cookies? Cute little girls should do that.'"

It was in these high school years that the troop/ship 11 girls began to exhibit the competence of the women we would become, the "career women of tomorrow," as recently predicted at the anniversary dinner celebration, and women of good character.

Photo from 1961 Carter High School *Eagle* yearbook
Front of Amon Carter-Riverside High School, where troop/
ship 11 spent its last three years of public school.

Troop/Ship 11 girls filled the student leadership of Amon Carter-Riverside High School. The training and confidence-building we had learned in Scouting were now propelling us into responsible positions and taking us in directions that would shape our futures. The directions we followed were as varied as our personalities, with perhaps one exception.

The main thing many of us were really interested in at this point was *boys*—football players mostly, but any good-looking male would do. Maybe he didn't even have to be good-looking: we simply had to think he was. Most of us talked about, thought about, dreamed about, and planned our lives around boys.

The physically beautiful girls of troop/ship 11 became cheerleaders and class favorites. Senior year Carole was voted Miss Carter High School (CHS), all-school favorite. Diane was runner-up. Elaine Walton and Linda Booker were finalists. Troop/Ship 11 owned the contest.

Photo from 1961 Carter High School *Eagle* yearbook
Carole Capps as pictured in *Eagle* yearbook as Miss Carter High School.

Photo from 1961 Carter High School *Eagle* yearbook
Diane Crawford was runner-up for Miss Carter High School.

Elaine, Linda Booker, and Diane were cheerleaders. Booker was band queen our junior year, followed by Diane as a senior. Elaine and Marilyn Ball were baseball queens.

Photo from 1961 Carter High School *Eagle* yearbook
Elaine Walton, front row, left; Linda Booker, front row,
second from right, and Diane Crawford, front row, right,
were cheerleaders our senior year in high school.

Carole was president of Cheerleaders Club, the school's largest club. Earline Campbell was junior class secretary, the year before. Ann was president of Music Appreciation Club. Jacque was secretary and I was historian in Future Teachers of America. Wanda was president of Spanish Club.

The most studious troop/ship 11 girls served as officers in National Honor Society. Ann and I were vice president and treasurer, respectively. Carole, Elaine, Jacque, Karyn, Margie and Mary Stoddard, and Wanda were members.

Five of us—Earline, Jacque, Linda Booker, Margie, and I—used the public service experience we had gained in Scouting to serve in National Junior Red Cross.

Photo from 1961 Carter High School *Eagle* yearbook
Linda Kay Killian and Ann Brown serve refreshments at the National
Honor Society Christmas party. Also pictured are Elaine Walton,
Jacque McNiel, and Margie Stoddard, left to right, bottom right of
picture. Additional troop/ship 11 girls in National Honor Society were
Carole Capps, Mary Stoddard, Karyn Hudson, and Wanda Elrod.

Some of us pursued areas of interest that we would follow throughout our lives.

Margie and Mary, active in business clubs, became successful accountants.

As long as I could remember, I had wanted to write. I was mostly interested in freelance writing, but my mother insisted that I should learn a skill with which I could support myself, so I chose journalism. I served as editor of the CHS newspaper, the *Eagle Record*. High school journalism was, indeed, the beginning of a lifelong writing career.

Others worked on our high school yearbook. Carole, Jacque, Margie, and Mary served as section editors of the *Eagle*, and Earline was business manager.

And some were budding poets. Five Troop/Ship 11 Scouts had poems published in the 1959 edition of *Yucca Yarns*, the CHS literary magazine. Three of us—Carole, Elaine, and I—wrote about friendship; Wanda wrote about Jesus Christ. Sandra Weiss, Marilyn's older sister, wrote a humorous essay about Marilyn, "The Tragedy of Having a Younger Sister." In this gem, Big Sis pokes a lot of fun at Little Sis. I like the humor and cleverness of Marilyn Ball's poem "His Bright Socks," reprinted here.

His Bright Socks
by Marilyn Ball

He had some colored socks.
Man! Were they a shock.
Purple, green, blue, and yellow,
You can imagine quite a fellow.
He had stripes, checks, plaids, and dots,
Some even looked like moon spots.
He wore the yellow ones to school,
And his green ones to the swimming pool.
He wore his blue ones to the show,
But his purple ones just had to go!
The stripes and checks were all right,
But the dots and plaids were quite a sight!

Some troop/ship 11 girls were active in athletics and earned letters in their sports.

Ann, Mary and Margie lettered in tennis.

Photo from 1961 Carter High School *Eagle* yearbook
Margie Stoddard, Ann Brown, and Mary Stoddard, back row,
first two on left and last on right, were on the tennis team. Karyn
Hudson was on the team her sophomore and junior years.

145

Jacque, Martha, and Linda Heaton were members of the Carter archery team.

Photo from 1961 Carter High School *Eagle* yearbook
Jacque McNiel, third from left, and Martha Still, far right, were on the CHS archery team. Linda Heaton was also on the archery team.

Jacque and Karyn were on the girls' A volleyball team, and Earline, Carole, and Wanda were on the B team. Jacque was also captain of the girls' rifle team.

Marilyn Weiss was active in sports at Birdville High School, to which she had transferred.

And at the end of senior year, when awards were passed out, Troop/Ship 11 Scouts took a large share of them.

When the Carter High School faculty chose Who's Who honors, three Troop/Ship 11 girls were selected: Ann for leadership, Linda Booker for school spirit, and I for citizenship.

Ann also won the citizenship award from the local chapter of the Daughters of the American Revolution (DAR).

Photo from 1961 Carter High School *Eagle* yearbook
Ann Brown won the citizenship award from the local DAR
chapter and the CHS faculty's Who's Who Leadership Award.

Margie won a scholarship from a local secretaries' organization.

Photo from 1961 Carter High School *Eagle* yearbook
Margie Stoddard won a scholarship from a local secretary's
organization for use in furthering her business education.

Linda Booker was the faculty's choice for the Who's Who School Spirit Award.

Photo from 1961 Carter High School *Eagle* yearbook
Linda Booker won the CHS faculty's Who's Who School Spirit Award.

My journalism teacher entered me in a competition for county female high school journalists. We had to take a test and undergo an interview. I placed first, was honored at a banquet, got my picture in the Fort Worth *Star-Telegram*, and won a college scholarship from Tarrant County's chapter of Theta Sigma Phi women's journalism fraternity.

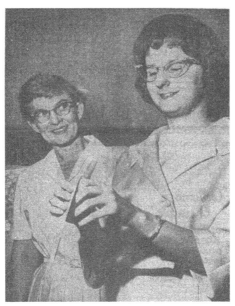

Fort Worth *Star-Telegram* staff photo
Linda Kay Killian was named top high school girl journalist in Tarrant
County. She received the Award from Mrs. Ann Leverich, left. Linda
Kay also won the CHS faculty's Who's Who Award for Citizenship.

Other troop/ship 11 girls were outstanding too. Beverly, Donna,
and Martha worked on the *Eagle Record* with me. Linda Heaton
was active in Cheerleaders' Club, Future Teachers of America, and
Spanish Club. Linda Simons was in Cheerleaders' Club and Music
Appreciation Club. Carole, Diane, and Wanda had leads in the senior
play. Joyce skipped a grade and graduated a year before we did.

Wanda and Ann sang in Girls' Sextet.

Photo from 1961 Carter High School *Eagle* yearbook
Wanda, first row left, sang in Girls Sextet.
Ann also sang with Girls' Sextet.

And what about academics? Were we so busy with extracurricular activities that we neglected our studies?

No way.

Ever the studious bookworm, I graduated summa cum laude. That meant I had made straight "*A*'s" throughout high school. Ann, Carole, Elaine, Jacque, Margie, and Mary graduated magna cum laude. And Diane, Earline, and Wanda graduated cum laude.

Joyce graduated magna cum laude in 1960.

That's eleven troop/ship 11 Scouts who graduated with honors. I call that impressive. And this doesn't take into account the girls who had left the troop before graduation, honor graduates who had been members of troop 11 but who had moved away.

Photos from 1961 Carter High School *Eagle* yearbook
Troop/Ship 11's 1961 senior pictures. We are top row, left to right,
Linda Booker, Ann Brown, Carole Capps, Earline Campbell, Diane
Crawford; second row, Wanda Elrod, Linda Heaton, Karyn Hudson,
Linda Kay Killian, Jacque McNiel; third row, Linda Simons, Martha
Still, Margie Stoddard, Mary Stoddard, Donna Throckmorton;
fourth row, Elaine Walton, Beverly Wilson. Marilyn Weiss was now
attending Birdville High School. Joyce Wakefield graduated a year
early. Marilyn Ball and Pat Cookus graduated the next year.

A few days after graduation, Girl Scout Mariner Ship 11, along
with our mothers, gathered at Fort Worth's Western Hills Hotel
for a farewell mother-daughter Hawaiian banquet. We dressed up.

Everyone received a real lei made of orchids. Amidst the fragrance of the beautiful leis, we ate Hawaiian-style food while we touched memories and shared future dreams. We had put Campfire Stew behind us: now we had graduated to poi, Hawaiian chicken, and rice. Whatever the menu was that night in this elegant hotel, we probably didn't taste it: we were too caught up in our emotions, be they excitement or sadness, to think of food.

Photos courtesy of Martha Still Littlefield
Left to right, Donna Throckmorton, Martha Still, Beverly
Wilson, Marilyn Weiss, and Earline Campbell at troop/
ship 11's farewell mother-daughter banquet.

Five of our number—Wanda, Marilyn Ball, Karyn, Pat Cookus, and Elaine—were already married. Two, Marilyn Ball and Karyn, were pregnant. Wanda would soon join her husband Hugh Crowder in Germany, where he was stationed with the US Army. The immediate futures of these girls were pretty well set. They were already somewhat launched.

Others of us had big dreams in different directions. We were headed for college, business school, nursing school, and business careers. Some also had marriage plans on the horizon. Most of us hoped marriage would be in our future somewhere, sometime.

It was a bittersweet celebration. I honestly thought I'd rarely, if ever, see these Scouts again. I guess the feeling was universal. It was the end of something very special and unusual—twelve years of Girl Scouting—experienced together. Not many Girl Scout troops have done that. Yes, graduation was the end of something.

Graduation was also the beginning of something, but we weren't sure what. The unknown seemed exciting and a little bit scary. Even so, we felt we were ready for it.

I'm not sure we girls considered what our leaders were feeling. Having now watched my children graduate from high school and leave home, I can imagine that Ellie and "Still" felt the same emotional mixture that every parent feels at the end of one life phase for a child and the beginning of another. Pride? Relief? Joy? Emptiness? Loss? Maybe all of these.

Ellie had always called us *her* girls. Multiply what she was feeling about Wanda's leaving by eighteen, and that's probably close to Ellie's feelings at the banquet. Do the same for Mrs. Still at having Martha leave, and we probably know Mrs. Still's frame of mind too. These women, the two shorter-term assistant leaders, and the rest of the mothers had given us such an amazing twelve-year run that they must have experienced some pride and sense of accomplishment. They must also have shed a tear or two when we weren't looking. Karyn was staying in town, so Mrs. Jeanette Hudson didn't have to say, "Good-bye," to her. Mrs. Esther Killian, my mother, didn't either because I would stay at home my first year of college.

What a past we had had. We had walked to Brownie meetings together, had learned how to do a multitude of tasks together, had gone on trips together, had camped and camped and camped together. We had loved each other most of the time, fussed among ourselves some of the time, and made it through the good times and the not-so-good times with our troop intact. Maybe we had not always done it in harmony and with magnanimity, but we *had worked together* and stuck with it.

Now we were going out to face our futures. We would do so equipped with confidence and numerous life skills because of our many Girl Scout experiences.

I like to say that the second smartest time in life is the senior year in high school, the first being the sophomore year in college. I taught sophomores as a graduate teaching assistant at The University of Texas at Austin, and I know how "smart" they are. Anyway, that night at the banquet as graduating seniors, I suppose we all felt optimistic and self-assured. But even so…

What would we be like on our own? Where would we go? What would we do there? How would we handle what lay ahead for us? How would we end up?

Would we make it through life without this group of girls? We could canoe and sail *in a group* on the waters of Eagle Mountain Lake. Could we navigate the turbulent waters of the adult world without these Scout sisters? Some of us—I among them—certainly was ready to try.

However, if we thought we'd indeed face the future alone and never see each other again, we truly had some surprises in store for us. As my mother used to say, "We had another think coming."

PART II

Launched into the Big Wide World

CHAPTER 10

Thirty-Eight Years of Slow Simmering

*It is 1986, twenty-five years after high school gradu-
ation. Troop/Ship 11 is thirty-seven years old. Most
of the "girls" themselves have reached the age of forty-four. We have met at Martha Still Littlefield's
house in Arlington, Texas, for our reunion.*

*All troop members are present, except Joyce
Wakefield Burks, who lives in California; Linda
Kay Killian Wood, who is in the process of moving her family from New Mexico to Maryland for
the year; Marilyn Ball Murray; Linda Simons Hill,
who has dropped out; and Margie Stoddard Terry,
who is already deceased. Twelve troop/ship 11 mothers also attend.*

A Fort Worth Star-Telegram *reporter and
photographer are present. A half-page spread on
troop/ship 11 will appear in the "Living" section of
the Tuesday newspaper. The reporter interviews the
various troop members and gets information he can
quote in his article. The photographer snaps pictures.*

*Beverly Wilson Greene and Karyn Hudson
Draper have come in their high school Scout uni-
forms: Beverly as a Mariner Scout and Karyn as a
Senior Scout. Everyone is amazed that they can still*

wear these garments. Beverly says she had to hold her breath to fasten her skirt. Karyn says her skirt has an elastic waistband, and that's how she managed to fit into it.

The troop sings "Johnny Appleseed" grace. Jacque comments on how our singing has never been very good. She is wrong, but the quote gets into the newspaper anyway.

The reporter is especially interested in the fact that troop/ship 11 did Mariner Scouting. "Did you really participate in aquatic activities?" he asks. He knows that Fort Worth is not near navigable water.

"You bet, we did," Carole Capps Steadham chimes in, "we swamped canoes—you wouldn't believe the bruises I got—and got our lifesaving badges."

Mrs. Minnie Ruth Elrod, who has moved to Florida, glows as she tells how "her girls" collected money and bought her a plane ticket to come to the reunion. "I didn't know whether to laugh or to cry, so I did a little of both."

Marion Hardy, recently retired executive director of the Tarrant County Girl Scout Council, is also present. She says, "I've seen some reunions, but I think this is the first time we've had this many girls and mothers get together at one time after this many years."

But the best quote is another one from Carole. "This will probably be the last [reunion]. I doubt we'll ever get everybody together again."

Well, Carole, would you like to place a friendly wager on that?

* * * * *

The 1960s were a time of upheaval in the United States. Girl Scout Troop/Ship 11 watched on our black-and-white TV sets, from our college dorms or our newly purchased family homes, as President John F. Kennedy was assassinated in Dallas by Lee Harvey Oswald (sadly, a fellow Fort Worther); as public demonstrations against the Vietnam War played out; and as African-Americans marched to obtain equal civil rights. American astronaut Neil Armstrong was the first man to walk on the moon—a bright spot in what we remember as a somewhat difficult decade.

In the 1970s and '80s, those of us who had put off marriage and children until after college and graduate studies were rearing our children in comfortable, modest houses. Our kids watched *Sesame Street* and *Mr. Rogers' Neighborhood* on color television sets. Bill Gates founded Microsoft Corporation, and Steve Jobs and Steve Wozniak unveiled the Apple II personal computer that made its way into many American homes. Iranian terrorists attacked the US Embassy in Tehran and held fifty-two American hostages for 444 days.

Troop/Ship 11 members watched as the US Olympic team boycotted the 1980 games in Moscow. Ronald Reagan was president eight years of that decade. On his inauguration day, Iran released the American Embassy hostages. Sally Ride became the first American woman to travel in space. The Berlin Wall came down, and Communism began to decline.

Troop/Ship 11 Scouts were living through and coping with these sometimes pleasant, sometimes turbulent times. Most of us still resided in Texas.

It didn't take long after high school graduation for Girl Scout Troop/Ship 11 girls to gravitate back to the troop. However, reconnecting didn't just happen: it took a lot of effort. Most of the work and organizing was accomplished by one Scout, Carole.

She's modest about it, though. "Since I had been getting our class of 1961 together, it made sense to me to get our troop back together too. So I had a goal, but it took the interest of the Scouts to make it happen."

In the beginning, it wasn't easy, but e-mail, which came available to us in the 1990s, has helped considerably. "E-mail has made it possible to stay, and pray, together," Carole now says.

It wasn't and still isn't as if we live in the same neighborhood and can easily communicate among ourselves.

Me? I had moved on—or so I thought. I'd spent a year and a summer at Arlington State College (now The University of Texas at Arlington) and then transferred to The University of Oklahoma, where I happily cheered on the ever-a-national-championship-contender football team and, in general, enjoyed the collegiate lifestyle. I figured the rest of troop 11 had moved on too. Frankly, I didn't think too much about them.

Well, of course, they *had* moved on. Some were married with children. Some, like me, were in college. Others had begun business careers.

Even Mrs. Elrod had established her own floral and catering business. Mrs. Thelma Still too had turned florist: she joined Ellie in her business and expertly arranged many gorgeous and fragrant creations. As always, the two of them worked as one. Wanda Elrod Crowder says, "Mother needed to hire someone reliable, hardworking, and trustworthy. Of course, Thelma Still was the answer."

Several troop/ship 11 Scouts got married in these early post-Carter High School years. Mrs. Elrod provided the flowers for several of these weddings. She did the catering and flowers for my wedding in 1965. She also prepared the flowers for Ann Brown's wedding in 1966.

Ann added another twist to her special occasion—wearing a pair of her Girl Scout shorts under her wedding dress. She tells the story as follows:

> I counseled at Timberlake in the summers from 1961 to 1966. In 1966, I headed up a primitive unit of high school girls. Either one of the girls or my assistant unit leader said to me, "You love Girl Scouting so much that I'm surprised that you're not wearing your GS shorts in your wedding." Then someone dared me to do so. That's all it took.

Photo courtesy of Ann Brown Fields
Ann Brown shows her Girl Scout Senior Roundup
shorts at her wedding in 1966.

Ann, indeed, continued to be active in Girl Scouting. In 1967, she was field advisor, responsible for Girl Scouting in one quarter of Austin, Texas, and five counties south and east of Austin. She was also assistant director of Girl Scout Camp Texlake in the Texas Hill Country.

She had come a long way from the Brownie who cried when her parents left her at camp.

Even though we had launched out into different careers and interests, most troop/ship 11 members still lived either in Fort Worth or in easy-driving distance of the city, so these stayed in touch with the group at least occasionally. And somehow, Carole managed to keep track of the rest of us. Those who didn't stay nearby lived at various times in Alabama, California, Florida, West Germany, Maryland, New Mexico, South Carolina, and Washington State. No matter, Carole found us. She was determined that no troop/ship 11 Scout would get away—and, only one, Linda Simons Hill, did.

Everything, of course, at that time came by way of the US Postal Service or long-distance telephone calls. Undaunted, Carole not only gathered us for luncheons and reunions; she kept us reasonably well informed on what was going on in each other's lives. If somebody had news to share—good or bad—we all got a note or call from Carole. Most of these years, out-of-town telephone calls were considered long-distance and added money to the monthly phone bill. So for Carole, it was a financial sacrifice.

Many of troop/ship 11's reunions were potluck lunches at a house of one of the members. Once we ate at Sammie's Bar-B-Q Restaurant in the Riverside section of Fort Worth where we had grown up. The savory morsels of barbecue "done right" (i.e., Texas style) delighted our palates. Sometimes, we celebrated Mrs. Elrod's birthday. There was always some good reason to gather.

One birthday party for Ellie took place in 1969, eight years after high school graduation. Troop/Ship 11 women gathered at the home of Donna Throckmorton Jones's mother, Mrs. Ollie Throckmorton. Many of the Scouts were married now and had children: they showed up with kids in tow. Some of troop/ship 11's mothers came too.

Photo courtesy of Donna Throckmorton Jones
Relaxing at Ellie's birthday party in 1969 are, left to right, Wanda Elrod Crowder; Mrs. Faye Simons (Linda's mother); Earline Campbell Wood's son Judd, Ann Brown Fields with daughter Charlotte in her lap, and Mrs. Dot Crawford (Diane's mother). The kids in front are Donna Throckmorton Jones's daughters, Janice and Susan.

Troop/Ship 11 members gathered at least once a year, occasionally more often. Sometimes our mothers came, sometimes not. Mrs. Elrod and Mrs. Still made it almost every year. Those of us who couldn't come wrote letters of regret that attempted to catch everyone up on our doings. Some who had come to the luncheon or party wrote back to us and sent pictures. Martha was especially good at doing this.

These years weren't all parties and levity for troop/ship 11. In 1981, we experienced the first terrible blow of our years together. On November 9, 1981, Margie Stoddard Terry passed away at the age of 38. We would always think we were too young to lose a Scout sister, but we definitely thought so when Margie left us.

Having received her degree from Arlington State College (now The University of Texas at Arlington), Margie was an accountant and a legal assistant in Fort Worth. She served as president of the Fort Worth Chapter of the National Association of Legal Assistants (NALA) and was active in the state NALA organization.

She was married to Mike Terry and had one son. Had she lived, she would have enjoyed having three grandchildren and one great-grandchild.

She was the twin sister of troop/ship 11's Mary Stoddard Hitt. We all deeply felt Margie's loss; but, without doubt, Mary's pain was by far the deepest.

Photo from 1961 Carter High School *Eagle* Yearbook
Margie Stoddard Terry in 1960.

But we recovered enough to put on the biggest bash of these years, the one in 1986 at Martha's house with the mothers, Marion Hardy (the only county Girl Scout executive director troop/ship 11 had ever known), and the *Star-Telegram* reporter and photographer.

By this time, most of the Scouts had adult children, some were grandmothers, some were proficient public schooteachers, and some were successful businesswomen. We had, at last, become Ellie's Campfire Stew, all the "girl" ingredients melding to make a marvelous concoction. The stew was simmering well and would continue to do so.

Fort Worth *Star-Telegram* staff photos by Norm Tindell
Earline Campbell Wood, Karyn Hudson Draper, Mary
Stoddard Hitt, Beverly Wilson Greene, Pat Cookus Haberman,
and Carole Capps Steadham opened Tuesday's *Star-Telegram*
on July 15, 1986, to find their pictures in the paper.

We greeted each other with our usual exuberance and hugs all around. Being together was now utter joy. We had grown up into gracious women. The pettiness of the teen years was long gone. We now knew what a marvelous gift we had been given—friendships closer than friendships, relationships better than anything we could have previously imagined.

Mrs. Elrod was pleased at how we had turned out. As she loved us and thought of us as her kids, she beamed at us and claimed to be justifiably proud. "They have become such beautiful women," she commented over and over, "and I'm not just talking about physical beauty either, but also inner beauty."

Perhaps we had matured far better than she had expected us to do. This whole reunion was an occasion for laughter, conversation, and maybe some nostalgic tears.

"Carole, can you eat hamburger now?" Mary asked.

"Well, it's still not my favorite thing," Carole answered.

"Jacque, I can't believe you told that reporter that we aren't good singers. Why did you do that?" Martha was a bit indignant.

"Well, that's my opinion, but ya'll certainly feel free to disagree," Jacque replied.

"Do you remember taking our final for the lifesaving badge?" Elaine Walton Lofland asked. "It was hard taking our clothes off in the water. It seemed silly, and the water was so cold."

"I didn't think we'd ever grow up," Wanda said, "but somehow we did. Amazing."

Who could have foreseen such togetherness back in 1949 at our beginning or even in 1961 at our high school graduation?

And Carole was wrong about this being the last reunion. The reunions continued to take place. She couldn't stop planning, and we couldn't stop coming.

In 1992 we celebrated Ellie's eighty-third birthday. Each girl wrote a letter to her, and Carole collected them into a spiral-bound book. The picture on the cover of the book was from a trip to Camp Timberlake and is the most complete one ever taken of the troop until 2019. Unfortunately, none of us can locate the original, so it doesn't print out very clear.

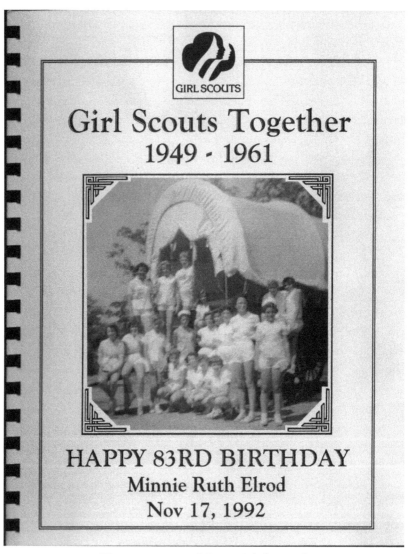

GIRL SCOUTS

Girl Scouts Together
1949 - 1961

HAPPY 83RD BIRTHDAY
Minnie Ruth Elrod
Nov 17, 1992

Photo courtesy of Gerry Odell Wood
The book Carole made to commemorate Ellie's eighty-third birthday. The photo on the cover is the most complete picture taken of the troop until 2019.

In 1997, we gathered for a luncheon at Carole's house. Most "girls" are age fifty-four.

Photo courtesy of Martha Still Littlefield
At Carole's house in Fort Worth in 1997 are, left to right, front row, Mary Stoddard Hitt, Elaine Walton Lofland, Ann Brown Fields, and Beverly Wilson Greene; second row, Diane Crawford Hill, Mrs. Thelma Still, Marilyn Ball Murray, Martha Still Littlefield, Donna Throckmorton Jones, Carole Capps Steadham, and Earline Campbell Wood.

The next year, 1998, troop/ship 11 convened for Mrs. Elrod's ninetieth birthday party, this occasion also at Carole's house. At fifty-five, we were now mature enough to appreciate the efforts of our competent leader. Mrs. Elrod was an outstanding woman, and we wanted to honor her as best we could. We were afraid that our opportunities would not go on forever. Life is fragile and over too soon.

"How did Ellie come up with so many ideas of things for us to do and learn?" Elaine asked at one of our luncheons.

"I surely couldn't do it," Diane Crawford Hill responded. "I tried but only made it a few years. It was hard, and it was sad when it didn't work out."

But Ellie did it: prepared activities every week of every month of every year for twelve years. We found such talent, love, ingenuity, perseverance, and pure unselfishness to be incomprehensible. We honestly didn't feel that any of us could do such a thing. Some of us—Wanda, Martha, Carole, and, of course, Diane—had tried leading troops, in most cases only to see their girls lose interest.

Photo courtesy of Donna Throckmorton Jones
In 1998, troop/ship 11 sang "Happy Birthday" to Ellie on her
ninetieth birthday before she blew out her tall candles.

As the post-high-school period zoomed by us, we lived mostly happy lives.

Of course, nobody sails through life without heartaches.

Ann's husband died of a heart attack in 1968, just before the birth of her daughter.

In November 1981, we lost our first Scout sister, Margie, to death at the age of thirty-eight. None of us saw this shock coming. We didn't consider ourselves old enough to experience the death of someone our own age. Mary, Margie's twin sister, was particularly hard hit, as anyone who has lost a sibling, understands.

Several of us lost parents to death during this thirty-eight-year period. Others by now had elderly parents to care for.

Some troop/ship 11 women went through the heartbreak of divorce during this period. Ever resilient, however, all of them recovered and went on to build better lives for themselves and their children.

Yes, life, as life will do, dealt us some blows, but armed with the strength we gained from God, our parents, and our Scout sisters, we have managed to stand tall in the face of everything that has whacked at us. We have stayed in touch over the miles and years.

And, yes, Carole, thanks to you and others and to our collective great delight, the reunions kept coming.

CHAPTER 11

Celebrating Fifty Years Together

Girl Scout Troop/Ship 11 has been together for fifty years. We are fifty-five and fifty-six years old. The year is 1999; the month, November. We are celebrating for an entire weekend. Even the girls who live far away are here in Fort Worth for the festivities.

We are spending Friday night in the new-to-us Lakewood Lodge at our beloved Camp Timberlake. We bring food to cook and share, including the ingredients for Campfire Stew and S'mores. Of course, we are delighted to be with each other again. It is always so nowadays.

We sing songs—"The Prune Song," "Little Red Caboose," and "Five Little Ducks," among others.

We pour over scrapbooks compiled by Carole Capps Steadham, Martha Still Littlefield, and Karyn Hudson Draper.

We pass around pictures of our grandchildren. We play Spoons.

We laugh at jokes and antics of Jacque McNiel Winkler and Linda Booker Webb, neither of whom, even now, can be serious or quiet.

When we finally get around to sleeping, we will do it with sleeping bags and bedrolls on cots in a big dormitory-like room. Some will complain that the springs on the cots don't go well anymore with their not-so-young bones. A few of us snore, keeping others awake.

But sleep won't come early. We have too much to talk about, too many jokes to tell, too many games to play, too many memories to mull over.

So we reminisce, telling the stories we remember, and we laugh…and we laugh…and we laugh.

A knock sounds at our door. We look at each other with questioning expressions. Who can be summoning us? Everyone who is coming to this part of the reunion is here. We feel safe. Everything— cooking equipment, plumbing—is working well in the lodge. No cyclones, tornadoes, or hurricanes are predicted. What's going on?

Wanda Elrod Crowder gingerly opens the door. The person on the other side is the leader of a Brownie troop that is also spending the night in the building. She hesitates, appearing a little apologetic. "I'm sorry to bother you," she says, "but our little Brownies are having trouble sleeping. Could you be a little quieter?"

Wanda does a double take, hastily and clumsily expresses a sincere apology, and assures the woman that we will try to make less noise. Then she closes the door and turns to face the rest of us.

We burst into laughter all over again, this time trying to do it quietly with our hands covering our mouths. Our faces turn red, as squelching a laugh is, well, painful. Some of us snort. Some of us have tears streaming down our faces.

Fifty years melt away in an instant. We are once more the giggly six-year-olds of 1949.

* * * * *

The 1990s brought some semblance of peace to Girl Scout Troop/ Ship 11. Scandals and bad news were still rocking the world around us. The Texas A&M University traditional pre-University of Texas football game bonfire structure collapsed, and twelve students were killed. The Cox Report alleged that China indeed was spying on the United States. Texas governor George W. Bush announced his run for the US presidency. The ever-popular *Star Wars* motion picture saga continued to captivate moviegoers.

However, Girl Scout Troop/Ship 11 soldiered on. Job successes, families, travels, and other personal triumphs and relationships filled our world.

In 1998, Girl Scout Troop/Ship 11 had celebrated its forty-ninth year with a birthday party for Mrs. Minnie Ruth Elrod's ninetieth birthday. We women had agreed at that time to do something extra-special for our upcoming fiftieth anniversary. We had several ideas.

As Karyn was driving home from the party, a notion came to her. "I was thinking how we are all intelligent women and how good this thing we have has been, but if we just keep it with *us*, it's not doing anything to pass on to future generations."

Karyn figured out a way to bless younger Scouts as we had been blessed. She shared her thoughts with the rest of the troop, and the project immediately took wing.

We would set up a "campership" at Camp Timberlake to help less fortunate girls attend camp activities. We would begin funding the campership with $10,000 that we would work to raise; we would call it the Minnie Ruth Elrod Endowment Fund.

It was a grand idea, and troop/ship 11 could make it happen.

Beverly Wilson Greene really was thrilled with Karyn's plan. "It [camping] was a real base for us, our most bonding time." Beverly had received a two-week campership when she was young—something we had not known—and she was grateful for that gift.

How would we raise the $10,000 to start the fund?

First, Martha had a garage and bake sale at her house in Arlington. Everyone contributed items for sale and baked goods. Jacque and Beverly worked particularly hard, baking cupcakes, pies, cakes, and scones.

"The goodies looked too yummy to sell. We wanted to eat them," Martha says.

The sale netted $1,120.

Two months later, Karyn organized a garage sale at her mother's house in the Oakhurst section of Fort Worth. "I thought that setting the sale in the part of town where troop/ship 11 girls had grown up—where we perhaps were known and remembered—might attract buyers."

Attract buyers it did, but Karyn relates an unfortunate incident that occurred.

> A man wanted to buy a small item and pretended that he had only a $100 bill. He scammed us out of the $100 by taking the change we had offered, the item he "bought," *and* the $100 bill. We instantly noticed the error after he drove off. Knowing there were other sales in the area that day, Earline tracked him down and confronted him. No, he did not return our money, but I bet he left the neighborhood after that. Go, Earline!

Photo courtesy of Karyn Hudson Draper
Karyn Hudson Draper demonstrates a stationary bike, and
Earline Campbell Wood helps with the Oakhurst sale.

One little girl possibly being cheated out of a "campership" notwithstanding, the Oakhurst garage sale pulled in another $693 for the Elrod endowment fund.

Carole Capps Steadham wrote letters to and visited businesses in the Oakhurst-Riverside area, seeking donations. Additional money came in from that endeavor.

Earline Campbell Wood had T-shirts printed with Karyn's childhood fishing picture on them. The picture can be seen on page 42 of this book. The shirts sold at a profit, mostly to troop/ship 11 Scouts and their families.

Photo courtesy of Martha Still Littlefield
Troop/Ship 11 members model their fiftieth anniversary tee shirts. Left to right, first row, are Martha Still Littlefield, Linda Booker Webb, Earline Campbell Wood, and Beverly Wilson Greene; second row, Elaine Walton Lofland, Ann Brown Fields, Carole Capps Steadham, Joyce Wakefield Burks, Karyn Hudson Draper, and Diane Crawford Hill; third row, Marilyn Ball Murray, Wanda Elrod Crowder, Linda Heaton Leonhardt, and Jacque McNiel Winkler.

Mrs. Elrod was so thrilled and touched by our efforts that she herself gave money to the fund and urged some of her family members to do so.

And Karyn wasn't done. She organized a benefit golf tournament at Eagle Mountain Country Club, near Camp Timberlake. People entered to play, paying a higher entrance fee than their game actually cost. Some people donated additional money by "sponsoring a hole."

"Golf is a big deal in Texas," Karyn says. "We had a good turnout." After expenses, the troop cleared $900 from the tournament.

Photo by Sharon Corcoran of Fort Worth *Star-Telegram* staff
Players warm up at Eagle Mountain Country Club
before the fund-raiser golf tournament.

And, of course, each troop/ship 11 member made a personal contribution.

Troop/Ship 11 did raise the $10,000. At our anniversary celebration in November, Karyn presented the check to the Fort Worth Circle T Girl Scout Council Executive Director Sandra Kautz.

Photo courtesy of Karyn Hudson Draper
Karyn Hudson Draper prepares to present $10,000 check and
commemorative troop/ship 11 album to Fort Worth Circle
T Girl Scout Council Executive Director Sandra Kautz. Left
to right are Ms. Kautz, Karyn, and Mrs. Jeanette Hudson,
Karyn's mother and assistant leader of the troop.

Over the years, we would continue to contribute. For example,
every time a troop member has lost a relative to death, we have made
memorial contributions in that family member's name. Some have
also found other reasons to contribute, such as forgoing birthday and
Mother's Day presents and giving the money to the fund.

With endowment fund activities underway, it was time to plan
the big anniversary weekend. Eight troop/ship 11 women met at
Carole's house to brainstorm.

After considering ideas, the women chose activities to fill the
three days—an overnight camp out at Camp Timberlake, a Saturday
lunch at Timberlake, an afternoon parents' visit there, a Christian
worship service on Sunday, a luncheon after worship, and a big
reception on Sunday afternoon with all family members included.
The selected dates were November 5–7, 1999.

Photo courtesy of Karyn Hudson Draper
Troop/Ship 11's fiftieth anniversary planners were, left to
right, first row, Martha Still Littlefield, Beverly Wilson Greene,
and Karyn Hudson Draper; second row, Earline Campbell
Wood, Carole Capps Steadham, Elaine Walton Lofland,
Diane Crawford Hill, and Jacque McNiel Winkler.

Plans made, venues reserved, food gathered and prepared, speakers booked, and families invited, the date for the event arrived.

Friday, November 5, we met at Camp Timberlake's Lakewood Lodge.

All but one troop/ship 11 member came to at least part of the weekend activities. Wanda, who was still living in Washington State, made a cross-country detour to Florida to escort Mrs. Elrod to Fort Worth. Ellie, who was having health problems, now lived with Wanda's sister Sharon Elrod Wallace in Lake Wales, Florida. Joyce Wakefield Burks came from California, Linda Booker Webb came from Alabama, and I came from New Mexico. The only post-high-school-graduation active troop members who weren't there were our beloved Margie, who had departed this life in 1981, and Donna Throckmorton Jones, who doesn't remember now why she couldn't come.

Photo courtesy of Jacque McNiel Winkler
Wanda Elrod Crowder flew cross-country and halfway back
to bring Mrs. Minnie Ruth Elrod to the reunion.

Friday night at Camp Timberlake, we talked and talked and talked. We laughed and laughed and laughed. We hugged and hugged and hugged. We played the games we used to play at camp when we were younger. We gathered firewood in boxes and carried them, two women to a box, back to the lodge. We built a fire in the lodge fireplace, ate delicious-as-ever Campfire Stew, roasted marshmallows for S'mores, and talked until most of us were hoarse.

"It's just like old times, isn't it?" Ann Brown Fields observed. "How can we not value what we've been given as a group? It's so special."

"We're not friends. We're sisters," Elaine Walton Lofland added.

"That's for sure," everyone agreed.

Photo courtesy of Jacque McNiel Winkler
Left to right, Martha Still Littlefield, Elaine Walton Lofland, Wanda
Elrod Crowder, Joyce Wakefield Burks, and Beverly Wilson Greene
play Spoons in Camp Timberlake's Lakewood Lodge on Friday night.

Time, as always, passed swiftly. The hour became late, but we were still going strong. Our noise level rose too high, so high that we disturbed the sleep of a troop of Brownies who were also spending the night in the lodge. We needed Mrs. Thelma Still to make us behave, but she wasn't there. So we meekly apologized to the Brownies, who forgave us and wanted their picture taken with us on Saturday. They couldn't imagine that women could live long enough to be in Girl Scouts for fifty years.

Saturday morning, we walked to our favorite campsites, Twin Oaks and Pioneer Village. Leaves and twigs crunched under our feet, and the trees emitted a clean forest smell. The camps seemed older and smaller, but otherwise just as we remembered them. We sat on felled tree logs and sang songs, including "Little Bunny Foo Foo" and "The Stormy Winds Do Blow." We admired the swimming pool that our cookie-sale money had helped fund.

Back at the lodge, Linda Booker and Ann clowned around, modeling some Girl Scout uniform paraphernalia that Martha, Karyn, and Beverly had brought. We again gazed at photographs and scrapbooks of our years together, indulging in some more "Remember when..." Jacque read a draft of Earline's new romance novel and pronounced it good.

We made a banner wall-hanging to leave in the lodge at the camp to commemorate our special anniversary. We all signed it.

Photo courtesy of Jacque McNiel Winkler
Jacque took the best picture of our fiftieth anniversary banner.

Saturday noon, we ate chicken-and-tuna-salad sandwiches for lunch. While we were eating, and for no particular reason, Carole announced, "These sandwiches are great. I don't do bologna."

"Yes, Carole, we remember that from the Colorado trip," Joyce said.

Carole had been quite vocal about her disdain for bologna then. Today she reminded us, and that set us off in recounting memories of that wonderful adventure.

In the afternoon, some of our mothers came to visit us at the lodge. They wanted to share the memories too. All of them had helped with our camp outs at one time or other. Camp Timberlake had been a big part of their lives for twelve years also.

Of course, our mothers weren't a bit surprised that we'd gotten ourselves in trouble by making too much noise the night before. They knew us too well.

"I'd have been more surprised if you hadn't caused a ruckus," Mrs. Dot Crawford, Diane Crawford Hill's mother, quipped.

Sunday, November 7, turned out to be another high-point day for troop/ship 11.

First, we met in a tent outside Oakhurst Methodist Church for morning worship service. This was the church where we had held our weekly meetings from first through sixth grades. Our parents, other family members, and friends attended with us. The church had moved down the street and had undergone some nice remodeling in the years since we had met there. It was very attractive.

Ann, our ordained Methodist minister, delivered the sermon for morning worship. She also presided over Holy Communion, which she says was a powerful moment for her.

"Wanda said to me with tears in her eyes that we had never had Holy Communion together before." It had taken us fifty years to get to that point.

Photo courtesy of Martha Still Littlefield
Partial audience at troop/ship 11's fiftieth anniversary morning church service. Left to right, first row, are Mrs. Minnie Ruth Elrod, Wanda Elrod Crowder, and Karyn Hudson Draper; second row, Earline Campbell Wood, Carole Capps Steadham, and Diane Crawford Hill.

Ann began with a prayer, then read her Bible text, Joshua 24:25: "Choose this day whom you will serve;…but as for me and my household, we will serve the Lord."

Photo courtesy of Martha Still Littlefield
Dr. Ann Brown Fields dons a microphone in preparation for
delivering Sunday sermon and presiding over Holy Communion
at Oakhurst Methodist Church, November 7, 1999.

She applied the passage to our need to serve God in the many "households" to which we belong—our family, our church, our work situation, our circle of friends. When she came to the "household" of troop/ship 11, she said the following:

> Girl Scout Troop 11 is one of those households for me. I'm pretty sure that I was not the easiest of kids to manage—either alone or in a group. I was pretty wiggly for one thing. We met in the fellowship hall of this church…Yes, it took a lot of patience to deal with me. And for years, I believed that Ms. Elrod and Ms. Still and all my friends in the troop deserved all the credit. Only in the last ten years or so has it become clear to me that it was not they alone who made the difference but the fact that they allowed the light of God in Jesus Christ to shine through their lives. It has always been clear to me that ours was a God-driven undertaking. What a gift. Yes, troop 11 has been a household for me, one which fears God and serves the Lord with sincerity and truth.

There was not a dry eye in the tent, needless to say.

At the conclusion of the church service, we and family members who could do so traveled to eat lunch at the Rose Garden Tea Room in Arlington. There we enjoyed a delicious lunch of soup, salad, and gourmet sandwiches—and we jabbered on and on about our families, our current interests, our health issues, and our aspirations. Conversational lapses have never been a problem for us.

Those of us who hadn't made it to many gatherings since high school jumped in wholeheartedly trying to get caught up with everyone. I wanted to know what everyone had been doing, so I brought a blank journal for the "girls" to write in.

My mother, husband Gerry, and daughter Julie came with me to the lunch. We four were impressed with the persons my fellow Scouts had become—beautiful, gracious, kindhearted women whose love for each other showed in every gesture and expression.

Photo courtesy of Linda Kay Killian Wood
At bottom left, Diane Crawford Hill signs my book at the luncheon.
Then moving clockwise around the table are Elaine Walton
Lofland, Carole Capps Steadham, Joyce Wakefield Burks, Martha
Still Littlefield, Linda Booker Webb, Ann Brown Fields, Beverly
Wilson Greene, and Gloria Wakefield Denson, Joyce's sister.

Long before we were ready to leave, someone glanced at her watch and informed us that we must rush to the main reception at the Fort Worth Botanic Gardens Deborah Beggs Moncrief Garden

Center. We quickly climbed into our cars and headed westward on Interstate 30.

When my family arrived, it was to hear a cacophony wafting down the passageways of the botanic garden visitor center. Upon entering the meeting hall, we saw an impressive gathering of fifty-six-year-old Girl Scouts, their living parents, their children, and their grandchildren.

The realization began to sink in for me that this wasn't only about troop/ship 11 but also about the numerous people who had touched the lives of the troop and the many people whose lives the troop had touched. My mouth flew open, my daughter's face showed wonder, my mother's countenance lit up like a Roman candle, and my husband whipped out his camera.

The room buzzed continually as we hugged each other, hugged each others' parents, hugged each others' siblings, hugged each others' children, and hugged each others' grandchildren. I didn't have grandchildren yet, but hugging those of others was fun.

I clung to precious Jacque, whom I hadn't seen in the thirty-three years since my wedding and hadn't heard from since my Christmas card bounced back several years previous, causing me to lose her address.

I also was able to thank Jacque's dad Jack for being a substitute father to me during the Scout years when my own dad was not in my life. Jack's eyes teared up, my eyes teared up, and, for perhaps the only time in his life, Jack McNiel—who always, always had a comeback, quip, or wisecrack—was at a loss for words.

The years came flooding back over me as Karyn and I reconnected. Cindy (Martha's sister) grabbed me and reintroduced herself. She didn't look like a little girl anymore. Circle T Girl Scout Council Executive Director Sandy Kautz reminded me that her mother had been my speech teacher at Riverside Junior High School. Fort Worth is a city, a rather large one really, but it's surprising how so many of us with connections to Fort Worth have connections to one another.

Martha and Karyn had arranged an impressive array of troop/ship 11 photographs, crafts, and uniforms on a long table. My daughter eagerly scrutinized every photo and craft item. I couldn't believe how interested she was in this part of her mother's early life.

Karyn and Martha asked me to read a tribute I'd previously written to Mrs. Elrod.

"Uh, really?" I asked in disbelief. "I can't remember what I said."

"Then just read it," they said.

I reviewed the paragraphs quickly before the formal program began. Ready or not, the presentations commenced.

Of course, a flag ceremony opened the occasion. Young Girl Scouts from several troops, in full uniform, performed the rite with all appropriate flags. Their uniforms were, of course, different from any we had worn, and the ceremony seemed a trifle different too, but it brought back many memories of flag ceremonies troop/ship 11 had muddled through.

Karyn took the podium to explain the Minnie Ruth Elrod Endowment Fund and present the check to Sandy Kautz.

Next, Wanda gave a tribute to her mother and our deceased parents, followed by my reading of the troop's tribute to Mrs. Elrod.

Photo courtesy of Gerry Odell Wood
Linda Kay Killian Wood reads a tribute to Mrs. Elrod from the troop.

Then, Sandy Kautz and Betty Roland from the Fort Worth Circle T Girl Scout Council office presented each Scout with a fifty-year membership pin. We went up one by one and gave the Girl Scout salute, which I didn't remember and fumbled around trying to accomplish. If anyone else had this problem, I didn't notice it. I do think everyone felt emotional and overwhelmed with our memories. Maybe that's my excuse.

Photo courtesy of Elaine Walton Lofland
Jacque McNiel Winkler receives her fifty-year Girl
Scout pin from Betty Roland and Sandy Kautz.

After we had received our pins, the young Scouts retired the colors.

The program ended, and we gathered for a group picture.

One of the surprising things about troop/ship 11 is that hardly ever in our years together have we managed to get us all in one picture. One exception may be the photo that Carole used on the cover of the commemorative book she made for Mrs. Elrod in 1992. The original photograph apparently no longer exists.

You'd think in fifty years we could get the entire group to pose for a picture sometime.

Again it was not to be so. Pat, who had come for the church service but didn't make it to the big reception, and Donna were missing in this one. Margie, of course, was deceased.

Still, the group shot taken that day is the most complete that we had managed to snap since graduation from high school. We feel pretty good about that picture. We thought we had aged rather well, but, then, we are Texas belles and do know how to fix ourselves up appropriately.

Photo courtesy of Gerry Odell Wood
Girl Scout Troop/Ship 11 at fiftieth anniversary celebration. Left to right, first row, are Earline Campbell Wood, Linda Heaton Leonhardt, Beverly Wilson Greene, Linda Booker Webb, Mrs. Minnie Ruth Elrod, Martha Still Littlefield, Karyn Hudson Draper, Diane Crawford Hill, and Marilyn Weiss; second row, Wanda Elrod Crowder, Mary Stoddard Hitt, Joyce Wakefield Burks, Linda Kay Killian Wood, Marilyn Ball Murray, Mrs. Thelma Still, Jacque McNiel Winkler, Elaine Walton Lofland, Carole Capps Steadham, and Ann Brown Fields. Missing from this picture are Donna Throckmorton Jones, Margie Stoddard Terry, and Pat Cookus Haberman.

Pictures taken, cake and punch consumed, and hugs once more exchanged, we began one-by-one to depart with our friends and families.

We had been together fifty years, and all but one of us had lived to celebrate that longevity. Certainly, few of us had thought such a lengthy association possible.

I was so excited about the joys of the weekend that I couldn't sleep that Sunday night. I know some other Scouts felt the same.

Beverly videotaped the entire weekend.

Photo courtesy of Martha Still Littlefield
Martha Still Littlefield snapped a picture of
Beverly Wilson Greene's videotaping.

A few days after the festivities were over and we had gone home, we received copies of this treasured keepsake. Beverly also included footage of photographs depicting troop/ship 11's many years of exploits. The video was and is a joy to watch, producing giggles at our silly antics and nostalgic tears at our fond memories.

Surely, fifty years would now be the end of it.

And in a way, it was. In the following year, we would lose Jacque to death because of heart failure. So I guess it *was* the last time we would *all* be together.

But, no, fifty years would not be the end for Girl Scout Troop/ Ship 11. We cantankerous, stubborn, strong, talented Texas women who loved each other more with every passing year weren't about to let such a good thing get away from us.

What did we do? We simply began working on the second fifty years of the troop. What else would we do? The first five decades had been glorious—well, mostly glorious. Maybe more adventures lay ahead for us.

So—like the Energizer Bunny®—we would just keep going and going and going.

PART III

Fifty Years?
Just the Beginning

CHAPTER 12

The Sixth Decade:
Too Many Farewells

Seven Girl Scout Troop/Ship 11 "girls" have gathered at Martha Still Littlefield's lake house at Possum Kingdom Lake, southwest of Fort Worth. The lake is located on the Brazos River mostly in Palo Pinto County, Texas. It is February 2004. Winters are usually mild in Texas, but the weather this February is chilly, blustery, and uncomfortable for most out-door activities. Everyone has brought warm clothes and jackets.

The weather does not deter us from gathering around a big campfire outside on the beach. In fact, Martha has carefully laid it out as we were taught to do in the 1950s by her mother and Mrs. Minnie Ruth Elrod—just the right size, just the right num-ber of logs and kindling, just the right log angles.

We are sitting around the campfire in a circle, digesting our Campfire Stew, roasting marshmal-lows for S'mores, laughing, talking, singing favorite camp songs (like "On Top of Old Smokey" and "The Grand Old Duke of York")—simply having old-time camping fun troop/ship 11-style.

All at once, we notice Linda Booker Webb "talking up-a-storm," as she always does. She is wrapped in her full-length mink coat. Smoke, ashes, and dust from the fire are blowing around, gooey melted chocolate from S'mores is dripping down most of our chins, and Booker's mink coat is dragging in the dirt.

We tell her that her coat is getting ruined, and Martha offers to get Booker an old coat from inside the house, but she merely blows us off.

"No big deal," she says and goes on licking her chocolate-marshmallow-covered fingers and telling the tale of the moment.

Few of us own mink coats, or even mink earrings, so we continue to worry about the coat, but we follow her lead and laugh at her story. We can always depend on Booker for a good laugh—always. And, as surely everyone knows, a good story is much more important than a mink coat.

* * * * *

After our fiftieth anniversary celebration, we of Girl Scout Troop/ Ship 11 sat back for what seemed like only a few minutes and took a collective deep breath. We watched Beverly Wilson Greene's video several times and basked in the joy and nostalgia of it.

But when Jacque McNiel Winkler died about a year later on November 14, 2000, we collectively gasped and got back to planning gatherings. We'd learned a valuable lesson: we weren't going to live forever, and we'd better not waste the time we had left.

Jacque had been a mainstay of the troop. She had supported us all. She was active, smart, strong, funny, and upbeat. Her wry sense of humor, inherited from her dad, had helped hold us together for fifty-one years. "That's about as funny as a train wreck," and "Well, that's so important, let's put it in the *Star-Telegram*," were two of her frequent sayings. Her sweet, loving nature, inherited from her mother, made her a close friend.

Nobody ever got mad at her. What was there to be mad at? *She* never got angry at anybody. She was Jacque, comfortable in her own skin and accepting of everyone else. She had a gift for peacemaking. Her absence was going to be hideously hard for us.

Photo courtesy of Martha Still Littlefield
Jacquelyn Ann McNiel Winkler with her two granddaughters, Kaitlin and Kerstin Winkler, at troop/ship 11's fiftieth anniversary, a year before her death in 2000.

In the end, it was heart failure that took Jacque away from us. She left behind her husband, Wayne; two grown children; two grandchildren; her dad Jack, her sister Sharon, and troop/ship 11. We were certain that the age of fifty-seven was way too young for such a thing to happen. However, as true followers of the indomitable Girl Scout founder, Juliet Gordon Low, we would persevere through heartbreak.

Every Troop/Ship 11 Scout would miss Jacque deeply, but she and I had been especially close friends since kindergarten. I can't remember a cross word ever passing between us in all those years. I *really* felt the loss.

On September 11, 2001, terrorists hijacked four American airliners and flew them into the World Trade Center in New York City, the Pentagon in Washington, DC, and a field in Pennsylvania. Almost three thousand people were killed. The country was severely wounded and shocked.

A few weeks after the attack, the Amon Carter-Riverside High School class of 1961 gathered for its fortieth reunion. I now wanted to reconnect with my high school friends, so I went. We fifty-eight-year-olds, of course, discussed 9/11 events ad nauseam.

The class reunion included a Girl Scout luncheon at Mrs. Thelma Still's house on Dalford Street in the Riverside neighborhood. Again, some Scout mothers attended.

I enjoyed sitting around the table, talking with my fellow Scouts and their moms about children, grandchildren, classmates, jobs, and recent Fort Worth events. Mostly we avoided discussing 9/11. We took refuge in the camaraderie we had that by then had caused our conversations to take on new meaning. I hung on every word.

My mother was at this time in Los Alamos, New Mexico, in a retirement home and not in good health. So that weekend, in addition to the reunions, I cleaned out her house so we could sell it to raise money for her nursing home care.

So it was a time of ups and downs for me, totally filled with memories. I shed tears over objects sent to the Goodwill Industries Collection Center, over saying farewell to my girlhood home, and over realizing how wondrously my entire life had been blessed by family, friends, and opportunities.

After the September 11, 2001 attacks, US President George W. Bush sent American troops to fight in Iraq and Afghanistan, and troop/ship 11 women went on with their lives.

In 2002, troop/ship 11 gathered for another annual luncheon at Carole Capps Steadham's house. I didn't get there, but Martha sent me a picture. Mrs. Still and Mrs. Jeanette Hudson came.

Photo courtesy of Martha Still Littlefield
Troop/Ship 11's 2002 lunch. Left to right, first row, are Linda Booker Webb, Linda Heaton Leonhardt, Karyn Hudson Draper, Mrs. Thelma Still, Earlene Campbell Wood, and Mrs. Jeanette Hudson; second row, Martha Still Littlefield, Beverly Wilson Greene, Elaine Walton Lofland, Mary Stoddard Hitt, Diane Crawford Hill, Ann Brown Fields, Carole Capps Steadham, and Marilyn Ball Murray.

In 2003, Mrs. Minnie Ruth Elrod, still living with daughter Sharon Elrod Wallace in Lake Wales, Florida, was too ill to make the trip to Fort Worth for a reunion. A frustrated Carole decided that since Ellie couldn't come to us, we should go to her.

So seven of us and Mrs. Still did just that. Wanda flew into Orlando from Washington State, Linda Booker drove from Alabama, I flew from New Mexico, and the "girls" living in Texas flew from Dallas/Fort Worth.

On Saturday afternoon, we helped Sharon host a reception for her mother at the Lake Wales Trinity Baptist Church.

Photo courtesy of Sharon Elrod Wallace
Seven troop/ship 11 women at the Florida reception honoring Mrs.
Minnie Ruth Elrod. Mrs. Elrod and Mrs. Thelma Still are in front.
Left to right, second row, are Linda Booker Webb, Ann Brown
Fields, Carole Capps Steadham, Wanda Elrod Crowder, Martha Still
Littlefield, Linda Kay Killian Wood, and Earline Campbell Wood.

Mrs. Elrod, since moving to Florida and, although not in good health, had been active in the church's senior citizens' group, the Keenagers. Still using her florist and ceramist skills, she taught them how to do flower arranging and make ceramic pieces. Her Florida friends loved her and were delighted to join us at this special reception.

Sharon and Wanda had created a display of photos, awards, and scrapbooks in honor of their mother, including troop/ship 11 paraphernalia. Guests enjoyed viewing these items.

At the reception, each Girl Scout took the microphone to thank Ellie for what she had done for us. As none of us had prepared a speech, we spoke off the cuff. We did well, no doubt because of Mrs. Kautz's speech class in junior high. Some Keenagers spoke too.

Then we had cake and punch and met Ellie's friends.

After the reception, the Keenagers took us to their craft room in the church building. They showed us the flower arrangements, wreaths, and ceramic pieces they had made under Ellie's tutelage. They sold their creations for charity projects. Also, they showed us each person's assigned workstation, including Ellie's. We each bought something as a memento of our trip and this special time with Ellie. The teapot and matching cup I bought appear on page 96 of this book.

We stayed in a delightful vintage motel by a lake, Lekarika Hills Golf Course and Country Inn. A former religious retreat, it was cozy, comfortable, and charming.

I had the joy of sharing a suite with Linda Booker. She, as always, was a hoot, filling our time with crazy antics and jokes. She particularly focused on tales from her cheerleading days at Carter High School. I learned about some of the scrapes she, Diane Crawford, Elaine Walton, and other cheerleaders had gotten into back then.

Also, Booker and I found time for seriousness. She had tragically lost a granddaughter in an automobile accident, and she shared with me her journey through her grief. I treasure our discussions.

Saturday night at dinner, as always, we sang "Johnny Appleseed" grace in the inn's restaurant before ingesting delicious fresh seafood.

Afterward, we played Spoons, Bunco, and other games in Carole and Earline Campbell Wood's cottage. We even bet money on our games, and I won one of them.

"Keep your money. I don't want it," I said over and over.

"Okay, give it to Wanda to put in the church collection plate tomorrow," Ann Brown Fields said.

So that's what I did.

When I said "good-bye" to my Scout sisters at Orlando International Airport on Sunday, I knew we had spent another memorable time together.

More significant, it was the last time we would see Mrs. Elrod. No one begrudges the effort to make the trip. We're just glad we could do it. Others, like Karyn Hudson Draper, whose mother was very ill in Fort Worth, regretted having to stay behind.

Mrs. Elrod passed away November 13, 2003.

Her funeral was held at Mount Olivet Chapel and Cemetery in Fort Worth's Oakhurst/Riverside area where she had lived for many years. Carole ordered a spray of flowers in green and gold with "Girl Scout Troop 11" on it.

I couldn't attend the funeral, but Carole asked me to write our tribute to be read by Ann at the service. Here's an excerpt:

> And just what do these sixty-year-old women think that Minnie Ruth gave to them? Well, the list is pretty long, but here is a short version.
>
> - She taught them everything they will ever need to know about camping.
> - She taught them many practical skills for living—how to cook, how to sew, how to decorate cakes, how to take acceptable photographs.
> - She provided numerous fun and educational activities—trips to Colorado and San Antonio, tours of Mrs. Baird's Bakery and the Dr Pepper Bottling Company.
> - She let them try many new things so that, through such sampling, they could develop their natural talents and abilities.
> - Most of all, she taught them how to accept, love, and interact with each other and the rest of the world.

Where and from whom did they learn many of the foundational skills that helped mold them into what they are at age sixty? Well, one godly woman nicknamed Ellie and her guidance of troop/ship 11 have to receive some of the credit.

Probably, neither Minnie Ruth nor anyone else on earth foresaw the outcome of her decision in 1949 to lead a Brownie troop. But for sure, when Minnie Ruth Elrod and troop/ship 11 have reunions in heaven, no one will be surprised.

Mrs. Elrod was a remarkable woman who did many things—graduated early from high school (having skipped a grade), worked at Leonard's Department Store in downtown Fort Worth, ran her own floral and catering business, served as Parent-Teacher Association president, made all her daughters' clothes, and headed an educational department at her church. Most important to the girls of troop/ship 11, she taught us innumerable skills and encouraged us to become accomplished, competent, and worthy women.

We owe her much. It's a debt we'll never be able to repay.

Photo courtesy of Wanda Elrod Crowder
Mrs. Minnie Ruth Elrod with son-in-law Larry Wallace at the Florida reception in May 2003. Mrs. Elrod passed away the following November.

My mother, Mrs. Esther Killian, also died in 2003, on December 30, Jacque's birthday. She had been living in Los Alamos, but she wanted to be buried with her parents and siblings in Fort Worth, so we flew her body there. Her funeral was at Lucas Funeral Home in Oakhurst, with burial at Rose Hill Cemetery, on the city's east side.

When I walked into the funeral home's chapel, I looked back at the sparse crowd. Mother had lived to be almost ninety-four and had been in Los Alamos for three years. Most of her friends and family were deceased or too infirm to attend the service. But the Girl Scouts filled two pews. Was I surprised? Not at all. Troop/Ship 11 Scouts always show up to support each other.

"Who are those women talking to Mother?" my son Paul wanted to know.

"The Girl Scouts," daughter Julie, who had attended our fiftieth anniversary, said.

My mother had been an assistant leader of troop 11 for the first three years of its existence. But, as mentioned previously, she resigned after that. An *A*+ mother, she continued to help with the troop, as did all the parents. I was gratified by the love expressed by my Scout sisters at her funeral and by their cards, flowers, and contributions to the Minnie Ruth Elrod Endowment Fund.

We Scouts often say that we turned out well because of our wonderful parents.

Esther Covey Killian was one of those parents. She was a straight-A student in high school (also graduating a year early) and college at what is now Texas Wesleyan University in Fort Worth. However, when the Great Depression hit the United States in 1929, she quit her collegiate studies to go to work and help support her family. She worked at Monnig's Department Store for twelve years. After her marriage ended, she raised her small daughter alone by selling magazines by telephone for Curtis Publishing Company, based in Philadelphia, Pennsylvania. She did so well that her superiors promoted her to sales manager. She also sewed expertly for the public and for us. Above all, she was a faithful Christian who never wavered in her love of God or her faith in Him or in her service to area Churches of Christ.

Photo by Olan Mills Studio
Mrs. Esther Killian, early troop 11 assistant
leader, before her death in 2003.

Troop/Ship 11's next excursion was to Martha's lake house on Possum Kingdom Lake in February 2004. Seven "girls" and Mrs. Still came to that one. It was our usual fare—a campfire, Campfire Stew, chatting, and, this time, a flag ceremony.

Photo courtesy of Martha Still Littlefield
Troop/Ship 11 women pose for flag ceremony at Martha's lake house.
Left to right are Mary Stoddard Hitt, Marilyn Ball Murray, Carole
Capps Steadham, Mrs. Thelma Still, Diane Crawford Hill, and Beverly
Wilson Greene. Martha is taking the picture. Booker is sleeping in?

While several significant things happened that weekend, Martha thinks the funniest moment was the one provided by Linda Booker and reported at the beginning of this chapter, a saga of a mink coat and amusing stories.

Once again, we had come together in love—still linked by an unbreakable bond that wasn't going to be severed by anything.

On July 10, 2004, we lost to death Mrs. Jeanette Hudson, another of our troop's able and dedicated assistant leaders. She had been a life-long resident of Fort Worth, and most of that time, she had lived in the Oakhurst neighborhood. She was a longtime member of Oakhurst Presbyterian Church and a thirty-five-year employee in the catalog department of Fort Worth's Montgomery Ward Department Store and Southwest Distribution Center. She was an active member of the Order of Eastern Star, a fraternal organization related to freemasonry. She had traveled extensively within the United States and to foreign countries.

Mrs. Hudson's first love, though, was always her family. She served as leader for the Boy Scout troops of both her sons and, of course, assistant leader of Girl Scout Troop/Ship 11 for her daughter Karyn. We of troop/ship 11 always admired her and loved her. She had a gentle way of instructing us and making us carry through. Tiny in build, she nevertheless knew how to get results. She seemed to be an expert on everything. We'll never forget the hammock-making session at Mrs. Hudson's house. She probably didn't forget either: her nerves were probably never the same after that.

Photo courtesy of Karyn Hudson Draper
Mrs. Jeanette Hudson in 1999

In this sixth decade, we also lost to death, Linda Booker Webb. Cancer was the culprit. She died on March 28, 2007.

Photo courtesy of Martha Still Littlefield
Photo of Linda Faye Booker Webb sporting her "Karyn" T-shirt
at Girl Scout Troop/Ship 11's fiftieth anniversary in 1999.

Booker had been a spark of energy that always brought smiles to our lips. She had been an effervescent leader in high school. After graduation from high school, she had attended Texas Technological University in Lubbock and had been a member of Delta Gamma sorority. Following graduation from Tech, she had been a public schoolteacher. Courageous in all life's circumstances, Booker was a loving wife, mother, and grandmother. She was an avid golfer and our troop clown. We would always miss the laughs she provided to us.

In August 2008, we got the word that our beloved Beverly Wilson Greene also had succumbed to cancer. This was our fourth Scout lost to death: we were, needless to say, stunned and bummed.

Beverly had always been energetic and healthy.

Photo courtesy of Martha Still Littlefield
Beverly Ann Wilson Greene in 1999 with her son and
grandsons at troop/ship 11's fiftieth anniversary reception.

Beverly had been a head of security at General Dynamics. A loving wife, mother, and grandmother, she had been a competent, capable survivor and always an avid supporter and vigorous "cheerleader" for troop/ship 11. How could she be gone?

Another gaping hole had been punched in our group and in our hearts. Maybe we had reached the age where death is a part of life, but we still didn't consider ourselves old enough for that. Perhaps no one ever does think they are ready, but age and accompanying losses come anyway.

It seemed as if we had barely blinked a few times until it was 2009 and time for Girl Scout Troop/Ship 11's sixtieth anniversary celebration. Barak Obama was now president of the United States and trying to find ways to shore up the nation's struggling economy. He was also working to get the Affordable Health Care Act passed and to solve the problem of drug and arms smuggling across the border with Mexico.

Time was going by so fast. How could it have been ten years since our fiftieth anniversary? Again the lion's share of the organizing work fell to Carole, partly because she's so good at it and partly because we've become accustomed to letting her do it. Martha, Earline, Diane Crawford Hill, Elaine Walton Lofland, and Karyn helped her though.

This time, we would spend an entire weekend together at the comfortable and attractive American Heritage House Bed-and-Breakfast Inn in historic Granbury, Texas.

Granbury, established in the 1860s, is a little town full of historic landmarks and located thirty-five miles southwest of Fort Worth. It's where Earline lives, so she was able to help Carole select the perfect settings and appropriate weekend activities.

The B&B's décor was vintage Southern charm. It was comfortable and had a meeting room with microwave oven and refrigerator, which we stocked with drinks and munchies.

Our hosts, Ron and Karen Bleeker, welcomed us warmly at 3:00 p.m. on Friday, November 13. We immediately stashed our belongings and gathered in the meeting room to talk—as usual.

As always, we had all brought pictures of our families to share, and those who had them brought pictures of our troop that dated back to our beginning. We perused pictures until late evening. Such gab-and-picture sessions have become standard fare at our gatherings.

"Marilyn, your dogs are beautiful," Wanda said. Marilyn Ball Murray breeds and shows championship Rhodesian Ridgeback and Havanese dogs.

"Anyone up for golf?" Ann asked. Karyn and Diane were.

"Does everyone have froufrou dolls in their room?" Joyce asked.

Photo courtesy of Martha Still Littlefield
At our sixtieth reunion, troop/ship 11 women stopped viewing
scrapbooks to pose for a picture. We are, left to right, first row, Joyce
Wakefield Burks, Diane Crawford Hill, Wanda Elrod Crowder, Linda Kay
Killian Wood, and Earline Campbell Wood; second row, Marilyn Weiss,
Ann Brown Fields, Martha Still Littlefield, Karyn Hudson Draper, Carole
Capps Steadham, Mary Stoddard Hitt, and Linda Heaton Leonhardt;
and, third row, Marilyn Ball Murray and Elaine Walton Lofland.

Carole told us that host Ron had built a campfire for us in the
backyard. We thought we'd enjoy that sometime during the weekend, but we ran out of time and energy, as it happened.

We munched on finger foods as we watched Beverly's video from
our fiftieth reunion, most of us getting weepy because of the memories the film brought to mind and because Beverly was no longer with
us. We laughed a lot too, but we missed Linda Booker's crazy antics
and Jacque's dry wit. Pat Cookus Haberman, who had planned to
come, fell ill and couldn't join us, so we missed her too. Again Donna
Throckmorton Jones wasn't there, and nobody remembers why.

Ann was my roommate. Having been best friends in high
school, we recounted old times and caught up on current doings. She
told me her daughter Charlotte was a successful lawyer in Houston.
I informed her about my family, which now included two grandchildren. Ann and I share a love of Austin and The University of Texas,
so we also spoke about goings-on in the Texas capital city.

Saturday was a busy day, packed with numerous activities. First, we enjoyed a delicious gourmet breakfast, elegantly presented. Afterward a reporter and photographer from *Granbury Showcase Magazine* met us at the B&B's gazebo. The publication planned to publish an article about us.

The reporter interviewed us so as to be able to write the story, and the photographer arranged us in the same order in which we had posed in an early Girl Scout picture, the one with the short-sleeved green uniforms. Unfortunately, everyone in the young Scout picture was not present at this photo shoot: otherwise the picture is the same.

Photo courtesy of *Grandbury Showcase Magazine*
The two-page spread in *Granbury Showcase Magazine*'s January/February 2010 issue featured an interview with troop/ship 11 members and old and new pictures of us standing in the same order. In the sixtieth anniversary photo, we are, left to right, first row, Earline Campbell Wood, Linda Heaton Leonhardt, Martha Still Littlefield, Karyn Hudson Draper, and Diane Crawford Hill; second row, Linda Kay Killian Wood, Carole Capps Steadham, and Ann Brown Fields; third row, Wanda Elrod Crowder, Mary Stoddard Hitt, Joyce Wakefield Burks, and Elaine Walton Lofland. The 1952 photograph is on page 51 of this book.

After the interview and picture-taking session, Diane yelled against Ann and me as we watched a football game between The University of Texas and Baylor University. Diane, an avid Texas Christian University graduate and fan, tends to root for small Christian schools, while Ann and I remain faithful to our alma mater.

In the afternoon, we shopped in some of Granbury's unique stores on the square.

"What a darling purse!" Carole exclaimed. "That would really go well with an outfit I have." Martha and Mary Stoddard Hitt, who were looking at jewelry, stepped over to see.

Earline liked some avant-garde throw pillows.

I bought a handmade metal windmill Christmas tree ornament.

That night, we ate a scrumptious dinner at Granbury's Café Nutt, located in the Nutt House historic hotel downtown on the town's picturesque square.

After dinner, we attended the *50s Reunion* musical revue at the Granbury Live Theater. The show was perfect for us because, of course, we were teenagers in the 1950s and remembered well the songs of Elvis Presley, Connie Francis, Chubby Checker, and Nat King Cole. The songs brought even more memories back to us to embellish the already memory-filled weekend. We found ourselves tapping our feet and singing along, then humming the tunes afterward.

When the show ended, we rode the Granbury trolley bus back to our B&B and, after talking some more, retired for the night. We were no longer able to stay up all night and jabber. Our bodies adamantly called us to sleep.

Sunday brought another, but different, gourmet breakfast at the B&B before we packed up and left the lovely place. We held hands and sang "Johnny Appleseed" grace at both B&B meals. How many times have we sung it? I wonder.

Our next activity was a reception for Mrs. Still, then living at Lakewood Village Retirement Community in east Fort Worth. Martha had reserved a private room, and her daughters had helped her plan a party.

Martha gave her mother a quilt made from squares that we and her family members had contributed. It was a thrill to be included as "family" in this heirloom. The variety of squares was striking: many stitches, many different ideas, many textures. My square was done with counted cross-stitch. Others drew fabric crayon pictures, embroidered messages, or made patchwork designs. The finished quilt was a masterpiece of love and creativity.

Photo courtesy of Paul Brandon Wood
Troop/Ship 11, Mrs. Thelma Still, and the quilt Martha made and we contributed to. Left to right, first row, are Mrs. Still, Earline Campbell Wood, Linda Kay Killian Wood, Mary Stoddard Hitt, Wanda Elrod Crowder, Linda Heaton Leonhardt, and Karyn Hudson Draper; second row, Martha Still Littlefield, Marilyn Ball Murray, Ann Brown Fields, Diane Crawford Hill, Joyce Wakefield Burks, and Carole Capps Steadham.

My son Paul and his family picked me up at the end of the party and finally got to meet the Girl Scouts. Just as Julie had done ten years before, my kids eagerly viewed the displays of photographs and memorabilia Martha had assembled.

My heart was touched by the love shown by my Scout sisters and Mrs. Still to my two-and-a-half-year-old granddaughter Sarah. They proved to me once again how our troop really is a family who cares for each other. Sarah talked to each Girl Scout and admired her "neckass" ("necklace" in adult parlance), fingering the pretty strands of beads around each neck. We *are* always and forever Texas belles, and Texas belles do like their jewelry, no matter what our age.

Sixty years. Reunions had become bittersweet now because we didn't know how much longer we'd be able to get together. The decade had been, in some ways, a hard one: we had lost three of our four leaders and three of our Scout sisters to death. Some of us were beginning to have health problems. Some of our children and grandchildren were having physical and emotional problems. These years had been filled with emotional peaks and valleys.

Carole issued instructions to us about what was to be done with her collected troop/ship 11 scrapbooks and mementos. "The last one of us left is to give all this to the local Girl Scout office, whatever it is named then or wherever it is located." We promised to comply.

Surely by now, we were beginning to set some kind of record for troop longevity. At least, we didn't know of any other troops that had been together so long. We knew, though, that we were in the process of forging something really special.

The Girl Scouts of Texas Oklahoma Plains, Inc., also honored troop/ship 11's sixtieth anniversary in *Spirit of the Plains*. They did a lovely job of describing us and our anniversary weekend.

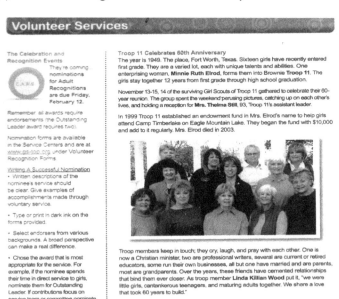

Photo courtesy of Gerry Odell Wood
Article honoring troop/ship 11's sixtieth anniversary
published in *Spirit of the Plains*.

However, we determined that troop/ship 11's death knell wasn't coming yet. We would meet as often as we could and enjoy every possible minute together. The reunions were not going to stop. In fact, we would get even more creative at planning them. We were still having a great journey together, and nobody wanted to get off the train.

And so, the first decade of the twenty-first century was almost behind us, and we had completed the milestone of sixty years together. Americans had survived the 9/11 attacks of 2001, and troop/ship 11 had lived through another decade of its existence. On to our next decade we went, with or without mink coats, but not without campfires, Campfire Stew, S'mores, and chattering. No, never, never without those things.

Photo courtesy of Martha Still Littlefield
The cake Martha Still Littlefield ordered for Girl Scout Troop/
Ship 11's sixtieth anniversary reception in 2009 at Fort
Worth's Lakewood Village Retirement Community.

CHAPTER 13

The Seventh Decade: a Fine Stew Indeed

It is a Saturday night in early November 2011. Girl Scout Troop/Ship 11 is celebrating its sixty-second anniversary at Azalea Plantation Bed & Breakfast Inn in Fort Worth's Riverside neighborhood.

After a full day of museum hopping, we gather around the fire that our host, Richard Linnartz, has built for us in the garden's barbecue pit. It's a beautiful setting on a small rise that overlooks a creek. Having filled up on dinner, we forego Campfire Stew but roast marshmallows for S'mores. We jabber about whatever comes to mind—Linda Heaton Leonhardt's latest trip, Carole Capps Steadham's son's new book, health problems of our remaining parents—as we always do.

We are talking, laughing, and munching on S'mores when the back legs of Ann Brown Field's chair slip off the brick patio. Before anyone can react, Ann is tumbling down the hill, backward, feet over head, toward the creek below.

Martha Still Littlefield jumps up immediately to try to help Ann, but the rest of us sit there staring with our mouths agape—like the giant stone wolves at Great Wolf Lodge in Grapevine, Texas, and we're just about as attractive too.

Fortunately, Ann isn't seriously hurt, just bruised in places, though the next morning she will admit to being sore. However, she has learned whom she can count on in a pinch—Martha. The rest of us are useless to her, first aid classes and hospital experience notwithstanding.

We are shamefully appalled at ourselves, but we were nevertheless inept. How many years have we been Girl Scouts, mothers, grandmothers? Lots of years. Did we take a first aid class? Yes, but a long time ago. Did we work in a hospital? Yes, but also a long time ago. Did we deal with camping emergencies? Yes, but a few years in the past too. Is one of us a nurse? Yes, but she has gone home for the evening. Did we come to the aid of our Girl Scout sister? No.

Earline Campbell Wood has an excuse: she's recently had knee-replacement surgery.

Ann, in her great capacity to forgive, loves us anyway, although she delights in teasing us unmercifully and probably will do so for years.

Wanda Elrod Crowder says, "Ann is the one in the best physical shape. The rest of us probably would have broken our necks."

* * * * *

Our sixtieth anniversary was our last time with Mrs. Thelma Still, for early in the next decade of Girl Scout Troop/Ship 11's life together, she passed on to the next world. We all treasured being with her once more. She was the last of our leaders to leave us. She was a great lady who loved all of "her girls" utterly. We were fortunate.

Even so, she had always been the "bad cop" when we were growing up. She was the disciplinarian, and most of us were a little bit afraid of her. However, when we girls reached adulthood, Mrs. Still must have figured that her authoritarian duties were finished. She relaxed and seemed to enjoy every minute with us. She often expressed her pride at our accomplishments and at the gracious women we had become. In our adult years, she developed into a teddy bear, and we lost all fear of her. We had fun with her on our trips and at reunions. Who could have guessed she would become the life of the party?

Ann particularly enjoyed how, later on, Mrs. Still had turned into such a teaser.

"Remember when you first went to camp as a Brownie and cried your heart out?" Mrs. Still would remind Ann. Then they'd laugh about it because in adulthood, Ann became extremely dedicated to all facets of Girl Scouting.

Mrs. Still was troop/ship 11's assistant leader the entire twelve years of our public schooling. The perfect complement to Mrs. Minnie Ruth Elrod, Mrs. Still was competent and talented. Anything she didn't know how to do, she learned and taught us.

Mrs. Still went home to her Lord on September 12, 2010. She was ninety-two.

After her daughters graduated from high school, she had worked for and with Mrs. Elrod as a florist. After retirement, she had volunteered at her church, Riverside United Methodist, and with Meals on Wheels. Her favorite hobby was quilting, and she won several awards on her designs. So the quilt we helped make for her had been the perfect gift—Martha, of course, knew that would be true. Although it was probably not the most beautiful of her quilts and probably wouldn't have won any awards, I suspect it was her favorite.

Photo courtesy of Paul Brandon Wood
Perhaps my most-beloved picture of Mrs. Thelma Still was taken at troop/ship 11's sixtieth anniversary reception. She tenderly talks to my granddaughter Sarah, as Diane Crawford Hill (right) and I look on. Martha Still Littlefield's quilt on the table next to her was the perfect gift for an amazing lady. Marilyn Ball Murray, Wanda Elrod Crowder, and Mary Stoddard Hitt are behind us.

Today, with all our leaders now deceased, we continue to be amazed at the number of activities they envisioned and implemented for us—twelve years, every week of the school year, many summer activities too. And our leaders didn't merely teach us how to do tasks: they taught us how to "play well" with each other and people we came in contact with. What degree of talent, love, dedication, perseverance, and grit could produce such a rich, longtime program for more than twenty girls? Answer: the kind of love that could cause those girls to continue to hold each other in high esteem and want to be together when they aged into their seventies—a very rare kind of love and dedication indeed. News broadcaster Tom Brokaw wrote a book about our parents' generation in which he called them the "the greatest generation."[28] I have to agree with him.

After 2000, with the help of e-mail and Facebook, Girl Scout Troop/Ship 11 girls easily have kept in touch with each other. We interact often and quickly, though separated by distance. Now, when Carole plans a reunion, she gets the job done more easily and less expensively than before e-mail came along.

So it happened that the Amon Carter-Riverside High School class of 1961 came upon its fiftieth class reunion. It isn't just troop/ship 11 that relies on Carole; our whole graduating class does. This time, her organizing committee included several of the Girl Scouts—Diane Crawford Hill, Earline, Elaine Walton Lofland, and Martha—and she would call on some more of us to appear on the program—Ann, Wanda, and me.

Our entire class has learned to acknowledge the contributions of Girl Scout Troop/Ship 11 and consider us a class asset. At least, they *act* as if they consider us an asset. I don't think they have much choice, we being the headstrong women that we are.

The reunion took place in May 2011.

However, this time a glitch developed in Carole's plans. Her husband Joe was hospitalized. More people needed to step in.

Diane took over the compulsory Girl Scout luncheon: we gathered at the Rose Garden Tearoom inside the historic Camp Bowie Mercantile antique mall in west Fort Worth. Helen Bowers, wife of one of our classmates, Bill Bowers, owns and operates the tearoom, as well as the one in Arlington where we went for our troop's fiftieth reunion lunch. We loved visiting with Helen, and we raved about the food and atmosphere. Carole didn't get to attend the luncheon, but the rest of us enjoyed it and missed her.

The luncheon was certainly a highlight of the reunion weekend. In fact, Marilyn Ball Murray said the Girl Scout luncheon was the main event she really wanted to attend.

The Carter High School (CHS) class of 1961 used to make a big deal about its reunions, partying the entire weekend. Festivities this

---

[28] Tom Brokaw, *The Greatest Generation* (New York: Random House, 2004).

time included a tour of the Carter High School building (which we all declared had shrunk since our days there) and a dinner at Mamma Mia Italian Grill and Pizza Restaurant on Friday; a golf tournament at suburban Mansfield's Walnut Creek Country Club in the day on Saturday; the main dinner/reception at the Gardens Restaurant of Fort Worth Botanic Garden Saturday night; and worship at Faith Methodist Church and lunch at Sammie's Bar-B-Q Restaurant on Sunday.

Troop/Ship 11 Scouts helped plan and implement everything.

Our Diane was the only woman who had nerve enough to enter the golf tournament. "So I guess I won on the women's side," she quipped.

Photo courtesy of Gerry Odell Wood
Girl Scout Troop/Ship 11 posed for lots of pictures at the CHS class of 1961 fiftieth reunion. At the Saturday night reception are, left to right, first row, Joyce Wakefield Burks, Elaine Walton Lofland, and Earline Campbell Wood; second row, Ann Brown Fields, Diane Crawford Hill, Wanda Elrod Crowder, Linda Heaton Leonhardt, Marilyn Ball Murray, Carole Capps Steadham, Linda Kay Killian Wood, and Martha Still Littlefield.

At the Saturday night reception, Wanda, Ann, and I led our classmates in the CHS alma mater and fight song. Carole, Martha, Earline, and Elaine also had parts on the program. I won a CHS polo shirt prize for getting my biographical profile submitted early. I have worn the shirt at class reunions I have attended since.

At the lunch on Sunday, we not only posed for more pictures; we sang "Girl Scouts Together" to the entire assembled group. The class simply has to put up with troop/ship 11 Scouts. As I said, they have learned to, at least, pretend to tolerate us, like us, and even be proud of us. Having known us for so many years, they are well aware that we have never been shy or quiet.

"I'd like to go back to the bed-and-breakfast for another Scout weekend," Joyce Wakefield Burks said at some point during our class reunion. Certainly, nobody disagreed. So Carol got busy planning another weekend at Granbury.

Unfortunately, the Granbury inn had closed because of the recession plaguing the United States at the time. Business had fallen off too much for them to keep going. So Carole found another B&B, and we began packing our bags.

First, though, we had another event to attend.

Amon Carter-Riverside High School turned seventy-five years old in 2011. Girl Scout Troop/Ship 11, among others, was honored at the school's celebratory reunion. From the auditorium stage most of us had stood on many times more than fifty years ago, Carole told the then-sixty-two-year story of our troop, and the rest of us, having sat together as a group, stood while the gathered alumni applauded. It was good to feel that Riverside folks of various ages were proud of us.

Afterward, we embraced all the people we remembered from our Carter years—teachers and students alike, then gleefully took off for our luncheon at nearby Azalea Plantation. It was nice to be minicelebrities, but we really wanted to be with each other.

After enjoying a gourmet lunch at Azalea Plantation Bed & Breakfast Inn, we decided it would be the perfect setting for our upcoming sixty-second reunion. Carole, as always, had made a great choice.

Photo courtesy of Martha Still Littlefield
Getting ready to sing "Johnny Appleseed" grace at the beautifully set luncheon table of Azalea Plantation in September 2011 are, left to right, Martha Still Littlefield, Linda Kay Killian Wood, Elaine Walton Lofland, Carole Capps Steadham, Marilyn Ball Murray, Wanda Elrod Crowder, and Wanda's sister Sharon Elrod Wallace.

That sixty-second reunion Joyce wanted took place in November 2011. Our hosts, owners Martha and Richard Linnartz of Azalea Plantation, welcomed us with total graciousness, and we settled in at their comfortable and well-appointed facility. Martha Linnartz again dazzled us with her gourmet culinary skills, and Richard built a fire for us in the barbecue pit outside, so we could roast marshmallows for S'mores.

We also enjoyed relaxing and gabbing in their public rooms. Diane brought some chocolate wine. I took one sip and knew I'd have to stay across the room from it: it isn't fair that an alcoholic drink should be that delicious.

On Friday night, we all went to dinner at nearby Fuzzy Taco Restaurant and gobbled down mouthwatering Tex-Mex food. After singing "Johnny Appleseed," we were our usual loud, exuberant selves. Others in the restaurant were noisy too—maybe noisiness is a Texas thing, not just a troop/ship 11 one. We can hope that no one was bothered by our noise.

Photo courtesy of Martha Still Littlefield
Before heading out for Saturday's activities, we gathered by Martha
Linnartz's beautiful dining table and a cabinet filled with chintz porcelain.
Sitting, left to right, are Earline Campbell Wood, Joyce Wakefield
Burks, and Carole Capps Steadham. Standing, left to right, are Wanda
Elrod Crowder, Mary Stoddard Hitt, Martha Still Littlefield, Diane
Crawford Hill, Marilyn Ball Murray, and Linda Kay Killian Wood.

When we're at Azalea Plantation, we always spend time admir-
ing Martha Linnartz's expansive collection of chintz porcelain.

Chintz began to be produced in England in the 1920s and cop-
ied cotton fabric designs from India. The patterns are usually flowers
and cover the entire surface of the serving piece.[29] Martha has rooms
full of it. She has so many beautiful patterns, colors, and shapes that
her collection makes us antique lovers go nuts.

Saturday was a full day of touring three of Fort Worth's fine
museums: the Modern Art Museum of Fort Worth, the Kimbell Art
Museum, and the Leonard's Department Store Museum.

---

[29] "Collecting English Chintz China: A Garden for the Table," AboutAntiques
Website, http://antiques.about.com/cs/ceramicsporcelain/a/aa051303.htm.

Our Modern Art Museum guide was Martha Stanton Lunday, whom we had known in high school, and our Kimbell guide was our own Elaine, a docent there.

At the Modern, we gained a better appreciation of modern art. That's not to say that we now wanted to fill our houses with it, but we did understand it better than before. The museum displays the work of some famous artists, including Andy Warhol, in its collection.

At the Kimbell, we toured the traveling Michelangelo Merisi da Caravaggio exhibit. Elaine narrated beautifully, giving us knowledge of the life and work of this important classical artist. She pointed out humor and details in his paintings we otherwise might have missed. I, who had never heard of Caravaggio before, increased my knowledge of fine art.

If we soaked up culture at the first two museums, we indulged in pure nostalgia at the third one, the Leonard's Department Store Museum. There we viewed and fingered memorabilia from our growing-up years. It's fun to revisit history that you remember.

Leonard's Department Store had been an amazing emporium that was located on several city blocks of downtown Fort Worth. It had a grocery store, a farm store, a drug store, an automotive repair department, plus all the other things that any modern department store is expected to have. It was even the first department store in Fort Worth to have escalators.[30]

Leonard's operated the M&O, the longest privately owned subway in the country, which ran from a parking lot outside downtown Fort Worth to the store's basement. The M&O was named for the two Leonard brothers, Marvin and Obie, owners of the store. You didn't have to buy a ticket or even show a purchase receipt to ride the M&O: it was free to park and free to ride, no questions asked.

When I worked part-time for the Fort Worth *Star-Telegram* newspaper between graduating from The University of Oklahoma and attending graduate school at The University of Texas at Austin,

---

[30] Victoria Buenger and Walter L. Buenger, *Texas Merchant: Marvin Leonard and Fort Worth* (College Station, Texas: Texas A&M University Press, 2008), 113–14.

I parked in Leonard's parking lot, rode the M&O into the store, and walked to the *Star-Telegram*. It was easier than trying to find a parking place closer to the newspaper—cheaper too. Other parking lots and garages charged fees.

Mrs. Elrod worked at Leonard's in her teen and young adult years. She studied up on the merchandise she sold. One of her assignments was working in the toy department, selling tricycles. One day, Marvin Leonard, whom for some reason she did not recognize, walked through the area.

"Why are some tricycles more expensive than others?" he asked.

"Some of the tricycle wheels have ball bearings and some do not," Ellie said.

The boss said he was impressed with her explanation, expertise, and sales manner.

Karyn Hudson Draper worked at Leonard's as assistant floor manager (basement) and accountant (advertising department) for six years.

"I still have many special memories of Leonard's," she says. So do we all.

One day in 1965, I was shopping in the store's fabric department for decorations for my wedding and encountered Karyn there. We had fun getting caught up with each other's lives. She was married and had a couple of daughters by then.

Besides the wedding items I bought that day in the fabric department, I ordered my wedding cake from Leonard's bakery. Usually, I'm not fond of white cake, but for white cake, Leonard's creation was delicious, and its decorations were gorgeous.

Every Christmas, Leonard's had a Toyland that surely competed with the best in the country: kids especially loved the monorail ride that ran around the ceiling.

The store's slogan was "More Merchandise for Less Money." If you could find what you needed anywhere in Fort Worth, it was probably at Leonard's. They stocked everything, and at reasonable prices.

My first semester at The University of Oklahoma, I nearly turned to an icicle (according to me) in the high winds that "come sweeping o'er the plains." I came home to Fort Worth and asked for a really warm coat for Christmas. Mother and I found it at—yes, you guessed it—Leonard's. It was a three-quarter-length quilted down-filled coat with a fur collar. When I wore it back at school, my friends called me "Nanook of the North." I was warm and cozy, however, and Leonard's had come through for me as it always did.

The closest thing to Leonard's today is Walmart, but I haven't yet seen a Walmart that sells tractors, hay, and livestock feed or has a subway.

At the end of each school year, the ever civic-minded Leonard brothers gave award pins to Fort Worth high school students who had made the scholastic honor roll all year long: bronze for first year, silver for second, and gold for third. Several troop/ship 11 girls received all three pins. Examples of the pins were on display in the museum. Mine are on my charm bracelet.

In 1974, Leonard's went the way of many locally owned United States department stores. That year, the Dillard's Department Store chain bought Leonard's, and even the downtown Dillard's eventually closed.[31] It was a trend: national chains bought local stores, and downtown stores moved to the suburbs. Still, none of us will ever forget Leonard's. It was really something special. I don't know how Fort Worth functions without it today.

Such were our considerable memories of Leonard's Department Store. We had grown up shopping in the store, all of us had loved the store's Toyland, some of us had worked at the store, some of us had received honor pins from the store, and all of us had ridden the store's M&O subway many times.

We thoroughly enjoyed all three museums, but the most squeals of delight over cherished memories definitely came during our visit to the Leonard's museum.

"Look, there are the pins we all got." Ann pointed out.

"I love the pictures of the M&O," Marilyn Ball said.

"I couldn't have planned my wedding without Leonard's," I said.

"It was a good place to work," Karyn added.

---

[31] Ibid., 193.

"You could find everything there," Martha said.

"I liked the tea room." Mary Stoddard Hitt remembered.

"There were always a million people in that store," Wanda said.

"My favorite was the Toyland," Joyce added.

"It certainly was one great store," we all agreed.

Troop/Ship 11 members also enjoyed a late lunch at the M&O Station Grill, adjacent to the Leonard's Department Store Museum. There we ate hamburgers and drank milk shakes that tasted like the ones we grew up on. The milk shakes, served in old-fashioned, tall, footed glass ice cream dishes, were so cold that we got brain freeze. Elaine said she wished she'd snapped a picture of me consuming mine. I'm still wondering why my slurping was so entertaining.

Saturday night, back at Azalea Plantation, we experienced the infamous campfire episode in which we almost let Ann fall down a hill into a creek. Besides being bruised and sore, she could have been wet and cold—gotten pneumonia even. Give us an *F* for effort that night, though Ann persists in calling the incident "funny."

Sunday morning, we worshiped together at Faith United Methodist Church in Riverside and then said our "good-byes." Leaving always is a weepy occasion for me. We share something so precious that it's hard to let go and return to everyday life.

Girl Scout Troop/Ship 11 decided to hold another weekend reunion the next year. So, in 2012, we gathered again at Azalea Plantation for our sixty-third anniversary.

This time, Carole included in our three days of activities two more museum trips, two restaurant meals, and Sunday worship.

Friday night, we ate a fabulous meal at Mamma Mia Italian Grill and Pizza Restaurant in Riverside. In fact, this charming restaurant is in the location that was a corner drugstore when we were growing up. It's situated at what we always called Six Points, an intersection of three cross-streets. The owners have kept the original stained-glass-enhanced windows that were in the drugstore, which, in my opinion, adds to the charm of the place. One of our classmates from 1961, Doyle Willis Jr., helped in the restoration of this gem of a building.

After dinner, we returned to Azalea Plantation for our inevitable gab fest. I learn more about my Scout sisters every time—mischief I never knew they got into, their respective views on politics, and more of their various achievements in life.

Saturday morning, we enjoyed one of B&B owner Martha Linnartz's gourmet brunches and then took off to visit two more of Fort Worth's excellent museums. If we have enough reunions in Fort Worth, maybe we'll get around to visiting all of its museums—and the city does have its fair share of marvelous museums, some of them world-class.

First, we went to the National Cowgirl Museum and Hall of Fame. This unique museum honors women who "shape the west... change the world." We had a guided tour of the exhibits, which included some women we had heard of and some women whose names were new to us. Among the honorees are authors Willa Cather and Laura Ingalls Wilder, artist Georgia O'Keeffe, Native American potter Maria Martinez, country singer Patsy Cline, Supreme Court justice Sandra Day O'Connor, actress Dale Evans, and Lewis and Clark guide Sacajawea.[32]

Exhibits also include a mechanical bucking horse and a mock chuck-wagon campfire where some cowgirls are undoubtedly about to enjoy a meal at any moment. Lots of visiting kids tried riding the bucking horse, but we confined ourselves to envisioning troop/ship 11 by the chuck wagon eating Campfire Stew.

The hall of fame maintains a cooperative program with the Girl Scouts of Texas Oklahoma Plains, Inc., and Girl Scouts of all ages receive discounted admission tickets to the exhibits. Among the kids at the museum that day was a young Girl Scout troop. Museum employees introduced us to them. We talked with them. Soon the girls' eyes glazed over, but their leaders seemed inspired by our troop's story. We encouraged the women to continue their hard work in planning troop activities, assuring them that they are giving the girls an unforgettable and worthwhile experience. We may have imagined it, but we thought we saw an added spring in the leaders' steps after our talk.

---

[32] National Cowgirl Hall of Fame website, http://www.cowgirl.net/.

Photo courtesy of Martha Still Littlefield
After brunch, we posed for a picture at one of Martha Linnartz's tables.
Left to right, first row, are Ann Brown Fields, Earline Campbell Wood,
Pat Cookus Haberman, and Elaine Walton Lofland; second row,
Martha Still Littlefield, Donna Throckmorton Jones, Mary Stoddard
Hitt, Wanda Elrod Crowder, Linda Heaton Leonhardt, Linda Kay
Killian Wood, Karyn Hudson Draper, and Carole Capps Steadham.

We had a few minutes between leaving the National Cowgirl
Museum and Hall of Fame and our scheduled tour at the next
museum, so we walked to the cafeteria of the nearby Fort Worth
Museum of Science and History for a light snack. While we sat
around our large round table throwing out ideas for what we might
do together on our next outing, Karyn said, "Those of us who live
here would like to travel to someplace else some year."

Wanda said, "I don't care what we do or where we go, as long as
we do it together."

Carole said, "Here's an idea. Maybe we could go to Savannah,
Georgia, and visit Juliette Gordon Low's birthplace." Juliette Low
founded the Girl Scouts of the USA.

"Oh, that's a wonderful idea," we chorused. "Let's do that."

So Carole spent most of the rest of the weekend brainstorming with us and planning our Savannah trip.

But first things first: we still had another museum to explore at this reunion. The Amon Carter Museum of American Art is named for the founder and first publisher of the Fort Worth *Star-Telegram*. Carter was a civic leader of and benefactor to Fort Worth for many years until his death in 1955. He unabashedly promoted Fort Worth all over the world and coined the city's slogan, "Where the West Begins." Our high school was named for him, as well as Texas Christian University's football stadium.

The Carter art museum's holdings include a superb collection of works by Frederic Remington and Charles M. Russell, two of the greatest artists of the American West. The museum features paintings and sculptures by these men. Both the permanent collection and the traveling exhibits also display art from other United States areas.

We spent most of our time that day viewing the exhibit, "To See as Artists See: American Art from the Phillips Collection" of New York. We learned much about American artists with which we previously had not been familiar: the exhibit was most enlightening. Then we simply had to spend time with Russell and Remington. These artists outstandingly captured the story of the West. And we women from "Where the West Begins" do like our western art.

After leaving the Amon Carter and getting our refresher lesson from Carole on walking down steps sideways (as reported on page 88 of this book), we drove to Lucile's Stateside Bistro for dinner. This charming restaurant features different kinds of cuisine and is housed in a historic building that was Finley's Cafeteria when we were growing up. My mother and I ate Thanksgiving Dinner there several years. Finley's was a local place that served down-home cooking. Now the decor is slightly fancier, but it has the same tiny tan-colored tiles on the floor, and ceiling fans still whirl above.

This was the second restaurant in which I had dined in two days where the buildings had been recycled from businesses of my childhood and where the new owners had kept some of the flavor of the original establishments. I felt so grateful for the past and for the fact that progress had preserved these special places.

Lucile's was having their annual "lobsterama," and a lobster dinner was as cheap as it ever is anywhere. I hadn't eaten a whole lobster before, so Ann taught me how. Needless to say, the lobster and the homemade bread were yummy.

We didn't do the campfire and S'mores at this reunion. Ann must have been relieved to avoid another tumble down the hill. We chose, rather, to sit in one of Azalea Plantation's public rooms and chatter. Troop/Ship 11's Martha had learned how to do massage, and she worked on all of us in turn until we relaxed and retired for the night. As usual, Martha was serving others—serving is one of her many gifts.

Sunday morning brought yet another yummy Martha Linnartz brunch, another singing of "Johnny Appleseed," and another worship service at Faith Methodist. Then it was off again for all of us. Carole's head was swimming with plans for our Savannah trip, and I returned to Los Alamos, New Mexico, to begin to write this book.

Needless to say, we were pumped for troop/ship 11's next adventure.

CHAPTER 14

Destination Savannah

It is Thursday, April 18, 2013. Girl Scout Troop/ Ship 11 has decided to celebrate our collective seventieth birthdays by traveling together to Savannah, Georgia. We are going primarily to visit the birthplace of Juliette Gordon Low, founder of the Girl Scouts of the USA. We are making the event a four-day weekend.

Seven of us are gathered in Terminal A of Dallas/Fort Worth (DFW) International Airport. Three are meeting us in Savannah. Two who are supposed to fly with us have not arrived.

It has not been a morning without stress.

Marilyn Ball Murray has failed to show up. We frantically try several times to phone her.

Finally, she answers. "Is it today?" she asks. "I thought it was tomorrow."

The rest of us wilt like fresh cut flowers out of water. Is there any way she can get to the airport before the plane leaves? She lives in Burleson, Texas, just south of Fort Worth. But our plane has been delayed because of stormy weather. Maybe she can make it. Failing that, can she take a later flight without being charged an exorbitant fee? We wring our hands, shake our heads, and moan. I get a hot flash and heartburn.

Soon, Marilyn calls back: she has checked her ticket, and it is for Friday, the next day. She has made her reservation for the wrong day. We are relieved that she has a scheduled ticket but sad that we will have one less day to spend with her, and she will have to travel to Savannah alone. However, she will get to come, and she won't have to spend any extra money. Most of us are retired women—we understand about budgets.

Adding to our stress is the fact that the stormy weather has delayed Mary Stoddard Hitt's flight from San Antonio. We worry that she won't make our Savannah flight. All of us have knots in our stomachs. DFW is one of the country's largest airports: getting from one terminal/gate to another can take a long time. When we are requested to board the plane and Mary is not yet with us, we grab our belongings with heavy hearts.

It's an American Eagle flight; the small plane holds only forty-four passengers. The seven of us make up almost a sixth of the group. Troop/Ship 11 members, most seated in a bunch near the middle of the plane, as previously mentioned, have never been known for our soft voices or reticent behavior. Everyone in the plane can hear what we say. We are "entertaining" the entire audience.

Wanda Elrod Crowder announces to everybody near us, which is just about everybody, that we are a Fort Worth Girl Scout troop that has been together for sixty-four years. She is certain that our fellow passengers will be suitably impressed. Some act as if they are.

We commiserate with each other, craning our necks every few seconds to see whether Mary has boarded the plane. When we finally see her come through the entrance, we burst forth in cheers and clapping.

Mary turns red, waves at us, and falls into a seat near the front—not too far away from us, of course, because it is a small plane.

The plane takes off.

Soon, the lone flight attendant comes to take our beverage order. When she gets to Diane Crawford Hill, the following exchange occurs.

Diane: "We have lunch reservations in Savannah at one o'clock. We were late departing. Do you think we'll make it?"

Flight Attendant, looking at her watch: "Ma'am, I doubt you will."

Diane: "Well, in that case, I'd like a cheeseburger, fries, and a milk shake, please." Diane has spoken loudly enough to be heard throughout the cabin. Everyone, including the flight attendant, laughs.

Yes, Girl Scout Troop/Ship 11 is headed for Savannah. The town is accustomed to Girl Scout visitors, but it ain't seen nothin' yet.

* * * * *

By far, the biggest and best Girl Scout Troop/Ship 11 excursion of our seventh decade was a trip to Savannah, Georgia. This was a trip back in time, away from the bustling, troubled modern world filled with terrorist attacks, social unrest, political intolerance, hurricanes, and earthquakes.

When April 2013 rolled around, Carole Capps Steadham had us organized and ready to go. She'd found us a bed-and-breakfast to stay in. She'd made reservations at Savannah eateries. She'd reserved for us a local bus sightseeing tour. She'd contacted the Juliette Gordon Low Birthplace to schedule our visit there.

We had our plane reservations. Nine of us—Ann Brown Fields, Diane, Joyce Wakefield Burks, Karyn Hudson Draper, Linda Kay

Killian Wood, Marilyn Ball, Martha Still Littlefield, Mary, and Wanda—would fly from DFW airport on the same plane. Three—Carole, Donna Throckmorton Jones, and Marilyn Weiss—would meet us in Savannah. Carole went early to celebrate her fiftieth wedding anniversary with her husband Joe. Donna doesn't travel by airplane, so her kind husband drove her halfway across country, and they vacationed en route. Marilyn Weiss, who spends much time in Hilton Head, South Carolina, tending to her sports-clothing business, was already nearby.

Problems notwithstanding, we eight made it to the charming Savannah airport.

The airport was just the beginning of charm: we were going to soak up some of the American South's best architecture, cuisine, history, and culture for the better part of four days. Best of all, we were going to do it together—twelve of us, anyway. Elaine Walton Lofland and Earline Campbell Wood had health issues that prevented them from coming. Pat Cookus Haberman was tied down by her interior design business and couldn't get away. Linda Heaton Leonhardt was on a cruise somewhere, as per usual.

First stop in Savannah was the lovely Zeigler House Inn, a handsomely appointed bed-and-breakfast establishment located in a building on the National Historic Register. The house was built in 1856 and sits on Jones Street, which *Southern Living* magazine has designated "the most beautiful street in North America."[33]

---

[33] The Zeigler House Inn Website, http://www.zeiglerhouseinn.com/index.php.

Photo courtesy of Zeigler House Inn, Savannah, Georgia[34]
Savannah's Zeigler House Inn where we resided most of four glorious days.

Innkeeper Jackie Heinz was a gracious hostess. She baked the most delicious pastries and happy-hour treats anyone could imagine. She ought to write a cookbook.

We had indeed missed our lunch reservation because of the delayed plane flight, so Carole and Jackie scurried to rearrange our weekend dining schedule.

Immediately after checking in and dropping off our luggage, we walked to Soho South Café, a retro-style restaurant, for lunch. The eclectic décor enthralled us.

"Look at that wooden bikini-clad woman hanging above our table," Karyn commented.

"I wonder whether she previously adorned the bow of a pirate ship or the entrance to a brothel," Martha said.

It was at Soho South that I began my campaign to eat seafood the entire weekend: this gal who lives in landlocked New Mexico gets

---

[34] Ibid.

Photo courtesy of Linda Kay Killian Wood
An example of Soho South Café's eclectic décor; this
wooden woman hung above our table at lunch.

some pretty hefty cravings for fresh seafood. First seafood order of
the trip was a crab-cake sandwich—yum.

Our tummies full and our palates happy, we walked across the
street to catch the Old Savannah Tours trolley bus. This open-air narrated riding tour takes visitors to Savannah's historic Victorian and
antebellum neighborhoods, riverfront, and market districts.

In 1864 during the American Civil War, Savannah city offi-
cials negotiated a peaceful surrender with northern General William
Tecumseh Sherman.[35] Preserving Savannah was Sherman's Christmas
present to US President Abraham Lincoln that year.[36] Consequently,
the town maintains its antebellum (pre-Civil War) charm. Along the
tour route, we saw not only historic sites, but we also saw and smelled
Azaleas in bloom and other luxuriant vegetation.

"Savannah's warm, humid climate must make it possible to simply stick plants in the ground and watch them grow," I said, accustomed to arid New Mexico where gardening presents a significant
challenge for black thumbs like me.

Back at Zeigler House, we relaxed a while before dinner.

---

[35] "Savannah, Georgia: History," Wikipedia Website, http://en.wikipedia.org/
wiki/Savannah,_Georgia#cite_note-8.

[36] Stacy A. Cordery, "Civil War and the Problem of Loyalties," *Juliette Gordon
Low: The Remarkable Founder of the Girl Scouts* (New York: Penguin Books,
2012), 16.

This trip, I roomed with Karyn. In addition to our significant conversations, we luxuriated in our fabulous accommodations, the Giverny suite, certainly one of the grandest in the inn. We had a sitting room, a bedroom, a complete kitchen, and a bathroom; and every inch was beautifully and tastefully decorated. The views from our corner windows were spectacular, encompassing tree-lined streets and elaborate old buildings. On our last day, Karyn and I weren't quite ready to leave this relaxing idyllic luxury and go home to doing dishes and laundry.

Our suite and another one were located on the fourth floor—actually the third because the main floor was called the second floor, as in Europe—and there was no elevator. So we seventy-year-old women got our exercise climbing the gorgeous old polished wooden staircases. Needless to say, we tried to minimize our trips to and from our rooms. Thankfully, Jackie's young helpers carried our luggage up and down for us.

Before we departed for dinner that night, Jackie gathered us all in the public living room of the house and treated us each to a glass of champagne. She wanted to celebrate our seventieth birthdays with us. She did special things like that the entire weekend.

After enjoying our champagne, Carole led us over brick side-walks and through two of Savannah's forty-four famous squares—small parks the size of a city block—to Jazz'd Tapas Bar.

Some complained about Carole's ability to judge walking distance.

"Her two blocks are really four, her four blocks really eight," Wanda, who was having knee problems, complained.

"Come on, girls, we must keep moving or our bodies atrophy," Carole retorted.

Jazz'd prides itself on reviving a centuries-old Spanish tradition of serving small food portions in a pub atmosphere. There we enjoyed such delicacies as she-crab stew, crab cakes, coconut shrimp, French onion soup, fire-roasted tomato bruschetta, and humus—melt-in-your-mouth fare. We ordered different things and shared them.

We were treated like royalty all evening. First, we were seated directly in front of the stage. Next, Jackie showed up and introduced us to some of her Savannah friends, including the owners of the restaurant.

Jazz'd has live music every night. Trae Gurley, who sang Frank Sinatra songs on Thursday nights, dedicated a song to us and presented us each with a complimentary vocal compact disk. The audience, most of whom seemed less than half our age, clapped for us.

Then a woman who had been on the airplane with us sent over a complimentary bottle of wine to our table—perhaps, sometimes, it pays to be loud and obnoxious on small airplanes. Everyone enjoyed a little bit of the wine, but our waiter was slow in bringing us enough glasses, so Martha gave up and drank out of the bottle.

Finally, the chef sent us a complimentary dessert, a death-by-chocolate concoction that had "Go, Girl Scouts" written in chocolate syrup on the plate. We passed the decadent thing around and everyone had a bite, which was plenty because the delicacy was so rich.

Photo courtesy of Martha Still Littlefield
The complimentary one-thousand-calories-a-
bite dessert Jazz'd gave us to share.

Next we walked back through the square parks and over the brick sidewalks to Zeigler House, where Jackie had put out sweets for our enjoyment. We devoured pecan-pie squares, meringues, sand tarts, and the wine of our choice. I had a taste of chocolate wine—just a taste.

Friday morning brought the highlight of our trip, the main thing we had come to do—our visit to the Juliette Gordon Low

Birthplace. Our tour guide was ready for us. First, we took turns posing with a life-sized cardboard cutout of Juliette Low. Then we viewed the house, but our tour had to be delayed because Joyce and Diane got lost on the way. They were talking—imagine that—and failed to see where the rest of us turned and crossed a street. Having no idea which way to go, they had to be rescued by Birthplace staff before our house tour could begin.

Photo courtesy of Martha Still Littlefield
Donna Throckmorton Jones poses behind Juliette Gordon Low cutout.

The Wayne-Gordon House is a mansion built in the Regency style in 1821 for Savannah's mayor, James Moore Wayne, and bought by the Gordon family later. Most furnishings are original. Four Gordon generations lived there.

Juliette's father, William Washington Gordon II, fought for the Confederate army during the Civil War. However, her mother, Nellie Kinzie Gordon, was from Illinois, a northern state. So when Savannah surrendered to the Northern army, Nellie entertained Northern General Sherman at the house. That must have been bold in a Southern town not at all in sympathy with Sherman's march across Georgia to the sea.[37] Later, the Gordons would also entertain, among other dignitaries, President William Howard Taft, in their home.[38]

Photo courtesy of Juliette Gordon Low Birthplace, Savannah, Georgia
Juliette Gordon Low Birthplace, the Wayne-Gordon
House of Savannah, Georgia. The first Girl Scout troop
met in the carriage house behind this mansion.

In 1886, Juliette's wedding reception was held in the elegant rooms and on the porch of the house. She married William Mackay Low (Willy), and they moved to England after a time.[39] Our tour guide told us that there was a slight social inequality between the Gordons and the Lows. Juliette's dad was a successful cotton merchant, but the Gordons were "new money" in American Savannah. The Lows were "old money" and from England. The Lows felt that

---

[37] Stacy A. Cordery, "Civil War and the Problem of Loyalties," *Juliette Gordon Low: The Remarkable Founder of the Girl Scouts* (New York: Penguin Books, 2012), 16.

[38] Ibid., "The Savannah Girl Guides," 209.

[39] Ibid., "Omens and Weddings," 91–104.

they were somewhat superior to the Gordons. So the stage was set for a less-than-happy marriage.

Willy was the only son of a millionaire, and because he inherited great wealth, he never had to work. He also was a playboy who was unfaithful to Juliette. Willy and Juliette were in the process of getting a divorce when Willy had a stroke and died in 1905. Juliette inherited his house in Savannah and some of Willy's money.[40] After his death, she traveled extensively but found herself at loose ends, trying to decide what to do. They had had no children.[41]

In 1911, when Juliette met Sir Robert Baden-Powell, founder of the Boy Scouts, she knew what she would do with her life. First, she helped found the Girl Guides in England.[42] Upon returning to Savannah, she called a friend, Nina Anderson Pape, and said her famous quote, "I have something for the girls of Savannah and all America."[43]

On March 12, 1912, the Girl Scouts of the United States of America came into being. The first troop was in Savannah and met in the carriage house behind the Gordon mansion. The first Girl Scout was Juliette's niece Margaret Eleanor Gordon.[44] Both Juliette and Margaret were nicknamed Daisy, which must have been confusing at times, as are the multiple *Linda*s and *Marilyn*s in troop/ship 11.

Of course, the Girl Scout organization would expand beyond everyone's dreams—everyone's dreams except Juliette's, that is—until millions of girls worldwide would experience the benefits of Girl Scouts and Girl Guides.

Juliette Gordon Low died of breast cancer in January 1927. She was buried in Savannah in her Girl Scout uniform.[45]

---

40 Ibid., "A Parting of the Ways," 150–66.
41 Ibid., "Journeys," 171–180.
42 Ibid., "General Sir Robert Baden-Powell," 181–200.
43 Ibid., "The Savannah Girl Guides," 201–219.
44 Gladys Denny Shultz and Daisy Gordon Lawrence, "Starting the Girl Scouts," *Lady from Savannah: The Life of Juliet Low* (New York: Girl Scouts of the United States of America, 1958), 305–16.
45 Stacy A. Cordery, *op. cit.*, "Epilogue: Long Live the Girl Scouts," 294–98.

Daisy, as most everyone called Juliette, was a powerhouse—energetic, unstoppable, unflappable, and competent. Until her death, she was a positive role model for the young women who would come after her. She envisioned girls who would develop into strong, capable, resourceful, industrious public servants. In fact, the Girl Scouts served so vigorously on the home front during both World War I and World War II that they established themselves as an organization the country could turn to and rely on in time of need.[46]

The Girl Scouts of the United States of America bought the Gordon house in 1953 and turned it into a museum that is visited by tens of thousands of people yearly.[47]

In preparing to write this book, I read two biographies of Juliette Gordon Low, *Juliette Gordon Low: The Remarkable Founder of the Girl Scouts* by Stacy A. Cordery, and *Lady from Savannah: The Life of Juliette Low* by Gladys Denny Shultz and Daisy (Margaret) Gordon Lawrence.

I have thought much about the woman Juliette Low was: her independence in exercising her abilities fully and her determination that never accepted defeat but turned effort into victory.[48]

After thinking about the Girl Scout founder, I considered the women of Girl Scout Troop/Ship 11. I decided we became the women Daisy would have wanted us to be; in fact, she would be proud of us. I believe, we personify her dream for Girl Scouts.

After our tour of the Gordon house, we moved to the back garden, where fragrances of Southern vegetation again assaulted our senses. While there, we participated in a ceremony reserved for special visitors to the house. We received pins for having visited along with our sixty-five-year Girl Scout pins (a year early).

---

[46] Ibid., "The Excitement of Girl Scouting," 221–40.
[47] Girl Scouts of the USA Website. http://www.girlscouts.org/who_we_are/history/birthplace/facts.asp.
[48] Shultz and Lawrence, *op. cit.*, "Epilogue," 383.

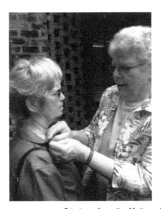

Photo courtesy of Martha Still Littlefield
Wanda Elrod Crowder attaches Martha Still Littlefield's pins
during a garden ceremony at Juliette Low's birthplace.

A young Girl Scout troop was also in the garden. When they heard our story and witnessed the pinning ritual, several of them asked if they could have their pictures taken with us. We were amazed that these young ones would want to do this. Even though we were flattered, we had to blink back tears from our eyes. It was still hard to imagine that young Scouts would look up to us.

After a quick look at the carriage house where the first Girl Scout troop met, we hurried off to a special lunch date, the one that had to be rescheduled after Thursday's late-flight arrival.

Our lunch experience was to be at Mrs. Wilkes Dining Room, a Savannah eating tradition since 1943, and we had reservations, which is not customary there.

The establishment is located on Jones Street only a few doors down from the Zeigler House Inn. The line begins forming early in the morning and expands down the block and around the corner by 11:00 a.m. when the dining room opens. We, however, thanks to our hostess, Jackie, did not have to wait in line but were taken in through the back door, as US President Barack Obama had been when he visited Savannah.

Mrs. Wilkes's employees serve the food boarding-house style. Tables seat at least ten. Diners in parties of fewer than ten sit with strangers around their table and pass the dishes to the right. Troop/Ship 11 was twelve in number and crowded around one table.

I counted twenty-three bowls or plates of different foods on our table, and I think I took a spoonful of twenty-one of them. There is no variation in the menu: you get what they serve you. But surely, with twenty-three dishes, no one goes hungry. Food is cooked Southern-style. Meats included fried chicken, meatloaf, beef stew, and sausage. Side dishes included green beans with bacon, sweet-potato soufflé, baked beans, okra gumbo, black-eyed peas, collard greens, macaroni and cheese, cabbage, and red rice. Breads were cornbread and biscuits. Desserts were fruit cobbler and banana pudding. Drinks were iced water and either sweetened or unsweetened iced tea.

"I think the sweet potato soufflé is my favorite," said Mary.

The food is tasty but heavy. The aromas mingle—bread baking, chicken frying, bacon-seasoned beans boiling. The atmosphere is busy and noisy: we had to speak loudly to be heard—never a problem for us. The décor and spoken accents at Mrs. Wilkes's are Southern. Mrs. Wilkes Restaurant is a truly Southern experience.

Photo courtesy of Linda Kay Killian Wood
Troop/Ship 11 women dine at Mrs. Wilkes Dining Room in Savannah.
Left to right, clockwise from left, are Marilyn Weiss, Diane Crawford Hill, Martha Still Littlefield, Ann Brown Fields, Joyce Wakefield Burks, Mary Stoddard Hitt, Carole Capps Steadham, and Donna Throckmorton Jones. At the table out of the picture are Marilyn Ball Murray, Wanda Elrod Crowder, and Karyn Hudson Draper. Linda Kay Killian Wood took the picture.

When we finished eating, we cleared away our own dishes, while the wait staff removed the serving plates and bowls and prepared our table for the next diners. Then we traipsed through two large dining rooms to pay for our food. Everything costs one price, and you must pay with cash: they do not take checks or credit cards.

We had entered through the back door, but we exited through the front, passing a display of tempting baked goodies and cookbooks for sale.

As we stepped outside, we heard someone in line say, "Oh, good, looks like a whole table opened up." We saw that the line really did extend down the street and around the corner. So we smiled at the hungry people, assured them that the food was good, and they were about to be served. Then we stepped sideways down the curved wrought-iron-decorated outdoor staircase. Carole was proud that we descended properly.

"If I ate like that every day, I wouldn't be alive," Ann said. We, as one, agreed.

Indeed, nobody had energy to play tourist after so large a meal, so we waddled back to our B&B, collapsed on our beds and "let things settle a bit" in our stomachs.

Following a brief rest, we prevailed on Marilyn Weiss, who had her car, to take us down to the waterfront area. After making two trips, she stayed to explore with us. Savannah's riverfront includes restaurants, hotels, shops, and historic buildings, such as the Cotton Exchange.

As if there weren't enough shopping temptations for us in Savannah itself that weekend, an "Arts on the River" crafts fair was taking place in the waterfront park. Naturally, I found some gift items to take back with me. Never could resist a crafts fair.

At the Candy Store, we sampled warm pralines—pecan and caramelized-sugar confections popular in some form all over the South. They are delicious enough at room temperature, but right off the cook stove at the Candy Store, they are the very definition of mouthwatering. Thanks to our enormous lunch, I was able to exit the store without buying anything. Several other Scouts, however, bought packaged pralines to take home.

We cut our waterfront visit short, as Jackie wanted us at Zeigler House Inn for "Wine and Cheese" and hors d'oeuvres.

Some of us thought it too far to walk, and rain was falling. So we rode back with Marilyn Weiss. Others took pedicabs. On a nice day in the right shoes, walking to the inn from the waterfront would be doable. But this day in these circumstances, Carole wanted no more comments about her perceived inability to estimate distance.

Photo courtesy of Linda Kay Killian Wood
Diane Crawford Hill and Carole Capps Steadham huddle in a pedicab to avoid the rain. They escaped getting wet, but their driver did not.

Back at the B&B, Jackie wowed us with more of her amazing goodies, every bite of which was delicious. While we feasted on brie baked in pastry and homemade cherry biscotti, we lounged in the public reception rooms and visited with other inn guests. Jackie had invited some of her friends to come and meet us. Everyone acted impressed with our longevity as a Girl Scout troop and, we hope, with our interpersonal skills.

After a wonderful breakfast that included homemade pastries, the lunch that was easily two meals, and the fabulous hors d'oeuvres Jackie served, nobody wanted dinner.

"I couldn't cram in another bite," Donna said. We all concurred.

So we simply lingered in the public rooms and talked until it got late enough to consider going to bed. It had been a spectacular day, packed with many unforgettable experiences, and we revisited them all in our conversation. Of course, as always, we got around to relating memories of all our years together. I was scribbling away, trying to get everything recorded for this book.

Photo courtesy of Martha Still Littlefield
We hashed over our Girl Scout memories and experiences in the Zeigler House parlor. Linda Kay Killian Wood at bottom left is furiously taking notes. Others in the picture, listening to Carole Capps Steadham, Martha Still Littlefield, or Wanda Elrod Crowder tell some tale, are, left to right, Mary Stoddard Hitt, Marilyn Ball Murray, Ann Brown Fields, Diane Crawford Hill, Joyce Wakefield Burks, and Karyn Hudson Draper.

Afterward, in our suite, Karyn and I each downed one pastry that was left from breakfast and retired for the night. Rumor had it that Jackie's employees would remove unused pastries the next day, and we simply couldn't let such a terrible thing happen. We'd worry about the calories when we went home. And besides, we had to guard against starving on this trip.

* * * * *

Saturday was a free day for us, so we went in different directions. Diane and Carole went shopping. Ann and Karyn walked around our beautiful neighborhood, visiting an old cemetery where they met a family that had just discovered the grave of an ancestor. Marilyn Ball, who hadn't toured the Juliette Gordon Low Birthplace yet, did that. Five of us—Donna, Martha, Mary, Wanda, and I—decided to take the Old Savannah Trolley tour for the second time. This is a hop-on-hop-off tour: today we would "hop off" and visit as many places as we could.

Our day was not without frustrations.

First, we "hopped off" at the Saint John the Baptist Cathedral. We had been told that it is especially beautiful inside, and we wanted to see it. However, it was closed for a wedding, so that scotched our plan there.

We saw on our city map that the Andrew Low house was in walking distance, so we headed toward it. We had seen the house where Juliette Gordon Low was born. Now we wanted to see the house where she died, the house that Willy had left her in his will.

The Andrew Low house is named for Juliette's father-in-law. When her husband, Willy, died, Juliette did come back to live in it for a time, and she died in the right front bedroom in 1927. This house too is a grand pre-Civil War Savannah mansion that was built in 1849. The Lows were wealthy English aristocrats who were successful in the cotton business.[49]

---

[49] The Andrew Low House Website. http://www.andrewlowhouse.com/.

Among famous people who visited the house were Civil War Confederate States commanding General Robert E. Lee and English author William Makepeace Thackeray.[50]

"The house was elegant, but they surely didn't mention much about Juliette," Donna fretted. "Daisy is our heroine, and I'm miffed that the Lows and our tour guide seemed to relegate her to the background."

"This *was*, in the end, Juliette's house," Martha added.

After touring the Andrew Low House, we climbed back on the trolley and went to the Pirates' House restaurant for lunch.

This historic structure has been serving up delectable fare since 1753. When first established, it was an inn for seafarers and travelers, but later it became a preferred haunt for pirates. Robert Louis Stevenson is supposed to have used this inn in his classic book *Treasure Island*. The house also sits on the site of the first experimental garden in North America. The sprawling restaurant operates fifteen separate unique dining rooms, and costumed pirates come around to "terrorize you" at your table.[51] We thought we had won the day when we coerced them to take a picture with us. They had the final laugh, however, when the picture didn't turn out.

Though the atmosphere is over the top, the food is amazing. We feasted on she-crab soup, chicken-salad sandwiches, and green salads. We raved over every bite. I was delighted to be eating seafood again: we couldn't have picked a better place to do so.

---

[50] Ibid.

[51] History of the Pirate's House. (September 13, 2010). The Pirate's House Website, 13 Sep 2010. http://www.thepirateshouse.com/index.htm.

As happened all over Savannah, we got acquainted with the people at the table next to us. Wanda, of course, told them, "We're a troop of Girl Scouts from Fort Worth, Texas, and we've been together sixty-four years…"

"Oh, I was a Girl Guide in England," a lady with a British accent replied. She was the mother and grandmother of the family next to us, and they were celebrating her birthday. She talked with us for some time, as we compared experiences in Girl Guiding and Girl Scouting. This lovely woman obviously enjoyed the exchange. Upon leaving, she said meeting us had made her day. What a joyful occurrence for us as well. The woman's son-in-law even snapped our picture. We didn't get his name, but he took the photo with my camera, so I took the credit.

Photo courtesy of Linda Kay Killian Wood
Happy to enjoy the atmosphere and delicious food at the
Pirates' House restaurant are, left to right, Martha Still
Littlefield, Linda Kay Killian Wood, Mary Stoddard Hitt,
Donna Throckmorton Jones, and Wanda Elrod Crowder.

Upon leaving the Pirates' House, we discovered that we didn't have time to visit any other places. We had dinner reservations and commitments that required us to return to Zeigler House. So we reboarded the trolley and rode it to a stop close to our B&B. We hadn't seen as much as we wanted to that day, but we had been together and had fun. That was the important thing.

The trolley ride was not uneventful, though. At one stop, an actor impersonating Johnny Mercer, prolific American musician and composer who hailed from Savannah, got on and gave us a spiel about Mercer's life in the city. At the next stop, a costumed "Katie Greene," wife of American Revolutionary War hero, Nathanael Greene, gave us a Savannah history lesson from that historical period.

At Zeigler House Inn, we again attended "Wine and Cheese" and devoured more of Jackie's never-ending culinary delights. We had a couple of little ceremonies too.

On their shopping spree, Carole and Diane had found some lovely scarves on sale; and they had bought one for each of us. We drew numbers and picked a scarf according to our numbers. Almost everyone got a scarf to match the outfit she was wearing. We Texas belles simply have to wear matching ensembles.

I chose turquoise, and Carole said that if I hadn't gotten that one, she was going to give me hers because it was the exact right color for my costume. Ann, a staunch University of Texas (UT) supporter got an orange one. Diane, of course, chose purple because of her alma mater, Texas Christian University (TCU). Burnt orange is one of UT's colors, and purple is one of TCU's colors.

Carole and Diane taught us how to tie the proper knots in our scarves, and after we lovingly fingered the soft fabric for a while, we donned our treasures to wear to dinner.

Then we called Jackie in and gave her a little globe statue from the Juliette Gordon Low Birthplace. The statue says "World of Thanks, Girl Scouts." She promised to keep the gift on her desk always. She said she'd never forget us. We won't forget her either: she was a perfect hostess, and we were going to hate to leave her.

Dinner was at the Olde Pink House. We rode there in golf carts that had been converted into small taxis. Going to the restaurant, it was still daylight, and the driver transported us in the open air. The weather had turned rather chilly: I nearly turned to an ice sculpture on the way. Coming back, the drivers had rolled down plastic windows to enclose the carts: I was more comfortable. The twelve of us fit in two of these carts.

The Olde Pink House and Tavern is another mansion located on a Savannah park square. Built in 1771 and covered with pink stucco, this house has served as a private home, a bank, a tearoom, and headquarters for one of Sherman's generals after the Northern occupation in the Civil War.[52]

Buildings in Savannah's historic district are limited as to the colors they can have on their facades. An owner must paint a house within the color palette used during its historical period, especially if it's an antebellum house. Although several of the houses we visited were pink, this one was the "pinkest" of them all; hence, its name.

We were seated in the restaurant's elegant grand ballroom, which boasted crystal chandeliers, gold appointments, floor-length brocade drapes, and large oil paintings.

Photo courtesy of Martha Still Littlefield
Seated in the grand ballroom of the Olde Pink House Restaurant and Tavern for dinner are, left to right, clockwise, Martha Still Littlefield, Diane Crawford Hill, Donna Throckmorton Jones, Marilyn Ball Murray, Ann Brown Fields, Wanda Elrod Crowder, Mary Stoddard Hitt, Carole Capps Steadham, Karyn Hudson Draper, Linda Kay Killian Wood, and Joyce Wakefield Burks. Girl Scout Troop/Ship 11 always eats well.

---

[52] The Olde Pink House Restaurant and Tavern Website. http://www.plantersinn-savannah.com/the-olde-pink-house/.

Because some of us had already eaten abundantly that day—Jackie's superb breakfast, the Pirates' House lunch, the "Wine and Cheese" hors d'oeuvres—our appetites didn't do the restaurant justice. Martha and I shared an entrée, crab-stuffed blackened grouper (yea! more seafood) with green beans and mashed potatoes.

The sharing worked fine until Karyn ordered three desserts for the group to sample—key lime pie, chocolate oblivion torte, and pecan pie. We sent the three delicacies around the table, and each took a bite of all three. Then we sent them around again. That did it: my stomach screamed at me, "You *will* stop eating—or else."

It does seem as if we did a lot of eating on this trip, and the food was *so* good. I'm told that calories consumed on vacation don't count. Sadly, I have not found this information to be true.

The Olde Pink House had a "house singer" who circulated and performed requests. She wore an elegant, flowing, floor-length black Southern-belle dress. She sang as well as she looked and acted happy to hang around our table to visit with us. She sold some of us her CDs. Wanda, of course, told her, "We're a troop of Girl Scouts," and the singer seemed suitably impressed.

Our experience at the Olde Pink House Restaurant and Tavern was superb. What a marvelous evening we enjoyed.

Back at Zeigler House, we sat in the parlor, where hostess Jackie joined us for conversation. We asked her questions about Savannah, and she wanted to know about us and where we lived, how we keep in touch, and how often we get together.

Sunday morning, Carole, Diane, Martha, Wanda, and I attended worship at the Cathedral of Saint John the Baptist. So Martha, Wanda, and I did, after all, get to see inside the building we had missed visiting on Saturday.

The first worship service in the present building took place on April 30, 1876.[53] The building is indeed gorgeous, as we had been told. The acoustics inside make the music sound heavenly: the choir and organ are located upstairs behind worshipers, causing the music

---

[53] The Cathedral of Saint John the Baptist Website. http://www.savannahcathedral.org/.

to float down upon the people in the pews. I found the glorious music conducive to heartfelt worship.

After mass, we went back to dine at Soho South Café for lunch, where I had my last seafood meal of the trip, a crab salad. Yummy.

As we walked back to Zeigler House, we stopped in several shops along the way and made our final souvenir purchases.

Finally, we finished packing; Jackie's employees carried down our suitcases, and we relaxed on the veranda until it was time to leave for the airport.

Jackie telephoned a professional photographer friend of hers, Jerry Harris, who came to take our picture. He gave it to us as a souvenir of our trip.

Jerry is a member of one of the first Boy Scout troops in America, which has kept going until today, obviously through several generations. He has a strong appreciation for all things concerning Scouting. He was excited to meet us, and we, him.

A few days after we returned home and back to reality, we received the photograph by e-mail. We had posed like Southern belles, without the billowing skirts, on the front steps of the beautiful and historical Zeigler House Inn. What fun. How special. What a wonderful souvenir.

Photo courtesy of Jerry Harris
Girl Scout Troop/Ship 11, pretend Southern belles, descend the front staircase of Zeigler House Inn. We are, clockwise from top, Wanda Elrod Crowder, Joyce Wakefield Burks, Marilyn Ball Murray, Mary Stoddard Hitt, Martha Still Littlefield, Ann Brown Fields, Karyn Hudson Draper, Carole Capps Steadham, Diane Crawford Hill, and Linda Kay Killian Wood. Notice our scarves given by Carole and Diane. Unfortunately, Donna Throckmorton Jones and Marilyn Weiss had already departed and aren't in the picture.

We have recently learned that the wonderful Zeigler House Inn has closed, and we are very sad about that. We are thankful for the superb weekend that we had there and extremely grateful to Jackie Heinz for all her many kindnesses. Savanna's loss is huge.

The return trip to the airport and the flight to Dallas/Fort Worth were uneventful. Everything was on time today; the weather, cooperative. Some of the people who had flown to Savannah with us were on our return flight too. We apologized for their having to deal with us both ways, and they simply smiled and laughed. Good sports, they.

We tried to behave ourselves on this flight. Some Scouts napped; we bookworms read the tomes we had brought with us, and others chatted quietly.

I said the flight was uneventful, but amateur golfers Diane, Karyn, and Ann got excited because professional golfer, Justin Leonard, and his family were on our flight. Leonard had won the NCAA individual championship while at The University of Texas at Austin in 1994, the US Open Championship in 1997, and Britain's Ryder Cup championship in 1999. His resume contains other victories as well.[54] After we boarded the plane, Diane worked up the courage to go and talk with him.

Back in Texas, those of us who were being met at the airport found our families. Others made their way to cars in the parking garage. But we didn't part before we had another round of hugs for everyone, hugs that always feel warm and soothing.

We hoped to meet the following autumn for lunch at Azalea Plantation, so we could visit with each other and the four Scouts who didn't get to come on this trip. Carole, not surprisingly, was already planning that luncheon.

Our fabulous four days together in Savannah were over. We really didn't want them to be over, but they were, and we had added yet more incredible memories to our ever-growing list. We had spent four days ignoring suicide bombings, urban air pollution, earthquakes, floods, and wildfires. We had seen a beautiful city filled with beautiful sites. We had eaten so much delicious food that now we'd have to diet for several weeks or buy new clothes. We hadn't eaten Campfire Stew, but, truthfully, we hadn't missed it. We don't have to eat it anymore anyway because, as we've said for years, we *are* Campfire Stew—a magnificent whole greater than the sum of its parts.

---

[54] Justin Leonard. (January 19, 2014). In Wikipedia, http://en.wikipedia.org/wiki/Justin_Leonard.

This marvelous trip might be over, but troop/ship 11's adventures would go on. No doubt, the memories would still pile up. No doubt, Carole would continue to plan reunions, and we would continue to come to them. Girl Scouts together—always—no matter what the world throws at us. We are not sidetracked by the ugliness that goes on in the world. We are bound by the beautiful love we have for each other.

"See you in November," we hollered to each other as we waved good-bye and blinked our misty eyes.

CHAPTER 15

Definitely Not Little Old Ladies!

"I hate it when I see an old person and then real-ize that we went to high school together," Donna Throckmorton Jones says.

It is January 2018. Troop/Ship 11 women are sitting in Martha Still Littlefield's living room in Arlington, Texas. We have come to Martha's house for dessert and chatter after a delicious lunch at Arlington's Rose Garden Tea Room. The tea room is a troop/ship 11 favorite gathering place.

"I know," Diane Crawford Hill says. "I don't feel like an old lady."

Linda Kay Killian Wood chimes in. "When my grandmother turned seventy, she was an old lady. She wore black dresses with lace collars and clunky black lace-up shoes. She put her long gray hair back in a bun."

We troop/ship 11 "girls" look around at our feet and observe fashionable boots of various heights. No clunky black lace-up shoes are in the room.

We consider the clothes we are wearing.

It's a basketball game day, and Diane wears a purple top and white pants in support of her beloved Texas Christian University Horned Frogs; Ann

Brown Fields and Linda Kay wear the burnt orange and white of The University of Texas Longhorns. We are glad that today our teams, though in the same athletic conference, are not playing each other.

Carole Capps Steadham has made her semiannual run to Chico's boutique and is her usual up-to-date stylish self.

Mary Stoddard Hitt, stunning in black and white, looks as if she has just come from a fashion magazine photo shoot.

Some of us wear jewelry made by our own Marilyn Ball Murray.

Nobody has on a black dress with a little lace collar.

Most hairstyles are short-to-medium-length. Most of us have gray in our hair, but some have chosen to color it, while others have not. None of us today have our hair back in a bun.

Everybody looks, in a word, spiffy.

We congratulate ourselves on not being "little old ladies."

We pass around cell-phone pictures of our grandchildren, great-grandchildren, and dogs. As always, we look back to our growing-up years, and we think we remember them accurately. We laugh at situations we thought were funny both then and now. We discuss our current projects, travels, and interests. We avoid politics because we don't all agree, and we don't want to get into unpleasant arguments. We can go on like this for hours. We thrive on this sort of thing and always have.

But finally, we begin to stand up. We sat too long: our knees, legs, and feet are stiff, and our backs don't want to support the lifting maneuver. We reach for something to hold on to—maybe the person next to us—and totter, just a little, not very much.

"Well, I may not be a little old lady," Ann says, *"but some of my body parts are certainly no longer teenagers."*

* * * * *

In the years after our Savannah trip, Girl Scout Troop/Ship 11 members have kept perking along pretty much as before. We may move a little slower now, and we try always to watch where we put our feet—we must avoid falls and broken bones. We're all in our seventies, but we rarely act like it.

Carole is still running her professional architectural placement business and coleading a Girl Scout troop with her daughter. Mary continues to work as an accountant. Marilyn Weiss has no plans to stop managing her sports-clothing line. Linda Heaton Leonhardt sends us postcards, as she travels the world in style. Ann works summers in national parks and rides in charity bike marathons. Earline Campbell Wood is caring for her aged mother and mother-in-law. Joyce Wakefield Burks continues to work for the University of California, Berkley. I keep writing and trying to publish books.

In the fall of 2013, Carole and our longtime friend, Janice Bell Fitzgerald, assembled a hard-bound photo book that tells troop/ship 11's story in pictures. We treasure it, as we admire the memory-filled illustrations and the attractive page layouts.

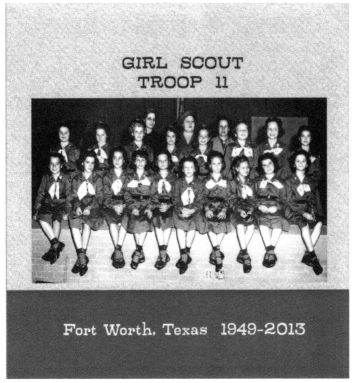

Photo courtesy of Gerry Odell Wood
Girl Scout Troop 11, Fort Worth, Texas, 1949–2013, the photo book
Carole Capps Steadham and Janice Bell Fitzgerald made for us in 2013.

Our Savannah jaunt was five years ago. Since then, troop/ship 11 members have celebrated several special occasions. For example, Earline Campbell Wood, Carole, Elaine Walton Lofland, and I marked our fiftieth wedding anniversaries, were honored at festive parties by family and friends, and have taken appropriate celebratory trips.

Several of the Scouts have had health issues to deal with. We've experienced kidney transplants and removals; shoulder, knee, and hip replacements; skin cancer removals; back surgeries; broken wrist repairs; and pacemaker insertions. We heal and, with the help of God and each other, we go on.

We had deaths of key family members, including Martha's and Elaine's husbands, Carole's mother, Diane's brother, and Joyce's sister.

In the midst of these trials, troop/ship 11 women supported each other in their usual style. In her home, one of us nursed a Scout sister after her surgeries. Several Scouts took in meals when others were sick, transported ailing Scouts to doctor appointments, and sat in hospital waiting rooms for surgeries to end. We all prayed fervently for our Scout sisters in every circumstance.

Troop/Ship 11 hasn't yet made any more group trips, but we're talking about it. Maybe it will happen. We have lots of ideas.

Through the years, it has been reassuring that Girl Scouts, past and present, in the Fort Worth area haven't forgotten about us. Two events in 2016 reminded us that we remain somewhat an inspiration to girls now coming up through Scouting.

In May 2016, troop/ship 11 members, along with others in Oklahoma and north and west Texas, were honored at a banquet in Arlington, Texas. Honorees had earned Girl Scouting's highest award, either today's Gold Award, or, in our day, the Curved Bar Award. At the banquet, we received certificates, etched glass plaques, and roses. We had our pictures taken together as a troop and with the other honorees.

As previously stated, troop/ship 11 is, of course, unique because we received our Curved Bar Award all together as a troop. That has never been a common event.

Photo courtesy of Gerry Odell Wood
Girl Scout Troop/Ship 11 was honored, along with others, for having completed requirements for Girl Scouting's highest award, in the 1950s, the Curved Bar. Left to right, front row, are Linda Kay Killian Wood, Marilyn Ball Murray, Wanda Elrod Crowder, Linda Heaton Leonhardt, and Ann Brown Fields; second row, Brenda Wilson Weir (Beverly Wilson Greene's sister), Karyn Hudson Draper, Diane Crawford Hill, Martha Still Littlefield, Carole Capps Steadham, and Donna Throckmorton Jones.

In addition, the November 2016 issue of *The Girl Scout Spirit*, magazine of the Girl Scouts of Texas Oklahoma Plains, Inc., published an article that featured our long-lived troop and our lifetime of worthwhile accomplishments.

Photo courtesy of Gerry Odell Wood
The first page of an article, "Troop 11: A Lifetime of Friendship," published in the November 2016 issue of *The Girl Scout Spirit* that showcased troop/ship 11.

On December 1, 2018, troop/ship 11 was honored at the nine-tieth anniversary celebration of Fort Worth's Oakhurst Elementary School. Carole again presented the troop's accomplishments, and the other women again stood to applause at their former school. Troop/Ship 11's latest project is sponsorship, both financially and socially, of Oakhurst's troop 1216. We are still "paying it forward."

In January 2018, twelve of us gathered to celebrate the year of our seventy-fifth birthdays. We ate lunch at Rose Garden Tea Room in Arlington and then moved on to Martha's house to chatter.

Photo courtesy of Carole Capps Steadham
Troop/Ship 11 members celebrating our collective seventy-fifth birthdays in January 2018 at Rose Garden Tea Room are, left to right, Ann Brown Fields, Linda Kay Killian Wood, Karyn Hudson Draper, Donna Throckmorton Jones, Marilyn Ball Murray, Carole Capps Steadham, Elaine Walton Lofland, Martha Still Littlefield, Mary Stoddard Hitt, Earline Campbell Wood, and Diane Crawford Hill. We were missing Joyce Wakefield Burks, Wanda Elrod Crowder, Pat Cookus Haberman, Linda Heaton Leonhardt, and Marilyn Weiss.

When we are together, as has always been the case, we spend time reminiscing. Sometimes we get caught up on what's going on with everyone, including the activities of our high school classmates.

Other times, we get to talking about what our many Scout years have meant to us, how the things we learned when we were young contributed to the women we became. Of course, as usual, everyone has something to say.

Carole begins. "Troop 11 gave me skills to lead a national volunteer organization in the design industry and gave me the leadership skills to start my own firm."

Diane became a competent public schoolteacher. She first learned how to teach and maintain discipline in Girl Scouts.

Never at a loss for words, I add my two cents. "I learned a variety of skills while working on the numerous badges we earned. I learned that it's okay to try new things and continue them if you like them and drop them if you don't."

Donna, always gracious, gives credit to our leaders. "We were lucky to have such wonderful leaders that were willing to invest their time in young girls for twelve years."

"Along with that," Karyn Hudson Draper reminds us, "is our Minnie Ruth Elrod Endowment Fund, which is evidence that we are generous and care about underprivileged girls—another thing we learned in Scouts."

"So many of the things we learned by earning all our badges have helped me in raising five children, teaching school, and owning my own engineering company," Martha says. "I couldn't begin to mention how many times the square knot has come to my rescue."

Marilyn Ball thinks our Scout adventures helped her in both of her chosen careers, first nursing and now jewelry-making. In both instances, she has set goals and achieved them through discipline, organization, and diligence.

"Scouting meant so much to me that I couldn't stop being a Girl Scout. I worked professionally in the Girl Scout organization for several years," Ann says.

Others highlight the relationships we had as youngsters and continue to enjoy.

Earline credits Carole for keeping us together through the years.

Mary values connections. "Two things stand out to me: (1) the friendships with my fellow Scouts and (2) the amount of effort our parents put in on us. We were so lucky. I would wish that for all young girls."

But when it comes to summing up, perhaps Elaine does it best. "Scouting with troop 11 gave me the curiosity to explore, the courage to try, the confidence to achieve, and, most of all, sisters to love for a lifetime."

We look back, we reminisce, we evaluate. Most important, we love each other. It's been a great journey and will continue to be so— seventy years plus whatever years are ahead of us. We are the nearly finished product of Ellie's Campfire Stew: we *love* to eat it, and we *are* it.

It may take us a little longer to accomplish tasks now than it used to. We may move a little slower than we did in the past. We have to limit spicy foods, even Campfire Stew, in our diets because of fussy stomachs. We don't have the sophisticated computer skills of our grandchildren, but we do persevere on computers. We remember dial telephones that plugged into walls for all uses, not just for recharging. When we were younger, we researched our term papers in encyclopedias and printed books, not on the Internet. We typed the finished products on typewriters, not computers.

We've witnessed enough current events and learned to use enough new inventions to define a lifetime. We experienced "duck and cover" exercises during the Cold War and heard practice air-raid sirens go off in our neighborhood. In the 1950s, we drove and rode in cars with large tail fins. We lived through the last half of World War II, listened on the radio as President Harry Truman fired General Douglas McArthur, watched the horrors of the Vietnam War on our TV screens, witnessed the fight of American minorities for equal civil rights, and coped with the lightning speed of technological development over seven decades. We have gone from party telephone lines to iPhones.

"We've seen it all," Karyn says, and she's not far wrong.

Yes, we have experienced a lot of things, but we continue to learn new things. Daily we exercise both our bodies and our minds. We are interested in many things and read incessantly. We socialize. Most of us still travel and have seriously long "bucket lists." We do the things books and television programs tell us will keep our minds and our bodies functioning as well as possible for as long as possible—eat healthily, get plenty of sleep, exercise, stay connected with friends, practice spirituality. We don't spend much time in rocking chairs.

In 2019, we gathered for a seventieth reunion celebration that included meeting with the precious little girls of troop 1216.

So, whatever other people may think, troop/ship 11 Girl Scouts are definitely not,
not,
not,
"little old ladies!"
Just ask us.

Photo courtesy of Martha Still Littlefield
All living members together for a photo at last, Girl Scout Troop/Ship
11 poses at their 2019 seventieth reunion on the front steps of Fort
Worth's Azalea Plantation Bed & Breakfast Inn. Pictured, left to right,
front row, are Joyce Wakefield Burks, Karyn Hudson Draper, Earline
Campbell Wood, Linda Heaton Leonhardt, Pat Cookus Haberman,
Elaine Walton Lofland, and Martha Still Littlefield; left to right, second
row, Linda Kay Killian Wood, Ann Brown Fields, Diane Crawford Hill,
Marilyn Weiss, Carole Capps Steadham, Marilyn Ball Murray, Mary
Stoddard Hitt, Donna Throckmorton Jones, and Wanda Elrod Crowder.

APPENDIXES

APPENDIX A

The Women of Girl Scout Troop/Ship 11

The main body of this book has presented the members of Girl Scout Troop/Ship 11 mixed together. Telling our story that way is appropriate because synergy, as it so often does, has made us greater together than we are individually. Nevertheless, at times, the reader may have found keeping all of us straight somewhat confusing and perhaps wished for more information about us as separate persons. Certainly, we are individuals and deserve to be considered that way as well. Yes, for sure, each troop/ship 11 member is unique. Here, then, is every girl and leader presented individually to the best of my ability. I am proud of us all—who we were and who we have become.

So I introduce to you each member of the Campfire Stew that is Girl Scout Troop/Ship 11. The leaders are placed in order of number of years they were active in leading the troop. The "girls" are placed in alphabetical order by their maiden names. The name in parentheses in each heading is the one we called them in troop/ship 11.

The Leader

Minnie Ruth Butler Elrod (Ellie)
November 18, 1908–November 13, 2003

1952   2003

Present town of residence: deceased

Marital status: married to Arthur Lee Elrod from 1933 until his death in 1964

Children: three daughters, Helen, who died at age four in 1944, Wanda, and Sharon

Grandchildren: seven

Great-grandchildren: twelve

Great-great grandchildren: two

Education: graduated at age sixteen from North Side High School, Fort Worth, Texas

Professional career path: salesclerk, Leonard's Department Store, Fort Worth, beginning in 1926; worker for the telephone company where her mother retired as a Bell Telephone Pioneer; employed five-plus years at Wolfe and Klar Jewelers; during her married years, a wife, mother, and homemaker; after the death of her husband, owner and operator, Elrod Florist, 1965–1983

Hobbies and interests: excellent seamstress, made her children's clothes; member, First Baptist Church, Fort Worth, and Trinity Baptist Church, Lake Wales, Florida; taught flower arranging and ceramics to Keenagers senior adults; traveled the United States, Europe, and the Caribbean

Achievements and awards: one of few Girl Scout leaders to keep troop together twelve years; Girl Scout district leader and organizer for Brownie troops in the 1950s; president, Oakhurst Preschool and Parent-Teacher Associations at Oakhurst Elementary School, Riverside Junior High School, and Amon Carter-Riverside High School; superintendent, children's Beginners Sunday School Department, ten-plus years, First Baptist Church, Fort Worth; member, Book Nook Study and Riverside Reviewers clubs; president, American Business Women's Association; member, florist associations; Minnie Ruth Elrod Endowment Fund honoree

Nickname: Ellie

Other pertinent information: Daughter Wanda says, "I don't remember Mother being mean to anyone. She helped the needy. She never yelled, displayed jealousy or vindictiveness, or cursed. She was truly a virtuous woman."

The Assistant Leaders

Thelma Frey Anglin Still (Mrs. Still)
October 19, 1917–September 12, 2010

1952   2004

Present town of residence: deceased

Marital status: married to Rudolph W. Still for sixty-three years until his death in November 2000

Children: two daughters, Martha Jane and Cynthia Sue (Cindy)

Grandchildren: ten

Great-grandchildren: nine

Great-great grandchildren: one

Education: graduate of Paschal High School, Fort Worth, Texas, 1936

Professional career path: Western Union telegraph operator, Stock Exchange, Fort Worth Stock Yards; during the Great Depression, sold magazines with her husband door-to-door in Texas and Oklahoma, sometimes taking chicken, eggs, fruits, or vegetables as payment, often eating one meal a day; in World War II, made quilts, blankets, and bandages for the war effort; after the war was a mother, volunteering for Sunday school, Parent-Teacher Association, Girl Scouts of the USA, and Meals on Wheels; served twelve years as assistant leader for Martha's Girl Scout troop and six years as leader for Cindy's troop; after rearing her girls, worked at Elrod Florist

Hobbies and interests: sewing (made most of her daughters' clothes through high school), bowling, quilting, gardening, reading, working puzzles, playing cards and dominoes, watching wrestling, golfing, enjoying her great-grandchildren, visiting Martha's lake house

Achievements and awards: several awards for floral arrangements; numerous awards for innovative, outstanding quilts

Other pertinent information: All her Girl Scouts were her special children. Even after we were grown women, she kept up with where we were and what we were doing. She loved seeing all "her girls" at reunions. She never forgot anything about us and treasured every contact with us. She often expressed her pride at the women we had become.

The Assistant Leaders

Jeanette I. Hudson (Mrs. Hudson)
February 13, 1917–July 10, 2004

1950   1999

Present town of residence: deceased

Marital status: married to Joe M. Hudson for fifty-eight years until his death in 1994

Children: two sons and one daughter, Karyn

Grandchildren: five, several step-grandchildren

Great-grandchildren: seven, several step-great-grandchildren

Education: graduate of Polytechnic High School, Fort Worth, Texas

Professional career path: worked thirty-five years in the catalog department of Montgomery Ward Department Store and Distribution Center, Fort Worth

Hobbies and interests: longtime member of Oakhurst Presbyterian Church; member of Eastern Star; leader in both Cub and Girl Scout troops of her children, worker in American Red Cross; traveler (to Europe, Africa, Canada, Mexico, and extensively in the United States); participant in activities of her children, grandchildren, and great-grandchildren

Other pertinent information: Mrs. Hudson was competent, loving, and gracious. We couldn't help but like her.

The Assistant Leaders

Esther Ellen Covey Killian (Mrs. Killian)
March 15, 1910–December 30, 2003

1949   1995

Present town of residence: deceased

Marital status: married to Fred Malcolm Killian for 19 years, divorced in 1949

Children: one daughter, Linda Kay

Grandchildren: two

Great-grandchildren: three

Education: graduated a year early in 1926 from Polytechnic High School, Fort Worth, Texas, was a straight-A student; teaching certificate from Texas Woman's College (now Texas Wesleyan University), Fort Worth, again a straight-A student

Professional career path: worked in the millinery department of Monnig's Department Store, Fort Worth, 1930–42; sales representative and later supervisor for Curtis Circulation Company, sales division of Curtis Publishing Company of Philadelphia, Pennsylvania, 1949–71, district office, Dallas; sales representative for preneed funerals, Lucas Funeral Home, Fort Worth, ten years; interviewer, Southwest Market Research Company, Fort Worth, ten years

Hobbies and interests: activities of her daughter and grandchildren; assistant leader of Girl Scout Troop 11, 1949-52; sewing (expert seamstress); doing embroidery; gardening; working crossword puzzles; cooking; teaching young women's Bible classes at Glenwood Church of Christ in 1930s; active in Riverside Church of Christ, 1941–66, Meadowbrook Church of Christ, 1966–95, and Midtown Church of Christ, 1995–2000, all in Fort Worth

Achievements and awards: numerous sales awards from Curtis Circulation Company

Other pertinent information: Esther personified strength and Christian faith, enduring many hard experiences in her life and never wavering in her devotion to Christ. In doing so, she set an inspiring example for all who knew her, especially her family.

The Girls

Marilyn Ann Ball Murray (Marilyn Ball)

1952   2013

Present town of residence: Burleson, Texas

Marital status: married thirty years to Gary Murray who died in 2008

Children: two daughters

Grandchildren: two

Education: graduated with a bachelor of science degree in nursing from Tarrant County Junior College (now Tarrant County College), 1972; graduated with a bachelor of science degree in gerontology from The University of Texas Southwestern Medical School, Dallas, 1987

Professional career path: registered nurse for thirty-one years; longest tenure was with the State of Texas, Department of Aging and Disability (DADS) for thirteen years; taught nurses-aide classes after retirement from the state

Hobbies and interests: making and selling jewelry and other crafts; breeding and showing Rhodesian Ridgeback and Havanese dogs; fostering dogs

Achievements and awards: In 2005, one of her Rhodesians, Riley, was sixth in the nation and Stud Dog with ten offspring who were also champions

Other pertinent information: Marilyn says, "I was one of the troop 11 Girl Scouts, and their support and companionship over the years have meant everything to me. It keeps me connected and a part of something bigger." Marilyn has weathered several hard things in her life; her strength and steadfastness is a constant inspiration to the rest of us.

The Girls

Linda Faye Booker Webb (Linda Booker or Booker)
November 17, 1943–March 28, 2007

1958   2002

Present town of residence: deceased

Marital status: married to Robert Michael Webb until her death from cancer in 2007

Children: one daughter, one son

Grandchildren: four, including one who died in an automobile accident

Education: graduated from Texas Tech University, Lubbock, in 1965, with a degree in liberal arts

Professional career path: public schoolteacher

Hobbies and interests: golfing, traveling, a member of Delta Gamma sorority

Nickname: Booker

Other pertinent information: Booker was troop/ship 11's clown, a constant source of laughs. She had strong interpersonal skills and an outgoing personality. She was liked by everyone. She was also strong and steadfast when her tiny granddaughter was killed in a car accident. Booker was both inspirational and entertaining. We miss her.

The Girls

Julia Ann Brown Fields (Ann)

1952   2013

Present town of residence: Austin, Texas

Marital status: married to Charles Fields until his death in 1968 of a
heart attack

Children: one daughter

Education: graduated with a bachelor of arts degree in Plan II Honors
Program with concentrations in American history and French
from The University of Texas at Austin (UT Austin), 1965;
graduated with a masters of education degree in counseling,
Southwest Texas State University (now Texas State University),
San Marcos, 1974; graduated with a doctor of philosophy
degree in educational psychology from UT Austin, 1980; graduated with a master of divinity degree from Austin Presbyterian
Theological Seminary, 1998

Professional career path: field advisor and assistant camp director, Lone Star Girl Scout Council, Austin, Texas, 1967–68;
teacher, counselor, supervisor, director of employee rela-

tions, and director of human resources, Austin Independent School District, twenty-nine years; ordained minister, United Methodist Church, 1995 till the present; vice president, Austin Presbyterian Theological Seminary, nine years

Hobbies and interests: actively involved in First United Methodist Church, Austin; working with Yellowstone Association in Yellowstone National Park; hiking; photographing the out of doors; bicycling; volunteering at Snow Mountain Ranch of YMCA of the Rockies; skiing; camping in her recreational vehicle; knitting; golfing; umpiring for adult softball games, including three national championships; actively supporting Conspirare Symphonic Choir, a nonprofit choral organization; participating in the Hill Country Ride for AIDS, Austin; cheering avidly for the Texas Longhorns

Achievements and awards: Girl Scouting Thanks Badge, the highest award for adults in Girl Scouting for service on the board of directors and for service as chair of the Girl Scout Scholarship Committee for twenty years

Other pertinent information: "Girl Scouting has been an important part of my life since 1950. I count the "girls" of troop/ship 11 as my sisters, and I am so very thankful that we continue to get together. My self-reliant lawyer-daughter has been able to build a fire and make Campfire Stew since she was a child. She herself is a former Girl Scout who was a camp counselor for many summers."

The Girls

Elizabeth Earline Campbell Wood (Earline)

1949   2013

Present town of residence: Granbury, Texas

Marital status: married to Alan Jerry Wood for fifty-six years

Children: three sons

Grandchildren: six, plus half-sister of granddaughter

Great-grandchildren: one, plus one by half-sister of granddaughter

Education: attended Arlington State College (now The University of Texas at Arlington)

Professional career path: coowner and operator (with Jerry), Sandra Gail Homes, Inc., home building company, Wichita Falls, Texas, 1962–85; real estate broker, 1965 to the present

Hobbies and interests: writing romance novels; playing Bridge; raising and running quarter horses; traveling (to Hawaii, Mexico, Spain, Switzerland, and her favorite, New Mexico)

Achievements and awards: awards for homes built by her company

Other pertinent information: Ever the faithful Christian, Earline faces everything that life throws at her with grace and good cheer. What an example she is to all who know her.

The Girls

Bette Carole Capps Steadham (Carole)

1953   2011

Present town of residence: North Richland Hills, Texas (suburb of Fort Worth)

Marital status: married to Joe Steadham for fifty-six years

Children: one son, one daughter

Grandchildren: four

Education: attended Arlington State College (now The University of Texas at Arlington) and Tarrant County Junior College (now Tarrant County College), receiving a degree in business administration

Professional career path: order interpreter, General Motors Corporation, and keypunch operator, Trinity Industries, both of Dallas, Texas; originator and teacher of English as a second language classes for Vietnamese children, Hurst-Euless-Bedford Independent School District; business, office, and human resources manager for Healthcare Environment Design owned by Baylor Hospital, Dallas; owner and manager, Placement by Design architectural consulting and recruiting service

Hobbies and interests: enjoying the couple's cabin at Red River, New Mexico, especially in the summer; hiking; fishing; gathering wild berries; cooking at both high and low altitude; country and western dancing; traveling (most major cities in the United States, Caribbean islands in winter); being active in White's Chapel United Methodist Church, Southlake, Texas

Achievements and awards: national president, Society for Design Administration (SDA); honorary membership, American Institute of Architects (AIA)

Other pertinent information: Carole is the person most responsible for keeping Girl Scout Troop/Ship 11 together for seventy years. Her gift for organizing has caused her to get saddled with planning our many reunions, a job she does graciously and without complaint. The rest of us are beyond grateful. Carole and her daughter Amy are now leaders of a group of Girl Scouts in the Fort Worth area.

The Girls

Lynda Pat Cookus Haberman (Pat)

1949   2013

Present town of residence: Irving, Texas

Marital status: married to Paul Louis Haberman, Sr., forty-four years

Children: one son, four stepchildren

Grandchildren: two, eight from stepchildren

Great-grandchildren: two

Professional Career Path: registered interior designer on commercial healthcare projects; worked thirty-five years in husband's architectural firm; established her own interior design business; retired; went back to work in husband's firm; still on-call

Hobbies and interests: taking care of two basset hounds, caring for her home, doing sewing and embroidery

Achievements and Awards: Professional Builder and General Contractor Association Interior Design Award for Skilled Nursing-Home Renovations; developing a deeper understanding of how interior design, color, texture and furnishings affect the well-being of the geriatric population; enjoying watching patients respond positively to their environment

Other pertinent information: Pat is never anything but positive when she is with us. She's a joy to be around.

The Girls

Carol Diane Crawford Hill (Diane)

1952   2013

Present town of residence: Fort Worth, Texas

Marital status: married to Leon Hill for forty-three years

Children: one son, one daughter

Grandchildren: four

Education: graduated from Texas Christian University (TCU), Fort Worth, with a degree in education, 1965

Professional career path: public schoolteacher and librarian, Fort Worth, Birdville (Texas), and Crowley (Texas) Independent School Districts, twenty-five-plus years; teacher, Fort Worth Museum of Science and History, six years

Hobbies and interests: playing golf; traveling (her favorite trip being to the Pasadena, California, in 2011 to watch the TCU Horned Frogs football team win the Rose Bowl; another favorite going to Disneyland in 2013 with her whole family, including her children and grandchildren); yelling for the Horned Frogs at football, basketball, and baseball games

Achievements and awards: making a difference in the lives of many children

Other pertinent information: Diane is a very upbeat Christian woman who is a constant source of encouragement to all of troop/ship 11.

The Girls

Wanda Lee Elrod Crowder (Wanda)

1949   2013

Present town of residence: Quinlan, Texas

Marital status: Married to Hugh Crowder for twenty years; divorced

Children: three daughters, one son

Grandchildren: six

Great-grandchildren: two

Education: attended Texas Wesleyan College (now Texas Wesleyan University), Fort Worth, Texas

Professional career path: assistant to a dermatologist, one year; secretary, the Boeing Company, Seattle, Washington, twenty years; operator of retail gift-item business, Crowder Accessories, for ten years; sales representative for ViSalus nutritional products

Hobbies and interests: the out of doors whether gardening or camping; making soap and candles; avidly reading, especially fictional mysteries; traveling in the United States, western Europe (eight countries), and China; residence in Texas, Germany, Alabama, and Washington State; making various crafts; caring for her dogs; active member of Terrell Bible Church, Terrell, Texas; spending winters with her sister and brother-in-law, Sharon and Larry Wallace, in Lake Wales, Florida

Achievements and awards: various awards while working with the United Fund and organizing airline conferences while at the Boeing Company

Other pertinent information: Wanda lived in Washington State for forty-plus years, maintaining a home and acreage in Randle for ten years of that time. She enjoyed the plentiful elk and deer on her five acres of pasture. She lived amid Mt. Rainier on the north, Mt. Adams on the east, and Mt. St. Helens on the south and loved this beautiful country surrounded by the Gifford Pinchot National Forest. However, she obeyed the summons within her to return to Texas in 2010. Wanda always was and still is an anchor of Girl Scout Troop/Ship 11. Her mother being the leader meant that Wanda participated in *all* the troop activities. Just as her mother did, Wanda loves and prays daily for all the troop members.

The Girls

Linda Gay Heaton Leonhardt (Linda Heaton, sometimes Heaton)

1952   2011

Present town of residence: Aledo, Texas

Marital status: married to Joy Lee Leonhardt

Children: two

Grandchildren: three

Education: graduated with a bachelor of arts degree from Texas Wesleyan College (now Texas Wesleyan University), Fort Worth, 1964; and with a master of education degree from Texas Wesleyan in 1987

Professional career path: teacher at Paschal High School, Fort Worth, Texas, before retiring in 2000

Hobbies and interests: traveling (almost everywhere: her favorites being London, Paris, Rome, Barcelona, Istanbul, Monte Carlo, Rio de Janeiro, and the islands of the South Pacific)

Nickname: Heaton

Other pertinent information: Linda just gets prettier as the years go by.

The Girls

Letha Karyn Hudson Draper (Karyn)

1952   2013

Present town of residence: Azle, Texas

Marital status: married to Harold Draper for twenty-three years, previous marriage for twenty years (previous spouse deceased)

Children: three daughters, two stepdaughters, and one stepson

Grandchildren: twelve

Great-grandchildren: one

Education: college hours in psychology and accounting

Professional career path: bookkeeper/accounting/office manager for several companies in Fort Worth, approximately twenty-five years; assistant floor manager (basement) and accountant (advertising department), Leonard's Department Store, Fort Worth, six years; owner and operator of business with her husband, manufacturing spa covers, twenty years; owner and operator of a retail store with her daughter in historic Fort Worth

Stock Yards district, four years; teacher of dancing for the city of Fort Worth, two years; owner of her own independent book-keeping service for several years; retired in 2008

Hobbies and interests: playing golf, bowling, supporting grandchildren's school and sports activities

Achievements and awards: greatest achievements are her three daughters—Lisa, Lauri, and Lesli—who have grown to be successful, caring, and wonderful women; also proud of laying the cornerstone and leading the fund-raising effort for the Minnie Ruth Elrod Endowment Fund ministering to needy Girl Scouts in Fort Worth

Other pertinent information: "Like all of my GS sisters, I know that my Girl Scout years with troop 11, besides giving me a world of different experiences and skills, prepared me to be open to life's opportunities and surprises. I learned to be strong, independent and to look for the goodness in everything. I learned love and acceptance."

The Girls

Linda Kay Killian Wood (Linda Kay)

1949   2012

Present town of residence: Los Alamos, New Mexico

Marital status: married to Gerry Odell Wood for fifty-four years

Children: one daughter, one son

Grandchildren: three

Education: attended Arlington State College (now The University of Texas at Arlington), Arlington, Texas, 1961–62; graduated with distinction from The University of Oklahoma (OU), Norman, with a bachelor of arts degree in journalism, 1965; graduated from The University of Texas at Austin (UT Austin) with a master of arts degree in communication, 1967

Professional career path: editor, *Oklahoma Daily* newspaper, OU, summer, 1964; part-time feature writer, Fort Worth (Texas) *Star-Telegram*, 1965; graduate teaching assistant, UT Austin, 1965–66; assistant editor, *Texas Medicine*, 1966–69; technical writer-editor, Los Alamos National Laboratory, Los Alamos,

New Mexico, 1992–2004; publicity chairman, Los Alamos Church of Christ, 1969–present; freelance writer, 1990–present

Hobbies and interests: writing; traveling (has visited twenty-eight foreign countries and all fifty states); doing counted-cross-stitch; reading; serving as an active member of Los Alamos Church of Christ; enjoying grandchildren's activities; cheering for the UT Austin Longhorns (any sport)

Achievements and awards: elected to Phi Beta Kappa, Phi Kappa Phi, Kappa Tau Alpha, and Theta Sigma Phi honor and professional societies; received *Reader's Digest* grant to cover National Republican Convention, 1964; received graduate fellowship from Fort Worth Theta Sigma Phi women's journalism fraternity, 1965; selected to Outstanding Young Women of America, 1974; received distinguished awards from Southwest Region, Society for Technical Communication (STC), 2002 (contributing writer, *Cerro Grande: Canyons of Fire, Spirit of Community*) and 2004 (coeditor, *Theory in Action: Highlights in the Theoretical Division at Los Alamos, 1943–2003*); received best-of-show award from Southwest Region, STC, 2005 (editor, *Laboratory Directed Research and Development*); published magazine articles and authored two as yet unpublished books

Other pertinent information: "I am an only child. Troop 11 girls are the sisters I never had."

LINDA K. WOOD

The Girls

Jacquelyn Ann McNiel Winkler (Jacque)

December 30, 1942–November 14, 2000

1949 1999

Present town of residence: deceased

Marital status: married to C. Wayne Winkler for thirty-eight years until her death in 2000

Children: one son, one daughter

Grandchildren: two

Education: attended Texas Wesleyan College (now Texas Wesleyan University), Fort Worth

Professional career path: homemaker

Nickname: Jacque (pronounced Jackie)

Other pertinent information: Jacque was another mainstay of troop/ship 11 who was loved by all of us at every point in our history. She got along with everyone and had an outstanding sense of humor. She was also very proud of being a lifelong Girl Scout. Her absence at our gatherings leaves a very large hole indeed.

The Girls

Linda Faye Simons Hill (Simons)

1953

Linda Simons was an active member of Girl Scout Troop/Ship 11 from first through twelfth grades. After high school graduation, she dropped out of participation in troop/ship 11 activities and reunions. As of this writing, all attempts to contact her have failed. We have all missed her and have wished to have her back among us. The last we knew, she was married, had three children, and had worked in a pharmacy.

The Girls

Martha Jane Still Littlefield (Martha)

1949   2013

Present town of residence: Arlington, Texas

Marital status: married to Eugene Littlefield for forty years until his death in 2015

Children: two girls

Grandchildren: five

Great-grandchildren: one

Education: attended Texas Women's University, Denton; Arlington State College (now The University of Texas at Arlington); and Tarrant County Junior College (now Tarrant County College); received license to be a real estate broker

Professional career path: cowrote curriculum for the first preschool at First United Methodist Church, Arlington; taught preschool, kindergarten, and developmental gymnastics, sixteen years; worked in physical therapy; president of B&L Engineering,

Inc., twelve years, a company she and her husband founded to perform gas and electric utility studies for manufacturing companies; buying houses to refurbish, sell, or rent; ready to retire

Hobbies and interests: oil painting; creating stained glass; sewing; quilting; woodworking; reading; remodeling houses; gardening; bicycling; kayaking; traveling (Europe, Canada, most US national parks, most of the fifty states); enjoying grandchildren's activities; spending time at her lake house; leading a Girl Scout troop

Achievements and awards: selected Teacher of the Year by First United Methodist Church, Arlington, 1985; selected Outstanding Business Woman by Arlington Chamber of Commerce, 1992; Girl Scout lifetime member

Other pertinent information: "Girl Scouting played a large part in who I am. Our troop's leader and assistant leaders kept us together for twelve years. They kept things exciting, interesting, and challenging. There was always something new and different to learn or experience. We were taught to look after each other and *never* do anything without a buddy. We learned so many things that I never thought would help me through life, but they did."

LINDA K. WOOD

The Girls

Margie Lou Stoddard Terry (Margie)

May 10, 1943–November 9, 1981

1952

Present town of residence: deceased

Marital status: married to Mike Terry

Children: one son

Grandchildren: three

Great-grandchildren: five

Education: graduated from Arlington State College (now The University of Texas at Arlington) with a bachelor's degree in accounting

Professional career path: worked several years as a legal assistant, accountant

Hobbies and interests: liked to cook, play racquetball, and travel

Achievements and awards: president of the Fort Worth chapter of the National Association of Legal Assistants (NALA), active in the Texas state chapter of NALA

Other pertinent information: Margie was a fraternal twin of Mary Stoddard Hitt. Both of them contributed much to the togetherness we experienced in the troop's early years and later.

The Girls

Mary Sue Stoddard Hitt (Mary)

1953   2013

Present town of residence: San Antonio, Texas

Marital status: married to Steve Hitt; divorced

Children: one son

Grandchildren: two

Education: graduated from Arlington State College (now The University of Texas at Arlington), Arlington, Texas, in 1965 with a bachelor of arts degree in history; attended St. Mary's University, San Antonio, Texas, completing courses in business and accounting

Professional career path: became a certified public accountant (CPA) in 1975; has worked for different companies as vice president of finance and administration and treasurer; currently employed at Central Catholic High School, San Antonio, as director of finance

Hobbies and interests: loves to travel and play tennis; is a member of a supper club and other social groups that involve food and wine

Achievements and awards: past president of San Antonio chapter of the Financial Executives Institute; long-term member of the San Antonio chapter of CPAs and has worked on various chapter committees

Other pertinent information: Mary is a fraternal twin with Margie Stoddard Terry. Mary has faced and survived many hard things. She continues to support troop/ship 11 in every way, almost never missing a reunion or trip and always offering encouragement when another troop member is facing a problem. She's another "girl" who gets prettier every year.

The Girls

Donna Sue Throckmorton Jones (Donna)

1949   2013

Present town of residence: Saginaw, Texas

Marital status: married to Jack Jones for thirty years

Children: four girls, one stepdaughter, one stepson

Grandchildren: seventeen

Education: graduated from Amon Carter-Riverside High School, Fort Worth

Professional career path: worked as teletype operator and miscellaneous office worker, Southwestern Bell Telephone Company, three years; worked in clerical positions at Buddie's Super Markets offices and Buddie's Credit Union, two years; held many clerical worker positions at the General Services Administration (GSA), twenty-seven years; the last fifteen of those years, administrative assistant to the regional administrator; bookkeeper, payroll officer, and general office manager for son-in-law's business, Tim Pulliam Concrete Work, nine years; retired in October of 2012

Hobbies and interests: round dancing (choreographs ballroom) and square dancing, serving as cue person and instructor for the round dance activity for fifteen years; traveling (Germany, Switzerland, Austria, Holland, Alaska, Hawaii, Mexico, Jamaica, Canada, and most of the fifty states); cruising (eight cruises)

Achievements and awards: received many bonuses and service awards while at GSA

Other pertinent information: "I was one of the ones that came to troop 11 from another troop. That troop folded, which turned out to be a blessing for me, because I think troop 11 is the best and most active troop I have ever heard about." Donna serves us all with love and sacrifice. She is a lovely Christian woman.

The Girls

Joyce Lynn Wakefield Burks (Joyce)

1953   2013

Present town of residence: El Cerrito, California

Marital status: married to William Creed Burks, Jr., for twenty-plus years; divorced

Children: one daughter

Education: graduated from Amon Carter-Riverside High School, 1960; graduated from Texas Tech University (TTU) with bachelor of arts degree in Spanish, 1963; completed coursework for master of arts degree in sociology from TTU, 1965

Professional career path: staff positions, University of California, Berkeley (UC Berkeley), ending as executive assistant to the dean of the Graduate School of Education; retired in 2008 after forty years of service; still working part-time at UC Berkeley

Hobbies and interests: reading; music; duplicate Bridge (Life Master); attending many Berkeley campus lectures in natural sciences, astronomy/astrophysics/cosmology, paleontology, archaeology, geology, and history/ancient history; participating in UC Berkeley retirees association's "Learning in Retirement" minicourses (presentations by UC faculty and emeriti); going on day-trips—including sessions about engineering and earthquake preparedness and a visit to new Bay Bridge (Oakland–San Francisco) while it was under construction; enjoying meeting and hearing more than ten Nobel laureates, various diplomatic and academic personages, a crown prince and princess, two Saudi princesses, statesmen (mayors and a US president), wealthy Berkeley campus donors, and university administrators

Achievements and awards: various campus awards/presentations, honor societies at TTU, and local awards

Nickname: Joycie

Other pertinent information: "I love those troop 11 reunions!" Joyce, with her rich, varied, and continuous educational background, has much to add to troop/ship 11 discussions. She is a joy to converse with and fun to be around.

The Girls

Charlotte Elaine Walton Lofland (Elaine)

1953   2013

Present town of residence: Colleyville, Texas

Marital status: married to Gerald Lofland for fifty years until his death in 2018

Children: two twin sons

Grandchildren: seven

Education: received bachelor of arts degree in marketing from Texas Christian University, Fort Worth

Professional career path: owner and operator of Jones of Dallas clothing manufacturing company; retired

Hobbies and interests: playing golf, playing tennis; playing Bridge; creating art; serving as docent, Kimbell Art Museum, Fort Worth; traveling (all over the world); skiing; scuba diving; gardening; decorating; entertaining; being active in White's Chapel United Methodist Church, Southlake, Texas

Other pertinent information: When Elaine was battling kidney disease, both Wanda and Ann offered to donate a kidney to her. "Girl Scouts together!" a grateful Elaine says. She's another troop/ship 11 Scout who never surrenders to defeat and, when knocked down, gets right back up. Kindness and gentleness are her hallmarks.

The Girls

Marilyn Kay Weiss (Marilyn Weiss)

1949   2013

Present town of residence: Fort Worth, Texas

Marital status: married to Cindy Kline, partner for twenty-seven years

Children: none

Education: graduated Birdville, Texas, (suburb of Fort Worth) High School in 1961; transferred from Amon Carter-Riverside prior to sophomore year but remained active with the troop/ship 11 Girl Scout troop; attended Arlington State College (now The University of Texas at Arlington), and the University of Hawaii; graduated from North Texas State University (now the University of North Texas), Denton, with a bachelor of science in health and physical education degree, 1965; received masters of arts degree from the University of Northern Colorado (UNC), Greeley, 1966; worked toward a doctorate in athletic administration at the University of Colorado, Boulder

Professional career path: coach, teacher, and supervisor of interns and student teachers, UNC Laboratory School, Greeley, Colorado, 1966–70; assistant athletic director and women's athletic director-coach, Utah State University (USU), Logan, Utah, 1976–81; associate athletic director and women's athletic director, the University of Florida (UF), Gainesville, 1981–85; president, Innovative Sports Sales, Inc., and vice president of Innovative Properties, Inc., 1991–present

Hobbies and interests: golfing; spending time in Hilton Head, South Carolina, and Ruidoso, New Mexico; traveling to and playing on many of the top golf courses in the United States; boating; water skiing; real estate investing

Achievements and awards: held national offices in Association for Intercollegiate Athletics for Women and National Collegiate Athletic Association; member, Colorado High School Coaches Hall of Fame; won national championships in volleyball, softball, and gymnastics while athletic administrator at USU and UF

Other pertinent information: Marilyn is a successful business woman and athlete. We are proud of her many accomplishments.

The Girls

Beverly Ann Wilson Greene (Beverly)

August 31, 1943–August 10, 2008

1952   2004

Present town of residence: deceased

Marital status: married to Lyndon Greene until her death in 2008

Children: three girls, three boys

Grandchildren: eleven

Education: attended Texas Wesleyan College (now Texas Wesleyan University), Fort Worth

Professional career path: administrative manager and head of security, General Dynamics, California

Other pertinent information: Beverly was a competent and ever-enthusiastic cheerleader for Girl Scout Troop/Ship 11. Life was not a joy ride for her, but she met every circumstance with grace and strength. She was an inspiration to us.

Appendix B

Beyond Campfire Stew: Favorite Troop/Ship 11 Recipes

Besides our beloved Campfire Stew and S'mores, recipes and instructions for which appear in the text of this book, Girl Scout Troop/Ship 11 has, through the years, compiled some additional favorite recipes. A few are our own, but others we have enjoyed at the bed-and-breakfast establishments we have visited. We share these recipes here for anyone else who would like to enjoy them.

Buddy Burner Pancakes

Butter
1 cup pancake mix
1/2 cup water
1 egg, beaten with fork
Chocolate chips, pecans, or blueberries, optional

Mix pancake mix, water, egg, and optional ingredients. Melt a pat of butter on Buddy Burner. If you don't have a Buddy Burner, use a skillet griddle on a stove. Spoon two tablespoons of batter onto top of buddy burner or skillet. Cook until top of pancake is bubbly. Flip pancake carefully with spatula so as not to drop it in the dirt. Cook for about a minute more until pancake doesn't stick to buddy burner or skillet. Remove pancake to plate and top with syrup or jam.

Two to three pancakes

Troop/Ship 11 enjoyed these pancakes on camping trips. After numerous tries, most of us became adept at flipping the pancakes onto the Buddy Burner.

Toad in the Hole

Butter
1 slice of bread with a hole cut in the center
1 whole egg
Salt and pepper
Grated cheese, optional

Butter bread on both sides and put on Buddy Burner. If you don't have a Buddy Burner, use a skillet or griddle on a cookstove. Cook on one side for about a minute, then flip it over. Break whole egg into hole in bread. Sprinkle with salt and pepper and, if desired, grated cheese. Heat on second side until egg and bread are cooked to your taste. Remove toast and egg with spatula and enjoy.

One serving

This was another troop/ship 11 camping favorite for breakfast. Several of us still like to fix it for breakfast at home. We found that our families enjoy it also. The kids kind of forget they are eating eggs and toast and think they're eating something special.

Tin Can Casserole

1/4 pound ground beef, browned and crumbled
1/2 potato, diced
Other vegetables to taste: onion, corn, green peas, green
        beans, tomatoes, squash
1/2 cup grated cheddar cheese, optional
1/4 cup water

Mix ingredients and pour into a twenty-eight-ounce tin can. Cook over open fire or in fire that has burned down to coals until all ingredients are hot and completely cooked, about thirty minutes. Remove from fire with long tongs. Cool for a few minutes. When the can has cooled enough, eat with a spoon.

One serving

This mixture is similar to Campfire Stew and delicious out-of-doors on camping trips. Troop/Ship 11 girls liked it almost as much as Campfire Stew. Troop members and their families also have enjoyed this concoction at backyard parties. If, like Carole, you don't like hamburger, leave it out or put in some other meat, such as cooked pulled pork. Probably, this recipe would also work well-cooked in a slow cooker.

Hamburger Stew in the Coals

1/4 pound hamburger meat, slightly browned
1 medium potato, cut up
1/4 medium onion, chopped
1 large carrot, sliced crosswise
1/4 green pepper, sliced, optional
1 small tomato, cut in wedges, optional
Salt and pepper to taste

Combine ingredients on a large square of foil. Fold foil over mixture and seal tightly. Place on open fire that has been burned down to coals for about thirty minutes or until meat is completely cooked and vegetables are soft. Eat right from the foil when the package has cooled sufficiently.

One serving

Troop/Ship 11 enjoyed this stew as another alternative to Campfire Stew. We especially enjoyed it on the primitive camping trip at West Farm, though I suspect real primitive campers didn't have foil. Perhaps they used banana or palm leaves. Obviously, this dish also can be cooked on a backyard grill. Easy cleanup too. Again, if you prefer another meat or no meat, adapt the recipe to your taste.

Porcupine Balls

1 1/2 pound ground beef
2/3 cup long-grain rice, uncooked
1/2 cup water
1/3 cup onion, chopped fine
1/2 teaspoon salt
1/8 teaspoon pepper
1/8 teaspoon garlic powder
1 fifteen-ounce-can tomato sauce or soup
1 cup water
1 teaspoon Worcestershire sauce

Crumble ground beef. Mix in rice, 1/2 cup water, onion, salt, garlic powder, and pepper. Shape mixture into 1 1/2-inch diameter balls. Place on ungreased two-quart shallow baking dish. Mix remaining ingredients and pour over meatballs. Cover and bake at 350 degrees for forty-five minutes. Uncover and bake fifteen to twenty minutes longer.

Four to six servings

Troop/Ship 11 enjoyed these meatballs at indoor parties. They do look like porcupines.

Pichams

1 slice Spam® (or cooked ham)
1 sliced pineapple ring
1 slice cheddar cheese (or American or Swiss)

Layer on a large square of foil with ham on bottom, pineapple in the middle, and cheese on top. Close foil and seal. Place on grill over open fire, or bake in 350-degree oven until heated through and cheese melts, about ten to fifteen minutes. Carefully unwrap and eat.

One serving

Many people have an aversion to Spam®. If you're among them, enjoy this entrée with real or processed ham. That's what some of our picky eaters in troop/ship 11 did. We also enjoyed this at camp. Oh, and for you younger readers, we are not talking about mass-distributed e-mail when we say "Spam®." It's a real canned meat on grocery store shelves.

Santa Fe Soufflé

(Courtesy of Martha Linnartz, Azalea Plantation Bed & Breakfast Inn, Fort Worth, Texas)

Whisk together in large bowl:

> 11 eggs
> 1 teaspoon baking powder
> 1/2 cup flour
> 1 stick melted butter
> 1 cup shredded Monterrey Jack cheese
> 1 cup shredded cheddar cheese
> 1 four-ounce can chopped mild green chilies (or four ounces frozen green chili)

Pour egg mixture into 9-inch × 13-inch pan (sprayed with vegetable cooking spray). Bake thirty to thirty-five minutes at 350 degrees, until slightly browned. Do not overbake. Cool five to ten minutes, cut into twelve or fifteen squares. Top each serving with a dollop of sour cream, half a cherry tomato, diced green onion, sprig of rosemary or cilantro. Presentation suggestion: cook pinto beans, spread beans onto large platter. Place soufflé squares on top of beans.

Twelve to fifteen servings

Martha served this dish with green salad and flour tortillas at a troop/ship 11 brunch.

Vegetable Casserole

(Courtesy of Martha Linnartz, Azalea Plantation Bed & Breakfast Inn, Fort Worth, Texas)

> 1 can French-style green beans, drained
> 1/4 cup chopped bell pepper
> 1 can shoe peg corn
> 1/2 cup chopped celery
> 1/2 cup chopped onion
> 1/2 cup grated sharp cheese
> 1 can cream of celery soup, undiluted
> 1/2 cup sour cream
> Salt and pepper to taste
> 1/2 stick margarine, melted
> 1/2 box cheese crackers, crushed
> 1/2 package slivered almonds

Preheat oven to 350 degrees. Grease a 13-inch × 9-inch baking dish. Combine vegetables, cheese, soup, sour cream, salt, and pepper in baking dish. In a separate bowl, mix melted margarine, cracker crumbs, and almond slivers. Sprinkle over vegetable mixture. Bake for forty-five minutes.

Ten servings

Martha served this as the perfect accompaniment to a mushroom-sauced chicken breast.

Cheesy Spinach

2 tablespoons butter
2 tablespoons flour
Dash of salt and pepper
1 cup milk
1 1/2 cup shredded cheese
2 ten-ounce packages frozen chopped spinach

Cook spinach according to package directions in a saucepan or microwave oven. Keep warm. Melt butter in saucepan over medium heat. Add flour and stir for one minute. Slowly stir in milk, then seasonings. Cook and stir until thickened about four to five minutes. Turn off heat. Stir in cheese until melted, thickened, and smooth.

Spoon a serving of spinach onto each plate and pour cheese sauce over it or mix sauce into spinach and serve.

Six servings

Troop/Ship 11 made this concoction in our cooking class at the Lone Star Gas Company in downtown Fort Worth. It was the dish that taught me to love spinach.

Biscuits on a Stick

Refrigerated canned biscuits, either large or small size
Long stick or skewer, 3/4–1 inch in diameter
Foil
Soft or melted butter
Cinnamon/sugar mixture, optional

Cover the end and at least six inches of the stick tightly with foil. Spear biscuit with foil-covered end of stick. Hold biscuit end of the stick over campfire until the biscuit is baked on the inside and golden brown on the outside. Roll in butter and, if desired, cinnamon/sugar mixture.

Caution: If you do not cover the stick with foil, the fire may cause the stick to catch fire.

One serving

Troop/Ship 11 enjoyed this biscuit variation on camping trips, both as a breakfast accompaniment and as a dinner bread. There's just something about a campfire that makes everything delicious. Needless to say, however, biscuits sometimes ended up in the campfire: place the dough securely on the stick and handle carefully.

White Chocolate Cranberry Biscotti

(Courtesy of Jackie Heinz, Zeigler House Inn, Savannah, Georgia)

> 2 cups all-purpose flour
> 1 1/2 teaspoons baking powder
> 3/4 cup sugar
> 1/2 cup (1 stick) unsalted butter, room temperature
> 1 teaspoon grated lemon zest
> 1/4 teaspoon salt
> 2 large eggs
> 3/4 cup pistachios, coarsely chopped
> 2/3 cup dried cranberries
> 12 ounces white chocolate, chopped

Preheat the oven to 350 degrees Fahrenheit.

Line a heavy large baking sheet with parchment paper. Whisk flour and baking powder in a medium bowl to blend. Use an electric mixer to beat sugar, butter, lemon zest, and salt in a large bowl to blend. Beat in eggs one at a time. Add flour mixture and beat until blended. Stir in pistachios and cranberries.

Form dough into a thirteen-inch-long, three-inch-wide log on prepared baking sheet. Bake until light golden, about forty minutes. Cool thirty minutes.

Place log on cutting board. Using a sharp serrated knife, cut log on a diagonal into 1/2 to 3/4-inch-thick slices. Arrange biscotti, cut side down, on the baking sheet. Bake biscotti until they are pale golden, about fifteen to twenty minutes. Transfer biscotti to a rack and cool completely.

Stir chocolate in a bowl set over a saucepan of simmering water until chocolate melts. Dip bottom half of biscotti into melted chocolate. Gently shake off excess chocolate. Place biscotti on baking sheet chocolate side down to set. Take remaining chocolate and drizzle over the top if desired. Refrigerate until chocolate is firm, about thirty-five minutes.

Makes two dozen

This is truly one of the utterly delicious concoctions troop/ship 11 enjoyed on our trip to Savannah, Georgia, a city full of delicious culinary offerings. Don't plan on losing any weight if you eat this yummy pastry very often. And, be warned, stopping with just one is almost impossible.

Mock Angel Food Cake

1 slice white sandwich bread
Sweetened condensed milk
Cinnamon, chocolate, and/or coconut sprinkles to taste
Cooking oil

Dip slice of bread in condensed milk. Sprinkle with cinnamon, chocolate and/or coconut sprinkles. Cook on greased hot griddle about one minute per side.

One serving

Troop/Ship 11 loved this easy-to-fix dish when camping or at house parties. It's a surprisingly delicious dessert that kids are sure to like.

Banana Boat

1 banana
1 heaping tablespoon chocolate chips
4–6 small marshmallows
1 tablespoon chopped pecans

Slice banana lengthwise. Stuff with chocolate chips, marshmallows, and pecans. Close together. Wrap mixture completely in foil, sealing tightly. Cook for ten to fifteen minutes on an open fire that has burned down to coals.

One serving

Troop/Ship 11 thought this the perfect ending to a camp meal and a delicious alternative to S'mores. The recipe should also work on a backyard grill. Being Texans, we preferred pecans—the pecan tree is the state tree, but the banana boat would probably be good with any type of nut.

Girl Scout Mint Tea

(Submitted by Carole Capps Steadham)

Mix:
6 cups of water
6 small or 3 large tea bags (decaffeinated, if preferred)
Boil tea and remove from heat
Add:
1 cup sugar (stir to dissolve)
3 large sprigs of mint
Let steep for ten minutes
Remove mint sprigs
Add:
6-ounce can frozen lemonade
6-ounce can frozen orange juice
4 more cups cold water

Great served at luncheons and freezes well too! Enjoy!

Carole served this tea at a troop/ship 11 luncheon. Diane's mother, Mrs. Dot Crawford, liked it so much that she named it "Girl Scout Mint Tea."

Bibliography

Brokaw, Tom. *The Greatest Generation.* New York: Random House, 2004.

Bryant, Weldon, ed. *The 1961 Eagle,* vol. 30. Fort Worth, Texas: Amon Carter-Riverside High School and Marvin D. Evans Company, 1961.

Buenger, Victoria, and Dr. Walter L. Buenger. *Texas Merchant: Marvin Leonard and Fort Worth* (Kenneth E. Montague Series in Oil and Business History). College Station, Texas: Texas A&M University Press, 2008.

Christiansen, Betty. *Girl Scouts: A Celebration of 100 Trailblazing Years.* New York: Stewart, Tabori & Chang, 2011.

Cordery, Stacy S. *Juliette Gordon Low: The Remarkable Founder of the Girl Scouts.* New York: Penguin Books, 2012.

Flemmons, Jerry. *Amon: The Texan Who Played Cowboy for America.* Lubbock, Texas: Texas Tech University Press, 1998.

Girl Scouts of the United States of America. *Girl Scout Handbook: Intermediate Program.* New York: Girl Scouts of the U.S.A., 1953.

Hoxie, W. J. *How Girls Can Help Their Country: Handbook for Girl Scouts.* Carlisle, Massachusetts: Applewood Books, 1913.

Jones, Marion, ed. *Very Personally Yours.* Neenah, Wisconsin: Kimberly-Clark Corporation, 1946.

Leman, Dr. Kevin. *The Birth Order Book: Why You Are the Way You Are.* Ada, Michigan: Revell, reprint edition, 2015.

Nichols, Mike. *Lost Fort Worth.* Charleston, South Carolina: The History Press, 2014.

Shultz, Gladys Denny, and Daisy Gordon Lawrence. *Lady from Savannah: The Life of Juliette Low.* New York: Girl Scouts of the U.S.A., 1988.

The Story of Menstruation. Burbank, California: Walt Disney Productions and International Cellucotton Company, 1946.

Willis, Libby. *Images of America: Fort Worth's Oakhurst Neighborhood.* Charleston, South Carolina: Arcadia Publishing, 2014.

About the Author

 Linda Kay Killian Wood, a charter member of Brownie Troop 11, has remained involved with Girl Scout Troop/Ship 11 throughout its long life.

She holds a Bachelor of Arts in journalism degree, with distinction, from The University of Oklahoma, Norman, and a Master of Arts in communication degree from The University of Texas at Austin. She was selected to Phi Beta Kappa, Phi Kappa Phi, and Kappa Tau Alpha honor societies.

Linda has been a feature writer for the Fort Worth (Texas) *Star-Telegram*, assistant editor of Austin-based *Texas Medicine*, and technical writer-editor at Los Alamos National Laboratory, Los Alamos, New Mexico. She is the author of numerous articles that have been published in national, regional, and local magazines and newspapers.

Linda has been married to Gerry Wood since 1965. The couple has two children and three grandchildren. The Woods are active members of the Los Alamos Church of Christ. They have traveled to twenty-eight countries outside the United States and have visited all fifty states.

CPSIA information can be obtained
at www.ICGtesting.com
Printed in the USA
LVHW071912100920
665534LV00022B/1800